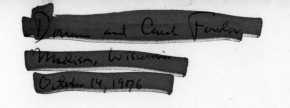

THE GEOGRAPHY OF RELIGION IN ENGLAND

The Geography of Religion in England

JOHN D. GAY

DUCKWORTH

First published in 1971 by
Gerald Duckworth & Company Limited
3 Henrietta Street, London WC2

© *1971 J. D. Gay*

ISBN 0 7156 0557 7

Printed in Great Britain by
Ebenezer Baylis & Son Limited
The Trinity Press, Worcester, and London

To Brenda

Contents

List of Maps

(pages 264–325)

Preface

During the course of its development geography has greatly extended its boundaries, but the field of religion has always been at the outermost margin. Religion is commonly thought to lie outside the scope of empirical enquiry and this may have deterred the geographer from ventures into what he feared would end up as metaphysics.

However it is not the task of the geographer to evaluate religious experience and neither is he concerned with assessing the validity or otherwise of religious claims and beliefs: this is the preserve of theology and the science of religion. The geographer should adopt the dictum that 'if men define situations as real they are real in their consequences', and then immerse himself in examining from a geographical viewpoint the empirical consequences of religion—its organized institutional expression.

Theology, the history of religion, comparative religion and the anthropological study of religion have all been successfully pursued in this country. In recent years the sociology of religion has come into the limelight. However the geography of religion remains a neglected field. The following pages are an attempt to remedy this neglect.

The approaches adopted by those few geographers who have tackled the subject of religion have varied according to the availability of the primary source material. Thus many of the studies made in the United States or in France could not have been undertaken in England. The first three chapters of this book are concerned with assessing the work of other geographers of religion and with evaluating the material available for a study of the geography of religion in England. This forms the vital ground-work for the remaining chapters which set out and offer explanations for the geographical distribution of denominational allegiance. This is but one approach to the geography of religion and I hope the work will form a jumping-off ground for future studies.

My greatest debt of gratitude is to Professor E. W. Gilbert, Emeritus Professor of Geography at Oxford. He has steered me through the many vicissitudes of my research with a clarity and wisdom I shall always remember. While he bears no responsibility for the contents, the work would have been appreciably worse but for his guidance.

I am extremely grateful to the Rev. W. L. R. Watson and Mr. F. V. Emery, both tutors at St. Peter's College Oxford, without whose initial suggestions and perseverance this work would never have been started. Also to the Rt. Rev. W. G. Fallows and the Rev. Prebendary G. T. Chappell who actively assisted the continuation and completion of my research.

My wife, Brenda, has been a constant source of encouragement and help to me. In addition she has saved the reader from countless lapses in clarity and grammatical eyesores. There are numerous people who have ungrudgingly supplied me with information and advice and have enabled me to glimpse the many facets of the religious scene in England. I would like to make particular mention of Dr. D. A. Martin, Mrs. M. Schmool, Mr. A. E. C. W. Spencer and Dr. B. E. Jones.

On the production side Miss M. Fletcher has painstakingly transcribed my handwriting into typescript. I am grateful also to Messrs. Darton, Longman and Todd Ltd., for permission to use copyright material from Boulard's *An Introduction to Religious Sociology.*

London
January 1971   J.D.G.

CHAPTER ONE

The Geography of Religion

Substantive and methodological writing that deals with religion within the field of geography is small in bulk and scattered among publications in several languages. Although geographers have long recognized that religious ideas and organization may play an important role in the way man occupies and shapes the land, important geographic studies focusing on this theme only recently have begun to appear.

D. E. Sopher[1]

THE STUDY OF RELIGION WITHIN THE GEOGRAPHIC FRAMEWORK

Although it is usual now to view the relationship between religion and geography in terms of the geography of religion, this has not always been the case.

Religious geography, in which the basic element is religion and the land is thought to or made to conform to it, has existed since the ancient Greeks. Thus Anaximander, the first known Greek map-maker, looked on the world as a manifestation of a religious principle, namely the inviolability of the spatial order. One of the major tenets of religious geography was that a correspondence existed between the events and structures of the heavens and those of the world of men. Even today we find religious principles underlying the lay-out pattern of many

Asiatic towns and field systems. However once the geographer was released from the religious world view imposed on him by the medieval church, he had little further use for religious geography. Isaac, in an article tracing the development in geographical thought from religious geography to the geography of religion, sums up the present position:

> With the possible exception of city and regional planning, which often seem to follow principles derived from some cosmic vision and certainly have little to do with the needs of those who live in the planned area, religious geography is not part of the western geographer's métier.[2]

There are two further variations on the relationship between geography and religion. Biblical geography was an early form of historical geography although today this subject is left to the archaeologist. Ecclesiastical geography is specifically concerned with mapping out the spatial advance of the Church in terms of its own institutions and the political territories allocated to it.

The geographical study of observable religious phenomena is normally labelled the geography of religion and falls within the broad category of social geography. In America it is included in the specifically American sub-section of cultural geography. In England particularly, geographers have been slow to recognize the importance of religion in the field of social geography and in three standard English geographical reference books[3] no reference to religion could be discovered. Even among American books I find no reference to the geography of religion in a work assessing the state of American geography published in 1954.[4] However by 1959, Broek, writing on the progress in the field of human geography, states that religion is a major element in any culture and deeply affects a people's way of life.[5] He then examines some of the geographical consequences of this.

Two definitive works on social geography written by English geographers each mention religion as a significant component of the subject. R. E. Pahl, in a recent discussion on trends in social geography, defines the field as

> the processes and patterns involved in an understanding of socially defined populations in their spatial setting.[6]

He sees social geography as the discipline which is fundamentally concerned with the spatial manifestations of social change:

> The social geographer is thus interested in the broad changes of population structure and distribution as the very necessary first stage in his analysis. From the basic demographic aspect, the analysis might proceed to such aspects as the geography of mortality rates, religion or occupational groups.[7]

A second definitive work on social geography, by J. W. Watson,[8] would also allow for a study of religion. He shows it is often thought that geographers should only concern themselves with the material element of the landscape, but he points out that if they do they forfeit their claims to describe the earth in terms of regional differentiation:

> The fact is, social geography is needed because geography, if it is to be successful, must describe the total relationship of a place, in comparison with other places. Not least among those relationships are social ones.[9]

Watson sees social geography as confining itself to social patterns, as opposed to sociology which is primarily concerned with social processes. The social geographer's first task is to note the material objects of the cultural landscape, such as cities, farms and churches. Then statistical data on population, race, language and religion can be fitted into the picture, and finally a study of the social groups and their activities is made. The vital criterion is the way these phenomena provide a distinctive character to the regions they fill.

There can be little doubt that the geography of religion fits squarely into the theoretical framework of social geography. So far however the geography of religion has been relatively neglected by geographers.

STUDIES IN THE GEOGRAPHY OF RELIGION

Much of the work carried out in this field is of a varied and diffuse nature. Despite the attempt by Sopher[10] to sketch out what has been described as a 'frontier territory', there is still a need for a collation of the studies dealing with the geography of religion. There follows a brief résumé of some of the most definitive studies, and an attempt has been made in the Bibliography to list all the available material.

France

Beginning in 1931 with the work of Gabriel le Bras,[11] France gave birth to a series of socio-geographic studies of religious distributions. Unfortunately these studies were described as religious sociology and were thus ignored by the majority of social geographers. They arose out of a practical desire to help the work of the Church by supplying an accurate picture of the Church's position within the general society. At first Le Bras's work was received with grave suspicion and he worked on his own for many years. Eventually he was joined by Boulard[12] who, in his capacity as organizer of the French Catholic Rural Movement, collected a vast store of information on the religious situation in rural France. They were later joined by Godin[13] and at last they managed to create an awareness of the usefulness of the studies.

Le Bras looked on the collection of statistical and demo-graphic data as the first stage in the long-term task of assessing the religious vitality of areas. This concept of religious vitality was undoubtedly one of the greatest contributions made by Le Bras to the geography of religion. He described this vitality as the degree to which overt religious behaviour is funda-mentally religiously motivated, and he contrasted this with religious observance (i.e. practice) which is frequently devoid of religious meaning, reflecting instead the strength of social custom. Le Bras had hoped that other researchers would take up the challenge of formulating techniques for assessing vitality, but he has met with little response. Nearly all the work has been concerned with the collection of attendance statistics and with attempts to establish correlations between attendance and the environment and between attendance and social class. This work has been labelled 'sociography'.

In 1954 the final version of the Religious Map of Rural France was published (Map 1). This is essentially a map of practice and not of vitality, that is of quantity and not necessarily of quality, and it is also a map of rural France (towns with over 200 persons per square kilometre were excluded from the survey). Three categories of practice are distinguished.

Category A are the areas of majority practice where 45–100% of the adult population (21 years and over) make Easter communion and in principle attend Sunday Mass. Adults were chosen because they create the religious climate of an area, whereas the practice of young people tends to fall off in adult life when they return from national service and begin setting up home.

Category B are the areas of minority practice and seasonal conformity. Below 45% of the adult population attend Easter communion and in principle Sunday Mass, but the population still retains its Catholic traditions and participates in the great religious events of life. People still observe the *rites de passage* (baptism, marriage, and burial) and usually the children make their solemn first communion.

Category C are mission areas partially detached from the ministrations of the Church, where a part of the population has deliberately dissociated itself from the Church. Statistically these areas are represented by a minimum of 20% of the children who are not baptized or attending catechism.

At the time of its publication the map was described as revealing great variety but not chaos. The regions of majority practice are the fringe areas—Brittany, the Pyrenees, the Massif Central, and the Jura, all of which are furthest away from the cities, and the great industrial areas. Zones of minority practice (Category B) include all the centre of France and part of the north, with Paris as its focus. There is also an area around Bordeaux, and a further one centred on Marseilles with an extension into Languedoc and Roussillon. Significantly there is no area of majority practice between Paris and Bordeaux. Mission areas are found in the Paris Basin and also along the line of the Garonne valley. A more detailed examination highlights the correlation between the 'de-Christianizing' of an area, and the existence of towns and important lines of communication.

Many Frenchmen, who had been accustomed to regarding religion as part of the private, individual sphere of life, were alarmed by this talk of a geography of religion. Boulard writes:

> Let us consider in more detail this fact that there is a geography
> of religion. It is a disconcerting fact, because we are so used to
> looking upon religious practice exclusively as an individual
> responsibility. Yet here we find that it is not only individuals
> whom we must classify as practising, indifferent, or cut off from
> the Church, but whole regions as well. It is true that we had a
> rough idea that there were Christian and dechristianized
> regions in France. Now we have this scientifically
> established. . . .[14]

Naturally this provoked cries of 'determinism', but it was
impossible to deny the powerful influence of the environment.
It was calculated that if 200 Bretons selected at random were
scattered round the Beauce, 150–160 of them would quickly
give up all practice of religion.

With the recognition of immense areas of minority practice,
explanations had to be concerned with general rather than local
causes. It was found that even in very religious regions, patches
of lower practice occurred and these were almost invariably
coterminous with industrial areas. Boulard held that the spirit of
secularism, which originates in the towns, arrives by the
agency of factories and industrial development, and also to a
lesser extent by the agencies of tourism and temporary migrations.

In his attempt to account for the geographical pattern of
religious practice in country areas, Boulard turned to historical
causation rather than to contemporary social problems. He was
able to produce four maps of the Diocese of Toulouse showing
the religious practice over the last 100 years. All four maps
reveal the same basic geographical pattern—the same isolated
areas have always had the highest practice, and the Garonne
Valley has always been the weakest. These maps pointed to the
conclusions that dechristianization was not new, and that
religious stability within areas was greater than was usually
thought.

A further way of analysing religious practice is according to
occupation group, for although a man belongs to a geographical
area, he is also part of a specific social milieu. Boulard found,
for example, that the working milieu of the French quarryman

was distinctly anti-Christian. The danger of focusing attention on the social milieu in any one area is that comparison between areas is eliminated. However by making a comparative study of the religious practice of one social group within different regions, the influence of geographical factors again becomes apparent. In general terms it was found that the same spatial distributions were to be observed for each of the social groups.

The work of Le Bras, Boulard and their contemporaries has shown that in France geographical regions have a religious tonality of their own. As a general rule an individual parish does not make progress independently of its neighbouring parishes. Based on the results of the sociographical work undertaken, its exponents have been enabled to speak clearly and definitively of a geography of religion in France.

Scandinavia

In the study of religion in Scandinavia, information of a geographical nature has been a by-product of sociological analysis, which in turn grew out of the work of church historians. Only Norway has a question on religion in her official census: Denmark omitted such a question in 1920 and Sweden in 1930.

In Norway therefore the census provides the raw material for any study of religious distributions. The population of Norway is strikingly homogeneous considering it is scattered over a country with tremendous regional differences between coastal and inland areas, the east and the west, the south and the arctic north. In his discussion of Protestantism in Norway, Vogt shows that since the Reformation the population has been exposed to the same official religion through the same sort of clergy and identical religious institutions. He writes:

> The very great differences in 'religiosity' between the various regions makes it an interesting test-ground for theories about the importance of geographical factors on religion, in particular of communication facilities, density of population, prevailing types of economic life, etc.[15]

So far, however, these theories have not been tested in any detail in Norway.

Work in Sweden has been extremely limited, and the small amount which has been undertaken has been the result of private initiative—primarily through the Religionssociologiska Institute in Stockholm. Its director, Gustafsson, has published a work on the geography of religious distributions in Sweden.[16] He assessed the present patterns on the basis of membership and communicant statistics and in his book he stresses the differences between the various regions and attempts to produce some tentative explanations.

Gustafsson emphasizes the necessity for continuous and exact statistical data in order to build up trend studies.[17] This concept of sequence is vital to the geography of religion for it provides a dynamic approach to the subject which the other methods do not.

Further information of interest to the geographer may come out of the Swedish work on folk religiosity. The Swedish religious scene is characterized by a minimal participation in divine worship, coupled with a maximum participation in religious ceremonies (*rites de passage*, and the big festivals). Folk religion conveys the basic religious themes by symbolic media, without the need for expression in words.

Once techniques can be devised for investigating folk piety and criteria discovered for measuring its variation in strength and vitality, it could well become a vital element in the social geographer's analysis of a region. It probably reflects an area's religious personality far better than any analysis of institutional practice.

The rest of Europe

Many of the studies undertaken on the continent of Europe have been of a sociographical nature modelled on the work of Le Bras. As early as 1952 a map of religious practice in Belgium was published,[18] based on Mass attendance statistics (Belgium is overwhelmingly Roman Catholic). It was found that the greatest abstentions from formal religious practice were in the provinces of Hainaut, Liège, and Brabant. In these provinces lie the large urban centres, and the big industrial areas based on coal, metallurgy and textiles. In general it appeared that people in French-speaking Belgium to the south of the linguistic divide, along with those in parts of Brussels, practised their religion less than those in Flemish-speaking Belgium.

Similar sociographic work has been carried out in the Netherlands. Traditionally the Netherlands has been regarded as a Protestant country, and the dominantly Puritan spirit of the peoples to the north of the rivers has stamped the national character. However, an analysis of the results of the 1960 National Census revealed there were more Roman Catholics in the Netherlands than there were Protestants. When the results were mapped it was found that the percentage of Roman Catholics in the total population base increased steadily from north to south, and that the two southern provinces of North Brabant and Limburg had percentages of over 85.

Studies along similar lines have also been undertaken in Italy and Spain, where the populations are almost entirely Roman Catholic. Because of the Protestant-Roman Catholic divisions with Germany, analysis of religious practice has not been so easy and instead the German geographers have concentrated their attention on the relationships between religion and the environment.

M. P. Fogarty[19] has taken all the available sociographic evidence in his attempt to analyse the geographical variations in religious practice over the whole of continental Europe. He delimits a belt of high religious practice running right across Western Europe from Holland, Belgium, French Flanders, and Alsace-Lorraine, through the Rhineland into South Germany and Austria, Switzerland and parts of North Italy—the so-called 'Christian Heartland of Europe' (Map 2). This belt contains a large Protestant as well as Roman Catholic population, and a high level of religious practice is common to both.

In Germany, religious observance among Protestants falls off fairly consistently from the west and south towards Berlin and the north coast. Similarly Roman Catholic practice is highest in the south and west and diminishes northwards and eastwards. It was in the north and east that during the Nazi period the paganized 'German Christian' movement made most progress.

There is a similar, though this time predominantly Roman Catholic zone of low practice, covering most of Italy, Spain, and France on the other side of the heartland belt. In discussing the pattern of religious observance in France, Fogarty disputes Boulard's interpretation. Whereas the French map, taken on its own, suggests a correlation between religious observance and fringe areas, when placed within the context of the European pattern of observance, a different interpretation is possible. The eastern and northern zones of high practice like Veneto and certain of the sub-alpine lands are part of the outer edge of the central heartland belt.

To the west and south of the heartland are the great sanctuaries of Lourdes and Rome; islands of intellectual and missionary activity such as Madrid and Paris; and even zones of high practice as in west France and north-west Spain. However the main impression, by contrast with the central belt, is of an uneven and usually low standard of religious practice. Interestingly the birthplaces of both Roman Catholicism and Protestantism lie in the 'religious wilderness'. Wittenberg in Saxony stands right in the eastern Protestant desert. Rome lies well to the south of the heartland and its proportion of practising Catholics is comparable to that in central France and well below the level of Holland or West Germany.

Some of Fogarty's work can be faulted. The statistical material upon which he bases his assumptions varies greatly in accuracy and coverage—he admits he has no information on the situation in Switzerland. Furthermore his work in this field is primarily concerned with establishing the numerical size of the Christian population base, which he uses in his analysis of Christian Democracy in Western Europe. He was not concerned with assessing in detail the geographical pattern of religious observance, although his concept of a central heartland is a theory which the geographer of religion should investigate.

Meyer and Strietelmeier[20] point out the obvious distinction between Protestant North Sea Europe and Roman Catholic Mediterranean Europe. Then they focus their attention on the area between the two and put forward an interesting theory:

> These two stronghold areas are separated from each other by a belt of religious interdigitation which extends through Central

Europe from the English Channel to the Netherlands, through Central Germany and north-eastward to the mouth of the Vistula. It is possibly significant that through most of this belt the physiographic pattern is a rather complex mosaic of hill masses and river valleys, conducive to the development of tiny political units which, under absolutist rulers, tended to become also religious units.[21]

Intensive and detailed investigations by geographers in these critical areas would certainly produce significant results for the testing of the heartland theory.

The United States

Work on the geography of religion in the U.S.A. is rather varied. Two classic studies by Zelinsky and Hotchkiss will be discussed in some detail as they contribute to the methodology of the subject. A recent publication by Sopher[22] has attempted to bring together much of the scattered material on the geography of religion but he has not carried out any further analysis of the situation in the States. Isaac's work has been concerned with the relationship between the landscape and religion and will be discussed on page 18.

In the late 1940s W. A. Hotchkiss[23] accepted the task of formulating a 'Master Plan for Protestantism in Cincinnati' as a way of testing the validity of geographical analysis in the field of organized religion. Being a geographer he saw the central concern of his research as being:

The significance of religion in the total geographic complex of an area.[24]

He advances the case for the study of religion within the framework of geography in the following passage:

The character of the religious institutions of a segment of the earth's surface is an integral part of the chorographic unique-ness of the area. Cincinnati's religion, for example, is as much a part of the uniqueness of the city as its machine tool industry, its Carew tower, or its *sangerfest*. The functional interrelationship of the religious institutions with all the other patterns, whose total character differentiates this urban area, is the point of departure from which this study was begun.[25]

He expresses each denomination as a percentage of the total religious community in each state, and by plotting these variations he is able to show the relative distributions. In discussing the patterns of location within the different denominations he asserts that there are two controlling factors: namely the distribution of the people whom the particular denomination wishes to serve, and the organizational theory of that denomination.

The Douglass Survey of Cincinnati[26] found that over half the churches making returns had compact parishes with over two-thirds of their members living within a mile of the church. A further 30% had moderately nucleated parishes, and only 15% had dispersed parishes with less than one-third of their members living within a mile of the church. These dispersed parishes were mainly characteristic of the smaller denominations and of the downtown city churches. By contrast the churches of the major denominations normally had compact geographical parishes from which they drew the majority of their members. Hotchkiss carried out a survey in one particular community and plotted the positions of church members in relation to their churches. The results revealed a tendency for a local church to serve its 'natural area' on an inclusive basis, irrespective of denominational labels.

Hotchkiss also dealt with the visible effect of religion on the Cincinnati landscape and looking down from the top of Carew Tower he observes:

> From this vantage point, the institution of religion is a rather prominent part of the landscape. The characteristic spires and towers of the downtown churches are recognizable in the midst of the more massive office buildings. Away from the central business district immediately around us, where the general level of the buildings is lower, the churches stand out more prominently, and on the top of the escarpment several church structures are the most prominent feature of the landscape.[27]

In conclusion Hotchkiss takes Hartshorne's interpretation of the nature of geography[28] and shows how his thesis has demonstrated each of these criteria in a specific situation. With regard to the differential character of religion, he has shown that the religious groups studied have an areal variation over the States as a whole, within Cincinnati itself, and even within the community selected for detailed study. He has also illustrated that religion is interrelated with other phenomena in space on the three levels of country, urban area, and local community; Finally:

> That organized religion as a geographic phenomenon has a significant areal expression has been demonstrated in two types of data. One, is organized religion as a visible part of the landscape, in the pattern and form of buildings used for religious purposes. Two, is organized religion as part of the activity pattern which is not directly visible in its areal expression.[29]

By activity patterns not directly visible, he was thinking of the location of members of specific churches, and also of the proportion of a certain religious group in the population of an area.

Hotchkiss's work provides the geographer with a most helpful methodology for the geographical study of religion within a given limited area, such as an English county or part of a county.

One of the few attempts at a systematic account of the geography of religion within a given country has been undertaken by W. Zelinsky.[30] He admits at the onset that a lack of adequate material and statistics has limited his work to an analysis of membership statistics as provided by the denominations themselves.

Denominational allegiance varied greatly in strength from place to place within the U.S.A. and it was on the basis of this that Zelinsky advanced his religious regions of the U.S.A. The Mormon area around Salt Lake City provided him with a classic case of a human geographical region in which religion was the originating factor as well as the reason for the persistent distinctiveness of the area.[31]

Part of the unique personality of south-eastern Pennsylvania is due to its large quota of 'peculiar people' and other staunch church members for whom religion has been a dominant force.

Certain small colonies of pietists have created micro-regions very different in form and function from their surroundings. The special regional character of New England is due in part to its 'quasi-theocratic past' and also to the unique blend of denominations working in the state.

Zelinsky admits that in most instances religion is not used to differentiate regions and that few Americans are aware of the regional variations in denominational allegiance. He attempts, however, to delimit religious regions based on patterns of church membership and suggests that there is a correlation between these and other cultural phenomena. He concludes as follows:

> From the scanty evidence available, we have reasonable grounds for proposing the hypothesis that religion is a significant element in the population geography of the U.S., in the geography of a number of economic, social, and cultural phenomena, and in the genesis and persistence of general cultural regions; but we have too little knowledge of the precise ways in which religion operates in these various directions. Devising ways to collect and interpret information for testing this hypothesis may prove to be one of the most difficult, but also potentially one of the most rewarding tasks awaiting the student of American cultural geography.[32]

Great Britain

Among British geographers the geography of religion has been almost totally neglected. There are however one or two exceptions: Emrys Jones's study of Belfast being one.[33] It is no coincidence that the official census of Northern Ireland includes a question on religion, whereas geographers in the rest of Britain have no such source material on which to draw. Concerning religion in Belfast, Jones writes:

> Here our main concern will be with the relative strength of the Protestant denominations in various parts of the city, as revealed in maps of their density. For the distribution of Presbyterians, Episcopalians and Methodists is by no means random.[34]

Before Jones's work, Estyn Evans, in an article on the site and city of Belfast,[35] had examined the distribution of religious groups in order to illustrate the importance of long-established factors for the social geography of a modern city.

Religious strife is an accepted feature of Belfast, and in order to measure this, Jones devised an Index of Segregation. He found that in broad terms segregation decreased with a rise in socio-economic ranking. His study of religion in Belfast has by no means explained the patterns of religious distributions, but it has pointed to significant correlations:

> The mapping of distributions and segregations does not completely explain these two phenomena. It does suggest correlations with the distribution of socio-economic data, but its main function is to illustrate differences in various sectors of the city, and these sectors themselves have historical and environmental characteristics of their own in which lie some of the complex factors governing religious distribution.[36]

It is doubtful whether similar work could be carried out in the rest of Britain. There has been no section on religion in the National Census since 1851 and so the basic information is lacking. Any one geographer is unlikely to have the resources to collect all the necessary information for himself. However Jones has pointed the way to lines of approach which could be adopted where the source material is available.

A number of studies on or relating to the geography of religion have been undertaken in Wales. The most significant and far reaching have been those of E. G. Bowen. Although he has dealt at length with the relatively recent phenomenon of Nonconformist Wales,[37] his main concern is with the early Celtic saints and the influence they have exerted on settlement patterns.[38] This aspect of the geography of religion has been taken up by D. Sylvester in an article entitled 'The Church and the Geographer'.[39] Further works by Sylvester,[40] G. J. Lewis[41] and J. E. Daniel[42] also add to the Welsh contribution to the geography of religion.

No other British geographers, apart from them, have embarked on a study of religion as the primary objective. A number of others have touched on religion in a secondary or incidental way, but the material is slight in amount and does not add significantly to the subject.

2

THE EFFECT OF THE ENVIRONMENT UPON RELIGION

The relationship between religion and the environment can be approached in one of two ways. The first is to investigate how the environment, including the people and the physical landscape, affects a religious form. This approach does not strictly fall within the scope of the geography of religion, and is better tackled by theology and by the science of religion, with geography furnishing the necessary particulars about landscapes, climates and regions. However several geographers have chosen to handle the subject in this way and so their results ought to be examined.

In three of his works, E. Huntington discusses questions of environmental determinism as relating to religion:

> Every religion is at least modified by its surroundings, especially those of its birthplace.[43]

The objects of worship themselves are frequently determined by geographical factors. Thus in India, where the rains are uncertain, the Rain God is one of the most prominent deities. For similar reasons the Nile was once an object of religious adoration in Egypt. Christianity originated in a dry region where sheep-herding was one of the chief occupations and this led to the widespread use in the Bible of the 'Sheep-Shepherd' metaphor.

Huntington also argues that Christianity flourishes best in regions of high climatic energy. Christianity is a religion which insists on high ethical and spiritual standards, and where old outliers of Christianity have persisted in geographical regions which are relatively unfavourable to human vigour, there has been a tendency towards the lowering of these standards, as the history of Christianity in South India and Ethiopia illustrates.

Huntington points out that he is not saying that 'high types' of religion are impossible in unfavourable climatic conditions, but rather that they require greater efforts than most people feel like making in such an environment. People of low efficiency seem to remain true to a 'high' religion only when they are stimulated by the presence of a stronger race.

The necessary effort to maintain the rigorous standards of a 'high' religion can be more easily made in North Sea countries, north and west U.S.A., and in New Zealand. Moving northwards from Ethiopia to Holland, Huntington shows that both Protestantism and Catholicism assume a higher form, whereby religion and ethics become more closely related, ceremonies assume less importance, and the keywords become self-sacrifice, service and self-control.

E. C. Semple[44] has also discussed the question of the effect of the environment on religion. The imagery and symbolism of a religion is greatly affected by its place of birth:

> The Eskimo's hell is a place of darkness, storm and intense cold; the Jew's is a place of eternal fire. Buddha, born in the steaming Himalayan piedmont, fighting the lassitude induced by heat and humidity, pictured his heaven as Nirvana, the cessation of all activity and individual life.[45]

Both Semple and Huntington have argued that the desert environment has been the determinant in shaping the monotheism of Judaism, Christianity and Islam. However this view is largely discredited now.

The Indian geographer, G. Kuriyan,[46] has continued the work of Semple and Huntington in the field of religion. For example, he conceives of a geographical explanation as to why Christ was unable to find disciples in his own city of Nazareth and instead had to turn to the fishermen of Galilee. The men of Nazareth were patient cultivators whose little gardens or hillsides were ringed by walls of stone. Like all cultivators they were rooted to the soil and could rarely move away from their homes as the land has to be constantly tended. The horizon of their minds was limited to the walls which shut in their corner of the earth and by nature they were against novelty and change. On the other hand the fishermen of Galilee were nomadic by virtue of their occupation. Fishing was a haphazard business and hence their readiness to uproot themselves and chance the integrity of a wandering teacher.

Meyer and Strietelmeier[47] rightly stress the fact that each religion has been greatly affected by its new environment on moving away from its place of origin. They raise the question as to how Christianity might have fared had it moved south into the tropics rather than north, or if it had developed in India rather than within the framework of Greek logic. They also emphasize that the cultural expressions of particular beliefs are primarily the products of specific environments. Thus the Jewish dietary laws prohibiting the consumption of pork made a great deal of sense in the warm Palestinian climate, even if today the laws appear to be archaic.

Few geographers are now concerned with examining the effect of the environment on religion. The earlier enthusiasm on the part of geographers to explain religion as the product of the environment has been largely abandoned.

THE EFFECT OF RELIGION UPON THE ENVIRONMENT

Fickeler[48] sees the task of the geography of religion as investigating the way a religion affects a people, a landscape, and a country. This is the approach which has been adopted by the majority of geographers who have considered the relationship between religion and the environment. It is certainly the most tangible and empirical line of study.

However there is a danger that such work can become merely a catalogue of landscape phenomena which have been influenced and altered in some way by religion. The large volume on the geography of religion by P. Deffontaines[49] is one such example. An article by P. Fickeler,[50] while having a useful analytical introduction, falls into the same trap. Descriptive cataloguing is necessary, but to be of any lasting value it must be accompanied by geographical assessment.

One of the main exponents of the effect which religion exerts upon the landscape is Eric Isaac. He defines the geography of religion as:

> The study of the part played by the religious motive in man's transformation of the landscape.[51]

> ... the task of the geography of religions is to separate the specifically religious from the social, economic and ethnic matrix in which it is embedded and to determine its relative weight in relation to other forms in transforming the landscape.[52]

In a number of articles Isaac gives a series of examples of the effect of religion upon the landscape. He makes the assumption, along with many other western geographers, that the landscape in west European and American Christian countries is much less influenced by religion than the landscape in Asian countries. This is a highly debatable issue and the prevalent view may well be the result of western geographers being more accustomed to church spires than to Hindu temples.

German geographers have been most prominent in the investigation of the effect of religion on the landscape. A. Sievers, in an article on Christianity and the landscape in south-west Ceylon, distinguishes between the dominant Buddhistic 'Dagoba landscape' and certain coastal stretches of Christian landscape. Of the Christian landscape he writes:

> This is expressed in the spiritual and social structure of the prevailingly Christian population, in the frequency of Christian church and lay buildings and the visible worship of Christian symbols and also in the many social, welfare and cultural institutions which extend their beneficial effects also to the non-Christian population.[53]

He illustrates his concept of a Christian cultural landscape by taking three examples from the hot, humid west coast to the north of Colombo.

In a discussion on religion and the landscape in Japan, L. Mecking is concerned primarily with the religious features which appear on the Japanese landscape[54]—temples, holy parks, holy bridges, tea houses for pilgrims and so on. In a similar article dealing with the Indo-Chinese landscape, W. Credner[55] describes the different types of cult buildings to be observed on the landscape.

H. Hahn has investigated the relationship between denomination social structure in the Hunsrück and Tecklenburg districts of Germany. In his conclusion he states:

> A social geographical analysis of the connexions between denomination and social structure shows beyond doubt that there is a different attitude of these denominations (Roman Catholic and Protestant) towards economic life. The denominations as social groups emerge in this way as landscape-forming agencies of the first order.[56]

In his work on Lebanon, W. Klaer[57] has illustrated that the varying religious beliefs of the inhabitants of various parts of the Lebanon have led to contrasting social structures and to related visible contrasts in the cultural landscapes of the areas concerned.

American geographers have also produced some good working examples. Hotchkiss's study has already been mentioned, as has the work of Eric Isaac. A specific study of a small area showing how religious factors have exerted a marked effect on the landscape is given by J. Warkentin[58] in a discussion of the Mennonite agricultural settlements of Southern Manitoba. The Mennonites, being an extremist Protestant sect from Russia, wished to insulate themselves from the outside world and felt the self-sufficient life of the agricultural village was their best form of protection. Despite the land being measured out according to the regular rectangular survey, on arrival in Canada the Mennonites were able to create the nucleated village pattern of the Old World. Although only seventeen of the original seventy villages remain, the religious convictions of the Mennonites are still revealed on the landscape:

> ... their (the villages') presence is revealed for miles around by the long rows of cottonwoods that rise from the flat plain and mark the village streets, and by the fact that the landscape in the immediate surrounding area is completely bereft of farmsteads.[59]

Mission establishments in pioneer areas have frequently played a dominant role in creating the present man-made landscape—e.g. the great Jesuit missions in South America. Similarly in California the Franciscan missions exerted a great formative influence on the landscape.[60]

Religion can also exert an indirect effect on the landscape through the injunctions it issues to its members. Zimpel's study[61] of the eastern Mediterranean landscape is a good example of this. He shows how religion affects demographic trends which in turn have a visible consequence on the landscape. Food taboos and ritual requirements (e.g. fish on Friday) are another case in point and are discussed in some detail by Sopher.[62]

Although a number of geographers have already tackled the effect of religion on the environment, it is a field which still offers great scope for exploration. So far most geographers have concentrated either on the supposedly more religious landscapes of non-European and non-North American countries, or on the more unusual aspects of religion in their home countries.

CHAPTER TWO

The Sources

It is one of the idiosyncrasies of the English people to regard enquiries into a person's religion as something unheard of.

M. A. J. M. Matthijssen[1]

INTRODUCTION

The empirical study of religion is fraught with difficulties. Objective criteria of measurement are necessary but extremely hard to obtain. One of the pioneer investigators, Charles Booth, concluded that spiritual influences did not easily lend themselves to statistical treatment and that if the statistics were trusted too much they could be very dangerous. The history of the empirical investigation into religion in this country over the last hundred years is littered with examples of dogmatic and general conclusions based on very shaky evidence. It is essential therefore to assess carefully any source material in order to discover its degree of reliability.

The availability of source material relating to religion in England is very limited. In many countries the state gathers statistics of the religious composition of its population through the agency of its population census: people are required to register their religious adherence on the census returns.[2] In England the census has never included any question on religious adherence largely as a consequence of the controversy that developed over the 1851 Census of Attendance at places of worship. There are only two occasions on which an individual is asked formally by the state to declare his religion: admission to hospital, and committal to prison:[3] and in neither of these cases are the statistics disclosed. Since the 1851 Census no further attempts have been made by the government to collect information on religious practice. The only official statistics on religion published by the state are related to marriages.

It is largely on account of this lack of census statistics that the geography of religion has been neglected in this country. The alternative approach of examining the vast quantity of other material is much more complex and involves wading through great piles of information which might possibly impinge upon the subject. Much of this material had to be rejected as being far too subjective and unverifiable. It is the residue which is now of concern.

DENOMINATIONAL STATISTICS

Each of the major religious denominations issues lists of its membership totals and these totals are broken down into geographical units—usually the county. These provide the geographer with a great potential of information but certain provisos are necessary. Membership figures tell little of how active a person is or what he believes. Some will lapse and remain on the books while keen attenders may never apply for membership. The statistics have been used for time studies going back into the 19th century but this is very difficult to carry out accurately as the criteria for membership also change with time. Each denomination defines its own requirements for membership and has its own internal discipline for seeing that members fulfil their obligations—a discipline varying in severity from the strictness of some of the evangelical sects to an almost total absence in the Church of England. It is difficult therefore to undertake comparative studies between denominations on the basis of membership statistics.

For a study of the geographical pattern of allegiance within a given denomination, membership figures are of tremendous

2*

value. Assuming the definition of membership and method of collecting the figures are constant over the whole country, then they will give a good picture of the varied allegiance to that denomination. As membership figures will be used extensively in later chapters a proper assessment on a denominational basis is necessary.

The Church of England

The Church of England has never officially defined its understanding of membership. From the time of the Reformation to the end of the 17th century it was a punishable offence to be regularly absent from worship at the parish church—everyone was assumed (and compelled) to be a practising Anglican. With the easing of restrictions in the 18th century, the *de facto* existence of Nonconformist and Roman Catholic communities was recognized, but the rest of the population was counted as Anglican. People had begun to suspect that for many, membership of the Church of England was very nominal and tenuous, and with the publication of the 1851 Census results revealing that $5\frac{1}{4}$ million lay outside the ministrations of the Church, this suspicion now rested on solid evidence. Yet there still lingered the feeling that all who had not deliberately dissociated themselves were in some way still members of the Church of England.

The whole issue of membership in the Church of England is bound up with Establishment. The nation granted the Church of England a privileged position and recognized it as the church which had prime responsibility for the spiritual welfare of the English people. On this basis it has been argued that all citizens of England living within the geographical boundaries of the Provinces of Canterbury and York are *ipso facto* members of the Church of England. However some citizens have consciously placed themselves outside her communion by joining other churches and it would be totally unrealistic to count them among her members.

Similarly what of the increasing number of people who have no effective church connection of any kind and yet still claim a right to her ministrations and would no doubt write 'C of E' on any form asking them to state their religion? The Church of England is not completely lacking in membership requirements and in Canon 21 parishioners have to receive Holy Communion 'at least thrice in the year (whereof the feast of Easter be one), according as they are appointed by the Book of Common Prayer'. Thus a minimum participation in public worship is required from her members. However this Canon dates from the time when virtually everybody would have been confirmed by a bishop and so able to receive Communion. Today there is a considerable group of people within the Church of England who attend regularly at non-sacramental worship (i.e. Matins and Evensong) but as they have not been confirmed they are unable to receive Communion. Any definition of membership which excluded this group would be of dubious value.[4]

This problem of definition was forced into the limelight in the early years of this century when it was decided to form a House of Laity as part of the Church Assembly, consisting of elected representatives of the Anglican laity. Who was to be allowed to vote? Eventually it was decided to admit to the Electoral Roll[5] all baptized persons of eighteen and over who signed a written statement to say they were members of the Church of England. Episcopal confirmation was not used as a test of eligibility. Useful as the Electoral Roll statistics might be in theory, in practice they are of little help. Many incumbents object to the concept of a list of members and so refuse to keep theirs up-to-date. Furthermore the Electoral Roll is used as a convenient loophole through the complicated marriage laws and a good percentage of names on many electoral lists will be of people who wanted to be married in that particular church but lived outside its geographical parish.[6]

Confirmation is the nearest equivalent in the Anglican Church to the Free Church procedure of admitting members, although its age limit is lower—candidates can be confirmed in their last year at Junior School when they are eleven. All candidates undergo a period of instruction, the contents of which are usually left to the discretion of the priest now that the Prayer Book Catechism is generally disregarded. The culmination is the confirmation itself when the candidate re-affirms the vows made on his behalf at baptism, and is admitted by the bishop into full communicant membership of the Church.

How valuable are the confirmation statistics to the geographer? Certainly the records are accurate, as the totals from the confirmation registers are sent in annually. However confirmation is a 'once and for all' occasion and there is no subsequent procedure for removing the name of a person who fails to attend church at some period in the future. So confirmation cannot be compared directly with Free Church membership, for whatever the inadequacies of the Free Church membership lists at least they are supposed to be revised annually. Furthermore it is difficult to believe that all confirmation candidates are going forward out of conviction, for in many suburban churches, in some Church of England primary schools, and in most public schools, confirmation is part of the social convention. Even if communicant status reflected active membership of the Church of England, the records would be of no help to the geographer, for there is no system of transferring membership from one church to another. Once the newly-confirmed person moves away from his home parish all trace of him is lost. We know there are nearly 10 million[7] confirmed members of the Church of England, but we have no method of assessing their geographical distribution.

Of even less value are the statistics for the number of baptized members of the Church of England—in all representing about 66% of the total population. Technically anyone who has been baptized in the Church of England can claim to be a member and is eligible to be included on the Electoral Roll. That only 13% of the baptized people aged 17 years and over bother to take this simple step of identification is a good indicator of just how nominal their membership really is.

There are no records of the actual size of the parish community who could be regarded as practising Anglicans and neither are there any Sunday by Sunday statistics of attendance. However, twice a year, at Easter and Christmas, the total number of communicants is counted and the figures are published for geographical units. As attendance at Easter communion is obligatory for Anglicans, these figures do give a general indication as to the size and distribution of those who take their duties seriously. It did not cheer the Anglican authorities to learn that only 6% of the total population has fulfilled the minimum requirements for membership as set out in Canon 21. Somewhere between this 6% and the 66% who were baptized in parish churches, lies the real membership of the Church of England (see Table 1).

On account of this lack of an accurate definition of membership and the duties of membership, in our assessment of the distribution of Anglicanism it will be necessary to use a variety of approaches.

The Roman Catholics

The overwhelming majority of Catholics are born into the Church and membership is formally bestowed on them through infant baptism. The Encyclical *Mystici Corporis Christi* laid down four conditions of membership of the Catholic Church: 'Only those are to be accounted really members of the Church who have been regenerated in the waters of Baptism and profess the true faith, and have not cut themselves off from the structure of the Body by their own unhappy act or been severed therefrom, for very grave crimes, by the legitimate authority.' At the age of seven or eight children are confirmed by a bishop and from then on are expected to attend Mass regularly.

During its eleven-year lifetime from 1953–64 the Newman Demographic Survey[8] tried to establish a proper system of membership statistics for the Catholic Church in England and Wales. The first task undertaken by the Survey was a study of all previously published statistics. They found that before 1911 the only available figures were for the numbers of clergy, churches and convents. Just before the First World War a tremendous effort was made to publish figures on a diocesan basis of infant baptisms, adult conversions, marriages, and total Catholic populations. The same four groups of statistics were still being collected in 1954 although several dioceses were also issuing figures of Confirmations, Mass Attendance, Paschal Confessions and deaths.

The Survey then attempted to assess the reliability of these statistics and the meaning that could be attached to them. It was found that each of the eighteen dioceses was using a different form, with different questions which were differently worded. Where notes were provided to help the parish priest understand what was required, these too varied between dioceses. Not all dioceses even gathered the four basic statistics from the same sources, the parish registers. At least two obtained their convert figures from Chancery records. It is therefore impossible to make use of any of these statistics for trend analyses from 1911 to the present.

The total Catholic population in each of the dioceses for the early 1950s was also examined by the Survey. Most of the dioceses merely asked the parish priest to state the 'Catholic Population' without any further explanation. One diocese in a holiday area asked for the number who lived in the area for the greater part of the year, and two in immigrant areas specified that foreigners were to be included. The texts of the documents sent out to parish priests made it clear that the definition of 'Catholic Population' was by no means uniform. Leaving the parish priests free to put on their own interpretation led to serious anomalies. Some excluded Catholics they regarded as 'lapsed', while others included unbaptized children of Catholic parents on the grounds that they 'ought' to be Catholics. In many cases foreigners, servicemen and temporary residents were omitted, and where the parish priest felt numerical totals affected various financial levies this tended to distort the returns sent in.

Since the late 1950s the instructions to the clergy include a standardized definition of 'Catholic Population' which incorporates all baptized Catholics normally resident in the parish, whether native or immigrant, practising or 'lapsed'.[9] However, despite this attempt at standardization, the figures are still essentially estimates by the parish clergy. Particularly in rural areas and high density loose-knit parishes these estimates can be little more than guesses. Furthermore it would be extremely difficult for most clergy to assemble the numbers of 'lapsed' Catholics. The arbitrary nature of some of the parish figures is revealed by the remarkable rise in the figure returned on the appointment of a new parish priest. Even if the Catholic

Population figures were accurate they would be of limited value in assessing the regional variations in allegiance to the Catholic Church, on account of their failure to differentiate between 'active' churchgoers and those who have severed all visible connection with Catholicism.

Of much greater value to the geographer are the figures taken by the Survey from the Parish Register Statistics for the number of people attending Mass. All the parishes were allocated to their appropriate county or county borough and the figures were given for these units, thereby enabling them to be related to the overall population. As attendance at Mass[10] is obligatory for Catholics it provides a reliable indicator of the quantity of overt support for the Church in a particular area. It is an easy test to apply, involving no qualitative judgments, but just simple head counting and recording. The degree of importance attached to Mass attendance is uniform thoughout the country and so the statistics can be safely used for areal comparison. However as these figures are only available for the period 1958–62 it is impossible to carry out any detailed studies of regional change in allegiance. Prior to the work of the Newman Demographic Survey one has to go back to the 1851 Census for comparable statistics covering the whole country.

The Free Churches

Each of the four major Free Church denominations publishes its membership figures on an annual basis, the figures being broken down into county or equivalent units. However, none assesses rates of attendance at Sunday worship, nor do they attempt to estimate the number of adherents who have not attained or requested full membership status. It is the declared membership figures therefore that are likely to be of value to the geographer. But what constitutes a member? How are the figures collected? How reliable are they? No general examination is satisfactory, for each of the main denominations is an independent unit with its own ways of operating. It is necessary to take each one separately and expose the definition of membership and the methods of collecting the returns to a critical examination.

The Baptists. Membership of all the Free Churches pre-supposes a definite personal conviction and certainly the Baptists are no exception. Indeed in some of the stricter chapels it would take the form of an explicit testimony. At first sight the requirements for membership appear to be extremely rigorous. Children are dedicated when young but are not baptized until they reach 'the age of conviction'. The so-called 'Believer's Baptism' by total immersion, which is the main distinctive feature of the Baptist Church, is rarely permitted under the age of 13, and stricter churches usually insist on a break of at least a year from leaving school.

Once baptism has been attained, the prospective member attends a course of prayer and instruction, at the end of which he is allowed to apply for membership. This application is duly considered at a private meeting of church members and if they are in favour, they instruct the minister to receive the person into membership at the next communion service and to enter his name on to the Roll of Members. However each Baptist congregation is independent and has the power to devise its own method of admitting members if it so wishes. The system outlined above is that adopted by the majority of churches, but the Baptist Union has no authority to insist on conformity. In general the churches of the 'closed' type are more selective and particular than those of the 'open' type.

Similarly the method of keeping the Membership Roll varies among churches. Strictly speaking the Roll is supposed to be revised once a year and this task is normally undertaken by the elders, as opposed to the deacons, sitting in private session. As soon as a member dies his name should be removed. If a member moves to a new district he can be transferred to his new Baptist church by means of a transfer certificate. If no request for such a certificate is made within a year his name is supposed to be struck off. A member can also be transferred to another denomination by this method. Any member who fails to attend a communion service once every three months would be visited by official representatives of the congregation and should he continue to absent himself he would be formally warned and then his name would be deleted.

If this procedure were observed in all churches, the membership statistics would provide an excellent guide to the strength of the denomination over the whole country. Unfortunately this is not the case and some Rolls are not revised for years on end. The Baptist Church has a weak central organization coupled with strong congregational autonomy, so little can be done centrally to insist on erring congregations improving their statistical book-keeping. Apart from a small number of very strict churches, most membership totals include elements of the following:

1 Non-Resident Members. There is usually a small proportion of people in any church membership list who keep their names on Roll for sentimental reasons instead of transferring their membership to a church in their new area of residence. This applies particularly to prestige churches.

2 Non-Attending Members—i.e. those whose membership has for one reason or another ceased to have much significance for them. In due time such names would be removed, but most churches are reluctant to do this while there is still any likelihood of the person resuming active church participation.

Although the membership figures, as recorded in *The Baptist Handbook*, may not be strictly accurate for any one particular church, they do provide us with a good working guide for the strength of the Baptists in a given area, particularly at a county level. There does not appear to be any reason why the method of roll-keeping should vary too much from region to region. Furthermore the provisos already mentioned fail to distort the basic picture of the Baptist Church which emerges and so we can safely use the membership statistics for areal comparisons by county.

The Presbyterian Church of England. The number of communicant members for each local church is published annually in the denomination's *Handbook*. Communicant member status confers the right to receive communion, and also the rights to vote in the meetings of the congregation, in the election of elders, and in the calling of a minister. A candidate for membership has to go through a course of instruction, the intensity of which will depend on the personal views of the minister and the maturity of the applicant. Full members of other denominations are usually received on 'certificate of transfer' without any further training. The lower age limit varies in practice but few members would be admitted under 15. Every member should be under the pastoral care of one of the elders and is therefore 'known'—he cannot lapse without this also being known.

Just how accurately do these communicant figures reflect the actual strength of the local congregation? The Session (i.e. all the elders plus the minister) has to revise the Membership Roll annually. Lapsed members who have failed to attend a communion service during the previous one or two years have their names removed unless there are extenuating circumstances. Clearly some Sessions will be stricter than others. In recent years financial reasons have caused a tightening up, as congregations now have their assessments for central fund payment based on membership figures. Most congregations can no longer afford to carry much dead wood.

After allowing for the chronic sick, the housebound and so on, the margin of inaccuracy is unlikely to exceed 5%.[11] Furthermore in most congregations there would be some loyal adherents, members in practically every respect but name and voting rights, who would make up for the inactive 5%. In all we can take the communicant membership figures as being substantially correct and providing a most useful indicator of Presbyterian allegiance.

The Congregational Church. Membership is by profession of faith, usually in the late teens, when the person is received into the congregation at a special ceremony and registered as a fully covenanted member. Most churches have a simple yet effective graduation system through the Sunday School into the Youth Fellowship and Sunday School teaching classes from where most of the new members are recruited. A small number come from other denominations by transfer certificate, usually occasioned by upward social mobility,[12] a neighbouring Free Church closing down, or a change in place of residence.

The responsibility for keeping a register of names, and submitting the membership totals to headquarters for annual publication rests entirely with the local church. Many churches do check through their lists on occasions but there is a marked reluctance to strike off any names. If a member moves away from the district and fails to request a transfer certificate, or if he remains in the locality but loses interest in the church, the probability is that his name will remain on the Roll. The Congregationalists have a similar system to the Presbyterians in using membership totals as one of the main factors in assessing payment quotas to headquarters and in recent years this has encouraged a greater degree of numerical realism. Where churches receive central fund grants for ministers' salaries accurate statistics are insisted upon.

Owing to the essential autonomy of the local congregation the basis of church membership is by no means standardized. The central body of the Congregational Church has set out a resumé of the privileges and obligations of membership,[13] but the responsibility for accepting and working out these principles in practice rests entirely with each local church. Nevertheless apart from a very few churches which would insist on strict theological tests, the *de facto* conditions for new members would be an active participation in the events of the church coupled with a commitment to support financially—both implied in the covenant relationship so essential to Congregationalism. Making allowance for a certain innate optimism in the majority of the returns (no minister is likely to underestimate the size of his flock), the author has come across no evidence which would invalidate their use for analysis of regional variations at a county level.

The Methodist Church. The organizational pattern of church life established by John Wesley, with its strong internal discipline, has resulted in a clearer definition of membership than is found in any of the other Free Churches. A person applying for membership has to show a sincere desire after salvation, produce evidence of this in his life and conduct, and be prepared to accept the duties and privileges of fellowship and the means of grace.[14] He will undergo a period of training and then be placed 'on trial' for a probationary period of not less than three months during which time he will be further instructed in church membership. At the end of this he will be received into full membership by decision of the Church

Leaders and is publicly recognized or 'Confirmed' at a service which concludes with a Communion Service. Few would achieve full membership before they were 15 and the rigorous training system ensures that most new members are sincere.

Once admitted, the new member is required to attend public worship, observe the two sacraments of Baptism and Communion, and attend, as far as possible, a Class Meeting or other assembly for Christian fellowship. It was the devising of the Class Meeting system which was Wesley's particular interest and contributed so greatly to the success of Methodism. It provided the vital link between the individual and the larger congregation, and the intensity of commitment and loyalty which could be generated in a stable group of ten or so people gave Methodism its essential cohesion. Through the Class Meeting also, a careful watch could be kept on any who were likely to fall by the wayside.

Records of membership totals are published annually[15] on a circuit[16] basis and it is the responsibility of each circuit, operating through its constituent class groupings, to furnish accurate returns. Members who die, move away from the area, or change denomination, would automatically be removed from the Roll. But how stringent is the procedure for removing the names of lapsed members? If the class leader realizes that a member has not attended his church for some time, this would be reported to the minister who would make pastoral enquiries. Such enquiries, and visits by the class leader with the member's quarterly Membership Ticket, could last up to eighteen months or two years. Finally the case would be brought before a disciplinary court consisting of the class leaders under the chairmanship of the minister who would declare the member had 'ceased to meet' and remove his name from the Roll.

This procedure is the norm throughout the country, although it tends to be applied with greater firmness in urban than in rural areas. In small rural chapels, families are often interrelated and it may be difficult to expel Mr. A., because he is the brother-in-law of the local steward, and so on. Thus the figures for rural circuits are likely to be slightly on the high side. Nevertheless the overall pattern revealed by the membership totals is an accurate reflection of Methodist allegiance, for the system of removing the names of dormant members is as efficient as any yet devised.

Other denominations

Owing to the diverse nature of the other religious groupings, their membership criteria and statistics will be analysed in the main discussion on their geographical coverage. Several general points, common to most of them, can be noted.

Many of the small groups are highly sensitive on the question of numerical size and strength and so it is rare to find ones which collect and make available statistics of membership and attendance. When asked for information of this kind, headquarters usually sent back a letter stating they were not worried about numerical size, only about intensity of commitment. The force of the argument, that a small band of twenty completely dedicated people is preferable to a nominal membership of 400, is very strong. The problem is that we have no effective way of measuring quality of religious belief and commitment. Particularly with the fundamentalist sects, their policy of exclusivism prevents the formation of a fringe of lukewarm adherents. You are either saved or damned, a sheep or a goat—there can be no half-way position.

While few publish membership data, most have lists of congregational meeting places and these lists are readily available. From them it is possible to plot the overall distribution of the sect concerned. Furthermore where a congregation has the services of a full-time paid minister or evangelist it would be safe to assume the congregation is of a reasonable size.

Along with Judaism, many of the new immigrant religions which are springing up in this country have a birthright membership and in so many of these instances it is virtually impossible to disentangle the religious factors from the national and cultural ones. However all these issues will be discussed within the context of the particular group concerned.

THE INSTITUTIONAL PRACTICE OF RELIGION

It is one thing to be on the Roll of a church, but it is another to attend regularly at services. Only the Roman Catholics collect any detailed information on church attendance and this provides a clear guide to Catholic practice. The Church of England's figures of Easter and Christmas communicant attendance are of limited significance as they are not representative of normal Anglican practice. From a geographical viewpoint they are suspect owing to the large number of people on holiday away from home at Christmas and Easter. The Free Churches have no records of attendance but they would rightly claim that their membership is to a reasonable degree in accord with their practice. With the stricter evangelical sects membership and active participation would be in almost complete coincidence—dormant members would be soon expelled.

Were it possible to obtain figures of institutional practice on a national basis, interdenominational comparisons would still be impractical, for the importance attached to church attendance varies so greatly. For a Roman Catholic to regularly absent himself from Mass is a grave sin: for an Anglican spasmodic appearances only are more easily excusable. This difficulty is often overlooked in local studies where a survey of attendance has been undertaken and the figures get presented as if they are directly comparable.

A consensus of a number of social surveys on religion shows that about 75% of the people in England believe it is possible to be a Christian without attending church. A clear dichotomy appears to have emerged between belief in religion and the institutional practice of religion. Some form or another of religion is almost universal in modern England, but attendance at worship and active involvement in the church has rapidly declined. Currently a debate is going on as to the exact nature and extent of secularization in England.[17] However until some definite conclusions have been reached and measurable indices agreed on there is little positive contribution the geographer can make to the debate. It does serve as a warning to him against relating too closely institutional practice and religion itself. There are many reasons why a person may or may not attend at church apart from purely religious ones.

Over the last fifteen years there has been a tremendous growth in the amount of information on religious beliefs and on church-going obtained by social surveys of various types. In the use of this material the geographer must be very wary for it varies greatly in quality and reliability. In some instances completely inadequate sampling methods are employed and in others the questions on religion are incidental to the main purpose of the survey.[18] The conclusions reached can only be as valid as the statistical material on which they are based and unfortunately the temptation to sensationalize inconclusive evidence is not always resisted.

A whole group of surveys which make use of a national sample have asked their interviewees to state their religious allegiance and averaging out the results the following percentages emerge:

Church of England	66%
Roman Catholics	12%
Free Churches	11%
No declared affiliation	5%
Jews	1%
Other religious groups	5%

That 95% of the English population claim to be members of a religious group is in itself highly significant, even if only a small proportion would be recognized as members by the churches themselves. Such a high degree of self-ascription should temper some of the over-confident talk about our completely secular society. As yet these statistics are not available on a county or regional basis and so there is no way of assessing how self-identification varies over the country. When they are available they will be of much interest to the geographer.

Surveys can also attempt to discover just how a person con-ceives of his religion, how much it means to him, and how far he carries out its precepts in his everyday life. However the techniques and problems of interpretation involved in all this are so complex that attempts to assess religious vitality have hardly begun. We are likely to have to wait many years before such information is available on a local basis to enable areal comparison.[19] The regional analysis of religious beliefs carried out by Gorer[20] should be treated with extreme caution for his basic source material is not accurate enough to support his conclusions. A much greater degree of sophistication will be necessary before trustworthy results can be obtained.

A second group of surveys are those which concentrate on one particular region or locality and study it in depth. Usually these set out to achieve a complete sociological analysis of the area, religion being one of the factors discussed. They vary considerably in quality from the very superficial and impressionistic to the extremely detailed and objective. In each case the method used was to read through the survey and where possible check its conclusions against any other available evidence. Where the results appeared to be valid they were filed for future reference. It was not possible to obtain more than a sparse coverage of the country by this piecemeal process. Nevertheless the evidence gleaned from these surveys has been of great value in helping to build up the overall picture of denominational allegiance and many of them are quoted in the succeeding chapters.

One of the main problems about the bulk of the statistical information on religion is that no details are given concerning the people themselves. Only in rare cases are the people categorized according to age, sex, occupation, or socio-economic class, and even in these some of the categories used are so broad or indeterminate as to be virtually meaningless. And yet this information is vital for any attempt to set the statistics of religious practice and belief in their proper demographic context. Owing to this lack of precision much care has to be exercised in the way the material is treated and dogmatic conclusions should be avoided.

MARRIAGE STATISTICS

Until 1836 all marriage ceremonies had to be conducted under the auspices of the Church of England, but the Marriage Act of that year allowed Roman Catholic and Nonconformist churches to be registered for marriages, and it also made provision for civil marriages to be conducted in registry offices. In 1844 the Registrar General began to keep statistical records of the type and number of marriages conducted and the analysed results were published[21] annually up to the First World War. Since then the results have been published on a five-yearly basis.[22] As this is the only information on religion collected and published by the State it is particularly necessary to discover just how far it can be used by the geographer.

All the figures are broken down to the county level thereby permitting areal comparison. Unfortunately the denominational groupings used right up to 1919 failed to differentiate between the various Nonconformist churches and so trend analyses going back to 1844 would be possible only for the Church of England, the Roman Catholics and the Jews. The value of such analyses are further restricted by the changing climate of opinion towards the marriage ceremony. Although marriages in non-Anglican surroundings were legal from 1836 onwards, they were still far from socially acceptable and the decline in the proportion of Anglican marriages during the last part of the 19th century is largely a reflection of a gradual change in social outlook. It is a dubious indicator of actual allegiance to the Church of England.

One of the rare attempts to assess the regional variations in denominational allegiance in this country has been made by *The Reader's Digest Atlas*. The *Atlas* has a section entitled 'The Strength of Religion'[23] containing a series of maps purporting to show the strength of each major religious group, and most of them are based on the Registrar General's marriage statistics. However, it fails to provide any explanation of how these statistics reflect the strength of religion and whether in fact they do so at all.

Despite the apparent popularity of registry offices, 70% of all marriages still take place in church (this proportion has not declined much since the end of the First World War when it was 77%). The reasons are not difficult to locate. The whole social rigmarole and the romantic connotations of a church wedding with its church bells, choir, white dress, wedding march, and so on, make it 'a must' for countless couples whose normal contacts with organized religion are minimal. Any parishioner has the right to be married in his parish church, irrespective of how nominal his identification with the church really is. Furthermore the parish church is usually the most picturesque religious edifice in the neighbourhood and so inevitably the Church of England marriage statistics are the least representative of actual allegiance. In rural districts, where the power of occasional conformity is strong, it is quite accepted for a couple who are staunch Nonconformists to desert their chapel in favour of the parish church for the wedding service itself.

In the case of the Free Churches the majority of the couples who are married under their auspices will have some connection with the denomination concerned, frequently through their parents. The stark or gloomy interior of many chapels is such that a strong sense of obligation is the only thing that stops couples from going elsewhere on their wedding day. A small element of the total is composed of couples who want a church wedding and have been turned away from the Church of England because one of the partners is divorced. Even where the couple does have a strong link with the denomination, often it is only through one of the partners (normally the girl, for it is her parents who would arrange the reception and hence the church). Thus although the Free Church marriage statistics are a clearer reflector of allegiance than the Church of England's, the possible margin of error within them is still wide.

The position within the Roman Catholic Church is somewhat different. At least one of the partners would have to be a baptized and, in theory, practising Catholic before a Catholic marriage could be envisaged. At one time mixed marriages were strenuously discouraged and even now the situation is not easy. In many instances the other partner becomes a Catholic before the wedding takes place. Failing this the non-Catholic partner has to permit any children they may have to be brought up as Catholics, although recently this has been relaxed a little. This strong marriage discipline imposed by the Catholic Church has meant that only an insignificant proportion of the people married in Catholic churches are not baptized Catholics and so the statistics are much more reliable.

It might be tempting to use the figures for civil marriages as indicators of explicit irreligion and rejection of the churches, but the causes which lead couples to the Registry Office are many. Apart from the desire to publicly dissociate themselves from organized religion, couples will have a civil ceremony because it costs less, because they feel it is more intimate and private, or because they have guilt feelings over their pre-marital conception—also most divorced persons are re-married in Registry Offices.[24] The religious factor is but one of several.

Despite the admitted inadequacies of the denominational marriage statistics, it is possible to make use of them in a general way, particularly to confirm the patterns which emerge from the membership maps. Least importance should be attached to the Church of England's figures, most to the Roman Catholic's. The Free Churches lie in the middle of the spectrum, but in many of the smaller counties the absolute totals are very low and so chance plays a big role in determining the relative proportions of marriages. Used with caution the statistics of marriages can be a helpful tool.

ECCLESIASTICAL PLANT

Extreme care needs to be exercised in any attempt to relate bricks and mortar to denominational allegiance, for there is no necessary connection between size of building and size of congregation. A large cathedral-like structure may well have a small garrison congregation whose chief *raison d'être* is to keep open the shrine of their forefathers. Conversely an expanding congregation in a new suburb may have to be content with hopelessly overcrowded, makeshift accommodation. Most of the church buildings in England were erected before the beginning of this century and so reflect the accommodation needs of bygone eras. Some were even unrelated to the needs at the time of their construction and instead reflected the patron's optimistic hope for the future. Particularly in Lancashire a few of the Nonconformist cathedrals were never filled, even in their heyday. It was not uncommon to find wealthy merchants building churches simply to perpetuate their own memory.

Within the Church of England and the Roman Catholic Church the building of new churches is reasonably controlled, and where new premises are required, outside financial help is available. This is not so in the Free Churches where a system bordering on free enterprise prevails. The local congregation has to bear the cost of the new building with little help from central funds. In practice this means that one or two wealthy bene-factors are virtually essential and so a large congregation may lack a proper church of its own simply because they have not found a benefactor. The complications of closing a redundant church detract further from the usefulness of statistics concern-ing ecclesiastical plant. In the Church of England the closure procedure is quite formidable and ensures that most buildings remain open.[25] Normally Free Churches only close when the congregations are no longer able to meet their running expenses and there are numerous instances of congregations dying shortly after the death of the wealthy benefactor.[26] Closure problems rarely affect expanding English Catholicism.

In a survey of a local area, where individual assessments of congregational size and vitality could be undertaken, informa-tion on church plant would be of value. In a study of the national allegiance pattern of any of the large denominations, the extraneous factors are too many and too influential for the figures to be of much significance. However within smaller denominations and religious groups the situation is different. Many of them are unable or unwilling to issue membership statistics and so information as to the disposition of their churches and meeting places becomes of greater importance. Furthermore the spectrum of congregational size within the minor religious groups is fairly small, at least in comparison with the major denominations, and so the overall pattern of meeting places accords in essential respects with the actual pattern of denominational allegiance.

OTHER DISTRIBUTION PATTERNS AND LONG-TERM TRENDS

It is a common fallacy in ecclesiastical circles to believe that in matters of religion attitudes of mind and long established customs can be changed overnight. This is not so. While individuals can undergo conversion experiences, social groups rarely do. In his study of a Lakeland parish Williams[27] showed how the present vicar was being held responsible for an indifference to religion which could be traced back to the Reformation! If the present patterns of denominational allegiance are to be understood, they have to be seen as part of a long-term dynamic process stretching right back into our past history. For instance any attempt to understand the presence of Roman Catholics in the Fylde district of Lancashire and in the north-east without reference to the events following the Reformation would be doomed to failure.

A reasonable general picture can be obtained from the standard church histories dealing with the different historical periods, and also from the recognized denominational histories. The problem with this approach is that so much of the material of geographical interest is only included incidentally and in a secondary context. Few historians write with the geographer in mind.

Attempts to assess the level of religious practice before the 19th century are fraught with difficulties. So far the evidence is conflicting and contrary opinions abound.[28] Fortunately there is much more information on the relative distributions of the different denominational groups. This is understandable, for in ages when it was illegal to be a Roman Catholic or a Nonconformist, it was natural for the government to keep a close watch on their distributions. Of particular value is the list of licences issued to Nonconformists under the Declaration of Indulgence in 1672 and also the estimates made by Usher[29] for 1603. The many other sources will be quoted as they are used in denominational assessments.

Information on church or chapel buildings can provide important clues as to former patterns of allegiance. Before the mid-19th century most non-Anglican groups only put up buildings when there was a flourishing congregation already in existence—finance dictated this. Thus the presence of a church and of a full-time minister would be a good indication of activity in that area. Of even greater significance is the length of denominational continuity in a locality, for in this way we can set the present pattern in its dynamic context. Several of the denominational handbooks provide the date of foundation for each local church and from this information we can calculate on a regional basis the span of continuity. That a denomination has maintained a presence in a locality continuously for three hundred years will greatly increase its chances of future survival in that area. On most issues concerning religion change comes but slowly and gradually.

There is one remaining statistical source, the Census of Religious Worship of 1851. Even today, with all the emphasis which is placed on accurate and full statistical information, we are less well informed about religious practice in our society than were the mid-Victorians after they had digested the results of the Census.

On account of its tremendous possible potential for the geographer a thorough assessment of the Census is necessary and will be undertaken in the following chapter.

CHAPTER THREE

The 1851 Census of Church Attendance

Scarcely anything, indeed, is more curious or puzzling, than the attempt to trace the causes why particular doctrines or religious parties should find one soil favourable and another adverse to their propagation and success. But, at all events, as far as facts are concerned, England furnishes a striking picture of sects and creeds almost supreme in one part and absolutely unknown in another.

Horace Mann, 1855[1]

INTRODUCTION

For the first time, in 1851, a section on religion was included as part of the National Census of England and Wales.[2] It was also the last time. The very uniqueness of this Census makes it of utmost importance to the geographer of religion, for if its results can be trusted it provides an excellent historical back-cloth against which to set present-day patterns of denominational allegiance.

The underlying reasons for including a section on religion were twofold; to discover how many people were outside the institutional church; and to show that the Church of England was still the church of the majority and therefore entitled to be the established church. The task of assembling the necessary information was entrusted to a certain Horace Mann, a prominent barrister.

Right at the beginning Mann had to choose between two alternative methods of obtaining the data.[3] The first possibility was to ask every person to record on the population census return the denomination to which he professed to belong. Mann considered this idea but rejected it on the grounds that it would give too vague an impression and also that it was too inquisitorial a method to be tolerated by the average Englishman. Furthermore he believed that most people would refuse to declare themselves atheists and so would claim membership of one of the denominations, most probably the Church of England.

The alternative was to collect information about religious acts and this was the approach finally adopted by Mann. He argued that the outward conduct of people gave a better guide to their religious convictions than a mere statement of profession. Anyone could put 'C of E' on a form, but a certain effort was required to attend services regularly.

He organized an elaborate religious census which was carried out on Sunday, 30th March 1851. Its aim was to discover four pieces of information:

1. The total number of attendances at each place of worship on Census Sunday.
2. The entire number of places of worship.
3. The particular sects to which these places of worship belonged.
4. The number of sittings provided by each sect.

In his Introductory Report, Mann states that '. . . for the first time, there is given to the country a full picture of the state of its religion as exhibited by its religious institutions'.[4] Never before had the Nonconformists been dealt with in a State Paper, nor had any serious attempt been previously made to assess the relative positions of the different denominations. This quality of comprehensiveness was one of the outstanding features of the Census. When the results of the Census were finally published in 1854 they quickly became the centre of a violent controversy, and many doubts were cast on the accuracy of the figures quoted.

AN ASSESSMENT OF THE ACCURACY OF THE
CENSUS

A Census return was sent to the clergyman or pastor in charge of every place of worship in England and Wales and these returns were supposed to be filled in and sent back to the Census Officer. The vital question was the one concerning the size of the congregations. The churches themselves were responsible for counting the numbers and sending in separate totals for the morning, the afternoon, and the evening services. Unfortunately no explicit instructions were issued as to how the counting was to be carried out. Some clergy counted heads, others made estimates, and some refused on principle to furnish any numbers at all.

It has been argued by Mudie Smith[5] that the Census was of very little value precisely because the churches did their own enumerating. Because the final results showed that the total attendances at Nonconformist chapels were slightly higher than those at Anglican churches, the accusation of deliberate distortion was thrown at the Nonconformist ministers and pastors. Mann examined these charges in an address given to the Statistical Society[6] in 1854. He reasoned that if the Nonconformists had grossly exaggerated their total attendances, then their proportion of attendances to sittings would have been much higher than the Church of England's.[7] In fact there was no significant difference between the two. In some measure the charges were an attempt by Anglicans, who were afraid of the challenge to their privileged position, to discredit the Nonconformists. The extreme integrity of many of the Nonconformist clergy who supplied the figures, along with the careful checking of the returns by 30,000 Census Officers, would have made any extensive falsification most unlikely. Mann concluded that there was no real substance in the accusations.

An alternative claim that the Church of England returns understated their attendances was also put forward. Three days before Census Sunday, Bishop Wilberforce, speaking in the House of Lords, reluctantly advised clergy not to complete the returns, and nearly 7% of the Anglican churches followed his advice. In cases where clergy refused to fill in the number of

3

attendances, the work was done for them by the local Census Officers. If by any chance there was insufficient information for an estimate to be made, then the average figure for the denomination concerned was inserted. Unlike the other sections of the Census, legal sanctions were not applied to force clergy to complete the returns.

The method of obtaining the attendance figures, which relied on the goodwill and enumerating accuracy of the clergy,[8] left much to be desired. Nevertheless the checking technique ensured that few gross errors would have escaped notice and the general validity of the Census remained intact.

As the date of the Census was known well in advance, accusation and counter-accusation of 'pew-packing' abounded. Mann pointed out however that there was no reason why one denomination should have indulged in this more than others. It would merely have the effect of boosting all the returns slightly, without leading to any distortion of regional or sectarian distributions. It could be argued also that anyone who could be persuaded to enter a church on Census day was sufficiently active to be counted as a supporter of his or her denomination.

The results of the Census revealed that a sizeable section of the population was not at church on Census Sunday and two reasons were put forward to try and explain away the absences. The first was the bad weather. However this was not much worse than the weather typical of winter months. Bad weather would obviously affect attendances in rural areas more than in towns and so had it been a clear day the urban/rural disparity would have been even greater. It is true that a Census in mid-summer probably would have found more worshippers in church and one in mid-December less, but the differences would have been small relative to the total.

The second explanation was that the Census fell on mid-Lent Sunday. In parts of the country, especially in Lancashire, Cheshire, and several of the Midland counties, it was thought many stayed away from church on account of the festivities attached to Mothering Sunday. It has to be admitted that these were all strong Nonconformist areas, but even so the activities would have affected all the denominations.

A further proviso to the accuracy of the Census has to be made. Each place of worship was asked to record separately the number of Sunday School scholars who were present at normal services, but many ignored this request. The numbers of those attending meetings exclusively for Sunday School scholars were to be excluded anyway. Where possible the returning officers would make an estimate of the number of scholars at normal services and deduct this from the total, but this was frequently difficult to achieve.

After a careful examination of all the objections to the accuracy of the Census, Mann concludes:

> Isolated errors doubtless may be pointed out, but not such a number of errors as would cause a noticeable alteration in the aggregate. That aggregate, I fully believe, may be accepted as a faithful statement of the numerical position of religious bodies in this country, so far as their position may be inferred from attendance on religious services.[9]

The Times for the 9th January 1854, came to the same basic conclusion: 'The result . . . may be taken as substantially accurate and trustworthy.'[10]

Two recent investigations into the Census by K. S. Inglis[11] and W. S. F. Pickering[12] both agree on the general reliability of the results, and this research has not produced any facts to throw doubt on their conclusion.

THE COLLECTION AND PRESENTATION OF THE ATTENDANCE STATISTICS

A Census return was sent out to every place of worship in England and Wales. However when the Census Report was published in 1854, the attendance figures were not listed under individual places of worship but were grouped into registration districts or poor law unions. Before the Census was undertaken, Mann had given an assurance that he would only publish the general results and not the individual returns, thus preventing the possibility of direct comparisons being made between individual parishes and churches. It was hoped this pledge would encourage the clergy to co-operate and return accurate statements and attendance figures. Unfortunately there was no convenient administrative division between the parish and registration district or poor law union and so the latter unit[13] had to be used.

In certain cases clergy completed most of the Census return but failed to include any figures for attendances on Census Sunday. If it appeared that a service was held on Census Sunday, the average number of attendants for that place of worship (assuming this figure was given on the return) was taken to be the number present. However 4% of all the places of worship failed to give even the average number of attendants. For these places of worship Mann decided not to make any estimate of the number present when he compiled the registration district tables and instead the omissions were recorded in footnotes. This would enable anyone to make their own estimates, while the tables themselves 'contain nothing beyond the original authenticated figures'.[14] In certain of the summary tables, however, Mann has included an estimate for the defective returns.

A random examination of a few of the registration district returns revealed that errors due to the failure of churches to furnish returns were occasionally very serious. In some districts as many as 25% of the Anglican churches failed to send in any returns. Errors of this magnitude would be sufficient to render invalid any conclusions based on the remainder of the returns for that district. It was decided unfeasible therefore to carry out a detailed analysis of the geographical variations in denominational allegiances for the country as a whole using the registration district as the basic unit.

Is there any satisfactory method of calculating a figure for a defective return? In his summary tables Mann merely inserted the denominational average and while this worked at the national and regional level, it cannot be applied accurately at a local level. However, even where churches failed to send in any attendance returns, the number of sittings in that place of worship is usually known. Using this number it is possible to calculate the percentage of the total number of sittings for that denomination in the registration district which are provided by the place of worship with the defective return. The number of attendances can then be grossed up accordingly.

Example. Two Roman Catholic churches in the Registration District of Preston failed to supply attendance figures and between them they accounted for 14% of the total Roman Catholic sittings in Preston. The original total attendance figure of 10,806 was therefore increased to 12,350.

Where the number of defective returns is not large this method can be used to calculate the approximate figure for the total number of attendances, and has been used to adjust the Roman Catholic figures in Lancashire, Cheshire, Northumberland and Durham, and the Presbyterian figures in Northumberland, Durham and Cumberland.[15] Fortunately in these instances nearly all the places of worship concerned made proper returns and so any possible error could only be very small.

Should it be desired to make a detailed study of the religious allegiance pattern in one small area, the Census returns themselves can be studied in the Public Record Office, and an analysis of the relevant returns in conjunction with 'on-site' historical enquiry, would reduce errors to a minimum. While suited to intensive local work it would be most difficult for one person to use this method to obtain a national coverage. Eventually perhaps when a sufficient number of local studies have been undertaken by different people, a detailed map will begin to emerge.

For this present book the county has been adopted as the basic unit. The Census report lists the attendance figures for each county by denomination, although no estimate is included for the defective returns. In order to minimize this error a method was devised whereby the number of places of worship failing to make attendance returns was expressed as a percentage of the total number of places of worship for that denomination in the county. Then the county Index of Attendance[16] was grossed up by this percentage.

Example   County: Cheshire.
               Denomination: Church of England.
  Total number of places of worship   252

Number not submitting attendance returns   18
Those not submitting attendance returns expressed as a percentage of the total number
  of places of worship   7·1%
Original Index of Attendance   24·3%
Original Index of Attendance grossed up by
  7·1%   26·0

When all the counties were totalled up (Table 2) the estimates
for the defective returns calculated in this way showed a
marked agreement with the estimates made by Mann on a
national level.[17]

The figures given in the Census report for the London region
required breaking down into their component registration
districts and redistributing in order to make geographical
comparison more meaningful. The county tables only list
Surrey, Kent and Middlesex, which between them account for
the whole of the metropolitan area, as well as large sections of
extra metropolitan territory. It was felt essential however to
have a set of figures just for the metropolitan area on its own.
Accordingly the metropolitan registration districts were
regrouped to make Metropolitan London, and sets of figures
were also supplied for the extra-metropolitan parts of Surrey,
Kent and Middlesex.

METHODS OF EXPRESSING THE ATTENDANCE FIGURES

The Census collected figures for the number of attendances at
the morning, the afternoon, and the evening services, but no
specific enquiry was made to discover just how many people
attended church more than once on that Sunday. It would be
necessary to know how many attended two or more services in
order to calculate the number of people (as opposed to the
number of attendances) who were at church on Census Sunday.

By a piece of intelligent guesswork, Mann[18] estimated that
50% of those attending in the afternoon had not been to church
in the morning, and 33% of those at evening services had not
been either in the morning or the afternoon. However, this was

only a 'guestimate', and it was not based on any statistical evidence. Mann defended the general fairness of his formula, although he did admit it was biased in favour of the Church of England who had their largest attendances in the morning. On the other hand the Dissenters tended to have their biggest congregations in the evenings and it is certain that well over 33% of them would not have been to a place of worship before on Census Sunday. The application of a national formula which is unable to take account of regional and sectarian variations is of little worth for geographical analysis. It would be of great value to know the number of actual persons attending services on that Sunday but the Census method failed to make provision for this and no amount of statistical juggling can remedy this initial defect.

The attempts which have been made to estimate the size of 'the entire worshipping community' [19] are even more unreliable and suspect. Mann tentatively suggested adding two-thirds to the number of Dissenting attenders and doubling the number of Anglican and Roman Catholic attenders[20] in order to find the approximate size of the total worshipping community. In all fairness though, Mann himself is not all that convinced about his method: 'It is just at this point that we are destitute of information, and, I fear, without the means of forming any very probable conjecture.' [21]

A. Hume however takes up the problem with much more enthusiasm and conviction: 'An allowance must be made for those who are *bona fide* worshippers but who were absent on the Census Sunday, as a similar number would be absent on any other Sunday. The question simply is—what allowance?' [22] According to Hume, Mann's formula is the answer, and using it he estimated that the entire worshipping community of England and Wales was 75% of the total population, while the remaining 25% had a passive religion.[23] Many of Hume's contemporary critics felt that 75% was too optimistic a figure. In defence Hume quoted from a study he carried out in his own parish in a poor sector of Liverpool. He kept a record of all the people who attended his church over a period of $2\frac{1}{2}$ years and he found the number of 'positive' church-going people, all of whom had attended worship more or less during the last few months of that period was four times the size of the average congregation. So for his particular parish the number of attenders would have to be quadrupled and not doubled to give the size of the entire worshipping community.

Hume was aware of certain deficiencies in his method and only claimed accuracy for his figures over a broad area. Even this assertion was highly questionable, but he then went on to state that his method was still valid for small areas, though not quite so accurate. Believing this to be true he calculated the total worshipping communities for each of the forty-four counties and the seventy-three great towns of England on a denominational basis (Church of England, Roman Catholic, Dissenters and Non-worshipping.) He provided maps for each of the four main groups, but no tables giving the detailed figures for all the counties. When these were calculated it was discovered that a few counties appeared to have a total worshipping community appreciably larger than the total population!

In his work on the 1851 Census, K. S. Inglis[24] computed what he called an Index of Attendance. He added together the morning, the afternoon and the evening attendances and expressed this total as a percentage of the total population for that area.[25] However, in view of the many double and triple attendances by zealous persons an Index of 100 would mean that just over half of the total population had actually attended.

In the following chapters it is proposed to use the Index of Attendance as a method of expressing the relative strength of denominational allegiance as it varies over the country.[26] While being a useful device for comparative work within one denomination, extreme caution is needed when comparing the Index of Attendance of one denomination with that of another. The emphasis placed on the need to attend church worship varied from one group to another, and furthermore a given number of Dissenting attendances would represent fewer people than the same number of Church of England attendances (i.e. Dissenters tended to go to church more often on Sundays than Anglicans did). Despite its limitations the Index of Attendance is of great value to the geographer as it enables him to relate the attendance figures to the overall population

base, and then to carry out an analysis as to how the strength
of a particular denomination varies from county to county.

GENERAL RESULTS OF THE CENSUS REPORT

When the results of the Census were finally published in 1854,
a shock hit the nation. Although the attendance figures were
considerable, Mann saw the position as an alarming one. A
total number of 10,896,066 attendances had been recorded at
places of worship in England and Wales on Census Sunday
(see Table 3) and according to Mann's estimate 7,261,032
actual persons had attended, an allowance being made for those
who had attended more than one service. Therefore 10,666,577
had chosen to stay away. Those with valid excuses (too young,
working, ill, looking after young children and so on) were
estimated by Mann as comprising 30% of the total population
of 17,927,609 and so out of the 12,549,609 people who were free
to attend a place of worship 5,288,294 had deliberately absented
themselves.

Mann describes the situation as follows:

> The most important fact which this investigation as to atten-
> dance brings before us is, unquestionably, the alarming number
> of the non-attendants. Even in the least unfavourable aspect of
> the figures just presented . . . it must be apparent that a sadly
> formidable portion of the English people are habitual
> neglecters of the public ordinances of religion.[27]

This was the first time that proper statistical evidence was
available to throw light on to two major issues of debate. In the
first place it was now apparent to all that a significant proportion of our population were no longer practising Christians and
a further analysis revealed that most of the non-religious
people were to be found in the large towns. Secondly the
results finally dispelled the myth that the Anglican Church was
the church of the overwhelming majority of Englishmen—it
accounted for under 50% of the total attendances.

3*

ACCOMMODATION PROVIDED BY RELIGIOUS GROUPS

From the time the results were published church leaders were haunted by the spectre of the 5¼ million absentees. But what would have happened if all those who could have attended tried to attend? About 1·6 million would have been unable to get in. Each church was required to state on the Census form the total number of people it could accommodate, and after a careful study of these statistics in relation to total population figures, Mann concluded that a further 1·6 million sittings were required before everyone who was able to attend could do so. Nearly all this extra accommodation was needed in the large industrial towns which had been mushrooming since the beginning of the Industrial Revolution largely unnoticed by the ecclesiastical authorities. The frenzy of church and chapel building in the 1860s and 1870s was partly a consequence of the Census findings.

One of the questions asked on the Census form was the date on which the building was erected or taken over for religious services. The dates for the buildings of each denomination were tabulated decennially on a county basis from 1801–51 with a column for those dating before 1801 and another for the number of those not stating any date.

It was hoped these figures could be used on a denominational basis to reveal differential growth rates during the first half of the 19th century. A sudden spate of church and chapel building is likely to be a clear indicator of success in that particular part of the country. However a detailed examination of the figures showed they were of little value except for a very general type of comparison. Thirteen per cent of the total number of places of worship failed to state any date and this percentage was high enough to invalidate any conclusions based on the remaining figures.

In the case of many of the Dissenting bodies, places which had only recently been occupied for religious worship were returned with the dates of their erection, instead of with the dates of their first appropriation to such uses. The same applied to chapels which passed from one denomination to another. There are many instances in the Census report of chapels belonging to groups like the Bible Christians, the Primitive Methodists and the Mormons, which claim to date from before the initial foundation of the denomination concerned. Although the Mormons were not formed until the 1820s and did not reach England until the late 1830s, twenty-eight of the Mormon chapels in England claimed to date from before 1801.

A further problem was that small groups of Dissenters would have to move to larger buildings when they expanded. No statistics of the number of churches and chapels which closed were available and so the rapid increase in church building after 1801 is partially a reflection of the mobility of Dissenting congregations. In all the information on the dates of church buildings is of strictly limited value to the geographer.

THE PATTERN OF OVERALL RELIGIOUS PRACTICE

When the attendance figures of all the denominational groups for each county were added together, a clear picture of the varied state of institutional Christianity emerged (Map 3). There were two distinct areas of high religious practice; first, the whole of the West Country extending east into Gloucestershire, Berkshire, and Hampshire; and secondly a large group of counties to the south of the Wash where both Nonconformists and Church of England attendances were at their highest. At the other extreme the lowest attendances were recorded in Metropolitan London, Lancashire and the three northern counties of Cumberland, Northumberland and Durham, and attendances were only a little higher in the belt stretching south from the West Riding to the Black Country.

It was the expanding industrial areas with the lowest attendances which had the least amount of accommodation to offer potential worshippers (see Map 4). The London area, Warwickshire, Lancashire, and the North East had the smallest percentages of population which could be accommodated. The slightly higher figure for the West Riding was due largely to Methodist chapel-building, while the lack of a Nonconformist alternative in the south-east kept the percentages lower. It is necessary to look in more detail at those areas of growing industry and expanding population which had the lowest attendances and the least amount of accommodation to offer.

URBAN PRACTICE

An analysis of the detailed results for the 623 registration districts of England and Wales showed that most of the absent millions were to be found in the towns. Mann compiled a special table for the seventy-three large towns which had populations over 10,000 and taking these towns collectively only about 25% of their inhabitants were in church on Census Sunday. The absentees were quickly identified as the working classes:

> while the labouring myriads of our country have been multi-plying with our multiplied material prosperity, it cannot, it is feared, be stated that a corresponding increase has occurred in the attendance of this class in our religious edifices. More especially in cities and large towns it is observable how absolutely insignificant a proportion of the congregations is composed of artizans.[28]

Many people had suspected this already and writing in 1844 Engels said: 'All the writers of the bourgeoisie are unanimous on this point, that the workers are not religious and do not attend church.' [29]

The Census produced the evidence which confirmed this view. The standard interpretation was that these $5\frac{1}{4}$ million had somehow managed to break out of the fold due to the negligence of the churches, but recent scholarship has shown it was unlikely that they were ever in it. The churches never had any real influence over the working class in the new industrial towns of the 18th and 19th centuries.[30]

In his discussion of the place of the churches in mid-Victorian working class England, K. S. Inglis[31] concentrated his attention almost exclusively on the large towns making use of the special tables for large towns provided by Mann. It was found that the rates of attendance were lower in the large towns than else-where[32] (the Index of Attendance was 71·4 for rural areas and small towns, but only 49·7 for large towns), and generally the larger the town the lower the attendance.

Three large towns, Colchester, Exeter and Bath (see Map 5) had I.A.s exceeding the average for rural areas and small towns. Each was in the south and scarcely affected by industry.

Eleven other towns[33] exceeded the average I.A. for the whole of England and Wales. All but Wakefield and York lie south of the Trent and only Wakefield was classified as a 'chief manufacturing district'.[34] The average population of this group was under 30,000. A further twenty-one towns[35] had I.A.s which were higher than the average for all large towns. Seven of these were classified as chief manufacturing districts (Rochdale, Huddersfield, Dudley, Warrington, Kidderminster, Wigan, and Wolverhampton) and a further two, Derby and Nottingham, were also industrial centres. The average population was around 50,000, considerably higher than that of the last group.

The remaining thirty-six towns[36] all had I.A.s below the average for large towns. They comprised the eight parliamentary boroughs of London, twenty-one chief manufacturing districts, five centres of industry, and the two ports of Hull and Gravesend. Included in this group were the four largest provincial centres of Liverpool, Manchester, Birmingham and Leeds; every large town in Lancashire, apart from Wigan and Rochdale; the two great hardware centres of Sheffield and Birmingham; all the large cotton towns and the two woollen centres of Leeds and Bradford; and every large coal town apart from Wolverhampton. It is these thirty-six towns which above all illustrate that absence from religious worship was greatest where the largest number of working class people lived.

An examination of the achievements of the various denominations in Industrial England was also undertaken by Inglis, based on the twenty-nine large towns which were designated 'chief manufacturing districts'. In only three of these, Warrington, Halifax and Kidderminster, did Anglican worshippers account for more than half of the total attendances. In a further eleven the Roman Catholics prevented either the Anglicans or the Nonconformists from reaching 50%, whilst in the remaining fifteen towns Nonconformists represented over 50% of the attendances. A detailed breakdown of the Nonconformist statistics showed that Nonconformity owed whatever hold it

possessed in the large manufacturing districts to the Methodists
(Table 4). There was one exception to this, London, where
Methodists were sparse and Congregationalists predominated
among the Nonconformists.

In the large towns of England, attendances were almost
invariably low, and furthermore there was generally an inverse
relationship between the size of the town and the proportion of
attenders at religious worship. Attendances were lowest of all
in London, in most of Lancashire and West Yorkshire, and in
several other great towns which were centres of England's
industrial expansion.[37] It was here, above all, that the absent
millions were to be found.

REASONS FOR NO FURTHER CENSUS ON RELIGION

None of the national censuses after 1851 contained a section on
religion. Why was this? The results of the 1851 Census of
Attendance were disconcerting for the Establishment and
could be interpreted as showing that half the nation was
Nonconformist. Therefore the Anglican majority of M.P.s
opposed any further census of attendance.

In 1860 the Cabinet discussed the Census for the following
year and proposed that the section on religion should take the
form of a census of profession. Every person would be compelled
by law to state his religion on the census return. Nonconformist
M.P.s, realizing that the majority of nominal Christians would
put 'C of E' on the form, objected to the proposal. They
demanded a census of attendance or nothing.

Both the Anglican and the Nonconformist M.P.s were strong
enough to prevent the views of the other group from prevailing
and so a deadlock was reached, and this was reinforced by a
large body of opinion which looked upon the Census as an
interference with religious liberty. The result was that the
Home Secretary dropped all reference to religion from the 1861
Census. Every ten years up to 1910 the whole subject was
raised, argued, and rejected, but after 1910 interest waned and
it seems that few people have bothered to raise the issue since.

GEOGRAPHICAL ANALYSIS OF THE CENSUS RESULTS

The statistical information contained in the Census report presents the geographer with a great potential for distributional analysis of religious allegiance, but so far little use has been made of the material. The original compiler of the Census, Horace Mann, was content to produce the basic information and restrict himself to a few general comments on the geographical variations in strength. In his address to the Statistical Society he listed the names of the strongest and weakest groups of counties for each of the major denominations, but he made no attempt to produce any distribution maps. He was very much aware of the variations in denominational allegiance in different parts of the country and he admitted he was greatly puzzled by this phenomenon. However, he did not commit himself to examining the causes or offering possible explanations.

Hume was the only 19th century scholar who tried to view the Census results geographically and he published a pamphlet in 1860 which related the attendance figures to geographical areas. Unfortunately he took as his basic statistical unit the total worshipping community and for reasons already given the accuracy of this has been called into question.

Four main groupings were distinguished, the Church of England, the Nonconformists, the Roman Catholics, and the irreligious, and the total community size for each was expressed as a percentage of total population, on a county basis. Using these percentages he compiled 'A Map, Illustrating the Religious Condition of the Country'—the first map of the 1851 Religious Census. On to the map he also inserted pie symbols giving the attendance percentages for the seventy-three large towns of England and Wales.

The map itself suffered from several severe defects which reduced its value. The categories used by Hume were arbitrary and vague and he failed to publish all the figures on which he based the map. A check was carried out by recalculating all Hume's figures and it was found he had made three serious errors. Essex, Dorset and Somerset were shown as having more than 50% non-worshippers, but in fact these three counties were overwhelmingly Anglican. Furthermore he failed to break down the figures for the London area. Had he done so he would have found it was only Metropolitan London which had over 50% non-worshippers, while the non-metropolitan area of Surrey was predominantly Anglican. It is a great pity these errors have been perpetuated in the significant volume by Sopher[38] on the geography of religion, especially as this was the only map used by him to illustrate the position in England.

Despite provisos, Hume's work was a bold pioneer attempt which gave the broad outline of the distribution patterns. It showed clearly that the Church of England was strongest in the old-English counties, especially those least influenced by commerce, mining or manufacture, and that the percentage of non-worshippers was highest in counties with a considerable number of large towns.

Hume also arranged the counties in rank order and found that of the twenty-two counties which had a high percentage of practising Anglicans, as many as thirteen had a high percentage of practising Dissenters. On a county basis (this did not apply to the towns) it seemed that religious groups thrived on competition . . . so that much more depends upon the moral and religious tone of any particular place than upon the success of one denomination over another.[39]

It is curious that over a hundred years were to lapse before the Census results were again examined geographically. In 1963 Rogan[40] looked at the figures from an Anglican viewpoint and quoted certain general conclusions, although he did not publish any detailed statistics or maps. Inglis's research was predominantly concerned with the large towns and not with the country as a whole.

The most recent analysis of the distribution patterns was undertaken by W. S. F. Pickering in 1967.[41] He took the total for the best attended service of the day (this would be the maximum minimum figure) and then related this to the total population for that county. Although reasonably satisfied with the general accuracy of the Census, he concluded that even if the degree of error was considerable, there was no evidence to doubt that the errors would have been equally distributed over the whole country. Therefore the results could safely be used for geographical comparison.[42]

His article contained four maps (Church of England, Nonconformists, Roman Catholics and All Denominations) which showed the distributional variations by county. There was no detailed information on the component parts of Nonconformity and the scales chosen for the maps appear to be arbitrary and not necessarily related to distribution clusters. However Pickering was writing as a sociologist, not as a geographer, and was attempting a task which ought long since to have been tackled by geographers.

In the following chapters it is hoped to remedy this deficiency. The general trustworthiness of the Census results can be accepted, certainly at a county level, and by use of the I.A. these results can be related to the overall population totals. The Census provides the geographer with a reliable and detailed historical backcloth against which can be placed the more recent patterns of denominational allegiance. The contemporary distributions of the various denominations are thereby seen as part of a dynamic process which has its roots in the past and which is undergoing continuous modification in the present.

CHAPTER FOUR

The Church of England

Viewed religiously, the number of worshippers may be held to be unsatisfactory, but considered socially it is formidable, and makes the Church of England by far and away the most important social institution in the land.

Leslie Paul[1]

From the period of the Roman occupation, when Christianity was first established in England, the Ecclesia Anglicana has exercised responsibility for the spiritual well-being of the English people. The early history of the English Church has been well documented elsewhere[2] and need not detain us here. Suffice it to say the struggles between the Roman and the Celtic Churches for the right to evangelize England resulted in the defeat of the Celtic Church which then retired to its Celtic heartland. Thus during the Dark Ages the Roman Church reigned supreme and was able to develop a system of territorial organization which has remained the norm ever since.

By 1300 this system had been mapped out.[3] The whole country was divided up into dioceses, archdeaconries, rural deaneries and parishes. Minor additions and alterations were to be made in the following centuries but the basic pattern remained unaltered right up to the 19th century. To modern man ecclesiastical divisions are very much of a formality and normally they only impinge upon him when he wishes to be baptized, married or buried. This has not always been the case.

Particularly in the Middle Ages when matters spiritual and temporal were inextricably intertwined, the parish, the archdeacon's court, and the diocesan authorities all wielded considerable temporal power and influence over the lives of their subjects. It was of great concern to the average inhabitant as to whose jurisdiction he came under. The ecclesiastical division of England into geographical units had a vital bearing on the social landscape of the times.

Little is known about the practices and attendances of the medieval Church. One assumes that everyone attended services because they were compelled to by law and because the feudal system rendered deviation impossible. Furthermore the parish church was in a very real sense the centre of the community and its life. People came to church not only to worship, but also for the scant welfare provision, to buy and sell goods at the market outside and often inside the church, and for the many secular meetings and entertainments which took place in the church.[4] Men had not been instructed to draw a distinction between the sacred and the secular and the church was willing to house both. The whole of the medieval community life came under the aegis of the Church.

THE REFORMATION IN ENGLAND

The break between the Church in England and the papal authority in Rome took place in the 16th century, but this was no sudden or unexpected event. Long before the Reformation the Church in England had manifested its lack of subservience to the Papacy. At the beginning of the Norman rule in England William I had refused homage and fealty to the Pope and from this time onwards there is a record of struggles between Pope and King, King and Church, and Church and Pope. Although the permutations of struggles were many, the one constant was the feeling of hostility towards the Papacy which ran continually and broadly through English life and opinion. The Pope was looked on as the person who exacted payments from everybody and who appointed foreign bishops and clergy to the most lucrative posts. Rarely was his spiritual position considered.

By the end of the 15th century the Medieval Church was riddled with abuses and corruption. The Church in England was no exception. Bishops were also temporal princes and state administrators and had little time to devote to their pastoral duties—most regarded their bishoprics as sinecures. Life in the religious orders was a common cause of scandal, and the practices of the secular[5] clergy left much to be desired. A new breed of 'Mass priests' had developed and their sole job was to say Mass for the souls of the departed rich. Most of the Mass priests were completely uneducated and repeated the Latin of the Mass in a parrot fashion, many having no understanding of what the words meant. Inevitably the status of the priesthood was debased. At the parish level pastoral responsibilities were rarely taken seriously and in the eyes of many thoughtful people the Church had become a fallible human institution (and also a powerful one). It was time for a change.

The immediate causes which sparked off the change in England were political. Henry VIII wished to marry Anne Boleyn and asked the Pope to declare invalid his previous marriage to Katharine of Aragon. Finally realizing he was not going to be granted the required dispensation, he decided to by-pass the Pope. The Reformation was already in progress abroad, so why not in England? He began by extracting a Submission from the two Convocations in 1532 and the legal process was completed in 1534 with the Act of Supremacy which declared the king to be the Supreme Head of the Church of England. Thus all the legal rights of the Pope were transferred to the Crown.

However this was only the beginning of the Reformation in England. It was one thing to change the legal constitution and control of the English Church, but it was much more difficult to gain acceptance for the changes at the grass roots level of the individual parishes. Most parishes were innately conservative and resistant to change. What was good enough for their forefathers was good enough for them. Not that they objected to the abolition of the power of Rome: this was gladly welcomed. It was in the realm of liturgical practice and doctrinal formulation that opposition was met. The disappearance of the Latin Mass and the visible changes in layout inside the churches caused the most controversy.

The Reformation in England, although initiated by Henry VIII, spanned four reigns and it was only with the Elizabethan Settlement that the newly emergent Church of England was finally stabilized. And yet although the theology and practice of the new church was different, it was still basically 'the old firm under a new name with a new managing director'. Over most of the country the life of the average parish went on much as in previous ages.[6] The parish church, stripped of its ornaments and altar, was still the focal point of community life. By and large the clergy were the same, only now calling themselves Protestant ministers and not Catholic priests. The essential continuity between the old Catholic Church in England and the new Protestant Church of England remained unbroken.

The Elizabethan Settlement was an attempt to establish the Church of England as the *via media* between Reformed Protestantism and the Church of Rome. Elizabeth and her advisers tried to make the Church of England sufficiently comprehensive to include all but the most ardent and determined Romanists and Reformers. Then, as now, the spirit of compromise was the essence of the Church of England. It was hoped that all moderate Englishmen would recognize the reasonableness of this Settlement, and by the Act of Uniformity in 1559 it was decreed that the Church of England was henceforth the only lawful church in the land.[7]

It is difficult to discover just how quickly and wholeheartedly people identified themselves with the new Church of England. Usher[8] attempted to estimate the proportion of the population who were actually supporting the Church 'with firmness' in 1603, and Map 6 is based on his conclusions. The highest proportions were in London and the Home Counties and the percentages gradually dropped to the north and west. Everywhere to the south of the Bristol Channel/Wash line (with the exception of Cornwall) the percentages were 50 or over, while in the west Midlands and the northern counties only a minority of the people were active supporters of the Church of England.

Two main reasons account for this geographical distribution. In the first place the machinery for enforcing conformity was more powerful in the areas within reasonable distance of London. Further away however the influence of local leadership was stronger, and as travel and communications were difficult the edicts from London seemed remote and were certainly hard to enforce. Secondly there were great differences in the quality of parochial life in the Church of England. Most of the benefices worth over £25 per year lay in an area east of Oxford and south of the Wash. Naturally these richer benefices attracted the learned and more intelligent incumbents, and although many benefices were held in plurality, the greater density of parishes in the south more than counterbalanced. In the south-west, the west and the north the position was very different. Parishes covered large geographical areas and the benefices were poorly endowed. In Lancashire, Westmorland and Northumberland the average benefice was only £5 per year and very few were worth more than £15 per year. Most of the clergy in these areas were poor and uneducated and were completely swamped by the task of making the Church of England the church of the masses. Particularly in the north Roman Catholicism remained the dominating force.

The 17th century was a period of uncertainty for the Church of England. At first everything seemed to go well and the determined policies of Archbishop Laud, backed up by the legal machinery of the Star Chamber, ensured that conformity to Anglican ways was widespread. All this fell apart during the Civil War, and under Oliver Cromwell the Church of England was officially disbanded. Nevertheless the majority of the population remained moderate Anglicans and there was no difficulty in restoring the old ways at the time of the Restoration. A further drama occurred during the brief reign of James II when an attempt was made to restore the rule of Rome, but the arrival of William of Orange eclipsed this. The Church of England survived these various vicissitudes of 17th-century life and settled into a period of relative calm—the Age of Reason was beginning.

THE EARLY 18TH CENTURY

In the period immediately before the Industrial Revolution the organizational structure of the Church of England was well suited to meet the needs of the people. The settlement pattern was dominated by the village unit and into this the parish system fitted ideally. England was still a green and pleasant land: the dark satanic mills had not yet appeared on the landscape.

The first population census was not undertaken until 1801, but estimates are available for years prior to this. Based on Brownlee's work, Deane and Cole[9] quote an estimate of 5·8 million for 1701 (England and Wales). Gregory King[10] drew up a statistical account of the 'State and Condition' of England and Wales for the last years of the 17th century. The picture emerging suggests that between 70 and 80% of the total occupied population was primarily engaged in agriculture. The strictly rural population, that is those who lived in hamlets and villages, was equal to about 75% of the total, while a further 10% was to be found in London and its suburbs.

The urban population was very small. At the beginning of the 18th century London had over half a million, but only three other towns had over 10,000, namely Bristol and Norwich each with over 20,000, and Birmingham with 10,000–15,000. It is doubtful whether the population living in concentrations of 5,000 or over amounted to more than 13% of the total population. England was overwhelmingly rural.

On the evidence provided by the parish registers and the hearth-tax returns[11] it looks as if the centre of population in 1700 lay well to the south. It was estimated that the seven counties of Middlesex, Surrey, Kent, Gloucestershire, Somerset, Wiltshire and Devon accounted for 33% of the total population. There were also considerable densities in the east (Norfolk, Suffolk, and Essex) and in Lancashire and the West Riding. The wealthiest district was that of the six agricultural counties to the north of the Thames—Hertfordshire, Bedfordshire, Buckinghamshire, Berkshire, Oxfordshire and Northamptonshire. Their position highlights the importance of London as an agricultural market at this time. By contrast the seven poorest counties were Derbyshire, Cheshire, Yorkshire, Lancashire, Northumberland, Durham and Cumberland. Indeed the assessment of the whole district north of the Humber (one-fifth of the total area of England) was no greater than the assessment of Wiltshire.

The Church of England was fully integrated into the social environment of the early 18th century. Village and parish were normally coterminous. Each of these village communities had a well ordered and generally accepted system of authority—a type of modified feudalism. At the apex was the lord of the manor who controlled the life of the village. Frequently he was also patron of the parish church and as such could appoint the incumbent. The habit of appointing the younger son or brother from the manor house was on the increase and as well as providing a job for one of the family it also ensured the fullest co-operation between rectory and manor house. At best everybody benefited from the sort of paternalism imposed by enlightened gentry such as Sir Roger de Coverley.[12] These village communities were tightly knit and static: people moved out of them but rarely. The church interpenetrated all aspects of village life. In conjunction with the manor, the church was the custodian and administrator of traditional authority. As most of the population lived in villages and hamlets the Church of England had a very real influence on the lives of the vast majority.

The geographical density of parishes was directly related to population distribution of the early 18th century. The great strength of the Anglican Church lay in the south of England and it was here that the majority of the population and wealth was to be located. Usually the parish and township were coterminous and good endowments ensured that most churches were properly staffed with clergy. Every settlement had its own church and so the population of each parish was of a manageable size.

In the north the parochial system developed along different lines. Most of the north came under the Danelaw and the typical Danelaw manor included several townships. As the lord of the manor usually built the parish church as well, the manor became the area of the parish. The appropriation of tithes by the large religious communities in the late 11th century and early 12th century meant that the appropriated townships had to be merged into neighbouring parishes.[13] In remote agriculturally poor areas the population of an individual township was unable to support its own church and priest and so several townships had to be grouped into one parish. Thus by the mid-12th century when the parochial system had crystallized, nearly all the northern parishes included two or more distinct areas of settlement within their boundaries. This pattern was to remain static until the changes initiated in the 19th century.

These northern parishes were not only large: they were also badly endowed. Consequently they attracted few clergy, and many livings were held in plurality or by non-resident incumbents. In 1743 out of a total of 836 parishes in the diocese of York, 393 had non-resident incumbents and a further 335 were held by pluralists.[14]

However the majority of the people lived in the south, not in the north. The fact that the Church of England's pastoral machinery was in a poor state in the north was of little consequence at the time.

THE CHURCH OF ENGLAND AND THE INDUSTRIAL REVOLUTION

Right up to and including the early decades of the 18th century the Church of England was able to cater for the spiritual needs of the people as a whole. Its parochial system was geared essentially to a population which earned its livelihood from agriculture and from commerce. But this milieu was soon to change.

The precise course and nature of the so-called Industrial Revolution are still the subject for lively debate, but it is now beyond dispute that the population began to increase steadily from 1740 onwards.[15] Deane and Cole have divided up the counties of England and Wales into three groups and assessed the population totals of each. It appears that the population of the agricultural counties nearly doubled in the period 1701–

1831; the population of the mixed counties slightly more than doubled; that of the industrial and commercial counties increased 3·3 times; and the population of the northern industrial counties of Lancashire, the West Riding, Durham and Northumberland, taken as a separate group, increased four times. The greatest increases therefore were in the newly industrialized northern counties, where in the 18th century there were no towns of over 5,000 people.

The population upsurge beginning in the 1740s radically altered the settlement patterns in the north, and had a disastrous affect on the Anglican Church's ability to maintain a proper pastoral oversight. In many of the ancient parishes such as Sheffield,[16] Preston, Manchester, Bradford, Leeds and Huddersfield substantial urban development took place in townships which had been subordinate to the head township. In most instances the subordinate townships did not even possess a chapel of ease, and the inhabitants were expected to make the journey, frequently of several miles, to the parish church in the head township. Even where chapels of ease had been provided, every effort was made to prevent them developing lives of their own. They were supposed to be adjuncts to the parish church, and the parish churches jealously guarded their historical rights. The elaborate legal procedure necessary for creating new parishes further hindered the ability of the Church of England to cope with the changing circumstances. The net result was that the Church of England almost completely failed to take any positive action until well into the 19th century. There were virtually no new churches built from the beginning of the 18th century to the time of the Million Act in 1818: during this period the population of the country doubled. For example, Leeds had a population of over 70,000 in 1831 and yet it was still served by only one parish church and two chapels of ease, and further instances could be found from over the whole of the expanding industrial north.

The diocesan system in the north was equally inflexible and unable to meet the new situation. There was not a single bishop based in Lancashire and the West Riding until 1836 when the Diocese of Ripon was created. Lancashire had to wait until 1847 when Manchester was given its own bishopric.

Throughout the 18th century, the whole of Lancashire, large parts of Cumberland and Westmorland, and the north-west part of Yorkshire were all included in the gigantic and unwieldy Diocese of Chester (see Map 7).

The process of urbanization, whereby the population of urban areas increased more rapidly than the overall population, which began in the latter half of the 18th century was to continue throughout most of the 19th century. Unfortunately the Census reports did not begin to differentiate between urban and rural population until 1851, and the use of administrative definitions is too inaccurate for effective delimitation. C. M. Law[17] has proposed a new evaluation of urban population growth based on the three criteria of minimum population size (2,500), a minimum density of one person per acre, and evidence of nucleation. Over the period 1801–1911 he found that while the total population had increased just over four times, the population classified as urban had increased nine and a half times. At the beginning of the 19th century one-third of the English population was living in urban areas; by the end of the century this proportion had increased to four-fifths. Furthermore the greatest growth was in the largest towns and cities. The percentage living in cities of over 100,000 grew from 11% in 1801 to 43·6% in 1901.

THE 1851 CENSUS

The Church of England was slow to recognize the full significance of the changes which were taking place in the population structure of the nation. True enough in the cities themselves the clergy were learning from bitter experience that the parochial system was ill-suited to an urban environment, but then the vast majority of the clergy were not working in the cities. In his pleasant country rectory the average parson could be forgiven for not appreciating the seriousness of the position. After all solid factual information was almost absent. However once the results of the 1851 Census of Attendance at Religious Worship were published nobody had any excuse for ignoring the realities.

From the Church of England's viewpoint the results of the Census came as an unpleasant shock. It was no longer the church of the overwhelming majority of Englishmen—indeed it accounted for only half the total attendances. When the attendances were broken down geographically it was found that the strength of the Church of England lay in the south (Map 8). South of a line from the Bristol Channel to the Wash the Church of England attendances were at their highest (the only exceptions being London and Cornwall). The highest percentage of attendances was in Dorset, followed by Wiltshire, Suffolk, Northamptonshire and Rutland. North of this line the picture was very different. There was still considerable support for the Church of England in the far West Midlands and in Leicestershire, but elsewhere it had lost its hold on the people. The position was particularly bad in the north-east, and not much better in Cumberland, the East and West Ridings, Lancashire, Derbyshire and Staffordshire.

In his analysis of the attendance figures for the twenty-nine towns which lay within the 'chief manufacturing districts', K. S. Inglis[18] found that in only three (Halifax, Kidderminster and Warrington) did the Anglican Church account for more than 50% of the total attendances. In seventeen of these towns the Nonconformists commanded a greater allegiance than the Church of England. It was in the largest industrial towns that the Church of England fared least well.[19]

Turning to the map of the percentage of the total population which could have been accommodated by the Church of England (Map 9), it is clear that in 1851 the Church had not caught up with the changing distribution of population. In Northumberland, Durham, Lancashire and London less than 20% of the total population could have been seated in Church of England buildings and in the West Riding only 22%. The situation in the Potteries and the Black Country was not much better. In the areas where population and industry was growing most rapidly the Anglican Church had failed to expand its parochial system and hence failed to gain the allegiance of the people.

THE RURAL PARISHES

It was not just in the large towns that the Anglican Church's position was serious. Writing of the early 19th century W. R. Ward[20] argues that the real tragedy for the Church was not her failure to meet the needs of the people in the growing cities, but rather her failure in the countryside where all her resources were concentrated. The excessive emphasis placed on the alienation of urban man from the ministrations of the Church of England has tended to deflect attention away from the situation in the countryside. So often the assumption is made that because things were going badly in the towns the position in the rural parishes must have been fine. But this was not true. Over much of rural England the Church's ministry in the early years of the 19th century was little short of a scandal.[21] Absenteeism and pluralism were still widespread, many of the church buildings were in a shocking state of disrepair, many of the livings were held by the younger sons of aristocratic families, while most of the work was done by overpressed and underpaid curates. Where Dissent could establish a foothold in a village, the competition from the Church was often at a minimum.

The tremendous advances made in the field of agriculture during the 18th century had the effect of reducing the popularity of the Church of England over large areas. In order to facilitate the improvements enclosure was necessary and to achieve this tithes had to be commuted for land. At a time when status was measured in acres, it was widely noted that the clergy were going up, and this was to a certain extent at the expense of the peasant tenants. Over most of the enclosure territory (the belt of country running from the south Midlands to Lincolnshire and Yorkshire) the Church of England lost the allegiance of many of the people and the Nonconformist alternative provided an effective counterbalance.

An even worse reaction against the Church of England resulted from tithing in kind. The collection of tithe in kind was regarded everywhere as the ideal way of alienating the parson from his people. It was a particularly regressive tax which hit hardest when large sums of money were being invested to increase yields and also at times when agricultural incomes were depressed. The real home of tithing in kind was in the south-eastern counties of Kent, Surrey, Middlesex, Hampshire and parts of Sussex (Map 24).

When the Corn Prices broke in 1814 and again in 1820 the area worst hit was the south-east. The regressive nature of tithing in kind became the focus for discontent and there followed a series of astonishing attacks on the Church of England by the farmers and farm labourers, culminating in the Labourers' Revolt of 1830. The farmers had convinced the labourers that wages couldn't go up until tithes came down. Thus in the south-east the group that was supposed to be closest to the Church of England, the agricultural community, became its fiercest opponent. The seriousness of the situation was revealed in the 1851 Census. Although Nonconformity had failed to establish itself in the south-east, the Church of England often attracted a smaller proportion of the people to its services than in counties which were overrun by Dissent (e.g. the I.A. for Northamptonshire which had a strong Nonconformist following was 47·3, while in Sussex chapels were few but the I.A. was only 42·1).

It is dangerous to generalize too much on the varied state of rural Anglicanism in the early 19th century. The factors involved are numerous and complex—many of them are unique to particular areas. It would need a series of intensive local studies, such as the one undertaken by Walker,[22] to establish just how far a specific factor operated in a given area. However it is beyond doubt that over large parts of rural England the Church of England could no longer command the allegiance of the overwhelming majority of its parishioners. The position was particularly serious in the south-east where there was no viable alternative to the parish church.

THE CHURCH OF ENGLAND IN THE LATE VICTORIAN AGE

By the middle of the 19th century the Church of England had begun to take active steps to reform its machinery. The Ecclesiastical Commission was set up in 1835 and it quickly suggested a number of long overdue changes, such as the equal distribution of bishops' finances, the overhaul of cathedral chapters, and the creation of the new dioceses of Ripon (1836) and Manchester (1847). The Tithe Act of 1836 abolished the payment of tithes in kind. By 1860 big changes had been initiated. New parishes were being created, churches were built, services were more frequent and better in quality, and the clergy had become more active. Undoubtedly the shock resulting from the publication of the 1851 Census results did much to boost this renewed activity.

In the towns and cities heroic efforts were made to reverse the effects of the Church of England's earlier neglect in these areas. The 'slum parsons' had now become a feature of city life. Unfortunately their strivings were usually negated by the lack of suitability of the parochial system in an urban environment. In a visitation charge to his clergy in 1872 the Bishop of Manchester wrote as follows:

> The parochial system, as ordinarily conceived, admirably efficient in rural parishes and among limited populations, where the pastor knows and is known to everyone committed to his charge, breaks down in face of that huge mass of ignorance, poverty, and wretchedness by which it is so often confronted in the thickly peopled areas of our manufacturing towns.

The results of reform and renewed activity were also apparent in most of the country parishes. The country parson had once again become a working parson: he was expected to do his job. The 18th century idea of ecclesiastical office as the polite acknowledgement of a family connection, or a return for services rendered, fell into disfavour. Pluralism and absenteeism were restricted by law. The total result of all this parish activity was that during the latter half of the 19th century the majority of the inhabitants of most villages would attend Sunday service. The Rectory had become the centre of village life around which everything else revolved. The rector himself, as the landlord of the glebe farm and the receiver of tithes, usually acquired the status of a country gentleman. Most villages had a large and comfortable Rectory run by a big domestic staff, and the rector, along with the squire, ruled the

village like a benevolent autocrat.[23] He was not only the master
and father bountiful of his parish: he was also its protector and
social reformer. But this golden age was too good to last.

THE TURN OF THE CENTURY

The decline in the power of the Church of England had already
set in during the last decades of the 19th century: the peak had
been reached by about 1870. In the urban industrial areas the
Church was resigned to a long and unrewarding struggle, but
these were regarded as missionary areas by the Church. The
Church's home was the countryside, the villages and hamlets of
rural England. Even today three out of every four parishes are
rural although only one in five of the total population lives in
them.

Unfortunately for the Church of England, the stability and
isolation of the village communities began to be threatened by
the end of the 19th century. The price of wheat had fallen so
low that by 1900 England's wheat acreage was only 50% of the
acreage in 1871, and this continued to shrink right up to 1914.
Consequently the rural labourers flocked to the industrial areas
in search of work. The parson's income, being partly dependent
on wheat prices, began to fall and so the educational and social
quality of the clergy dropped accordingly. The internal com-
bustion engine broke down the self-sufficiency of village life,
and the advent of effective trade-unionism, the welfare state,
and universal education took away the leadership monopoly of
the squire-parson-schoolmaster trio. The early 20th century
witnessed the beginnings of the erosion of the Church's influence
in the countryside.

THE PRESENT

It is difficult to find accurate criteria which relate to the
strength of the Church of England's influence. After the
publication of the 1851 Census results there was a dearth of
reliable information right up to the present decade. The

recently established Statistical Unit of the Church of England now publishes figures for confirmations and also for Easter communicants.[24] Both sets of figures are related to total populations and expressed on a diocesan basis. The distribution of Easter Communicants (Map 10) and the distribution of confirmations (Map 11) taken together give a good indication of Church of England allegiance as it varies over the country.

The areas of lowest allegiance centre round the large urban complexes of London, Birmingham, the Potteries, the north-east Midlands (Leicestershire, Derbyshire and Nottinghamshire), and the north. The power of Anglicanism is at its height in the north-west (Carlisle and Blackburn dioceses), in the far West Midlands (Hereford, Worcester and Gloucester dioceses), in the West Country apart from Cornwall, in East Anglia and Lincolnshire, in the Oxford diocese, and along parts of the south coast.

What explanations can be offered for this pattern? When Map 10 and Map 11 are compared with the distribution of population density (Map 12) it is quickly apparent that an inverse relationship exists between population density and allegiance to the Church of England. Broadly speaking the dioceses with the highest population densities are those which fare least well. It is the rural dioceses with low population densities which can command the highest allegiances, and the two dioceses with the lowest densities (Carlisle—187 persons per square mile, and Hereford—137 persons per square mile) also have the highest allegiance rates.

When the present position is compared with that operative in 1851 (Map 8) interesting changes can be noted. With the geographical expansion of Metropolitan London there has followed a spread of secularizing influences into Essex, Hertfordshire, Surrey and Kent, whereas in 1851 Church of England attendances were low only in Middlesex and the County of London. In 1851 the largest I.A.s were recorded in the southern half of England and it is in this area that the breakdown of traditional village life has proceeded fastest— any village within commuter distance of London has long since undergone transformation. Today, allegiance to the Church of England is greatest in those geographically isolated

4

areas where village life will have experienced least modification
—parts of the West Country, the far West Midlands, and the
north-west.[25]

CONCLUSION

The history of the Church of England over the last three
hundred years has been one of a gradual movement away from
the centre of national and social life. The system of territorial
organization built up over the centuries met the needs of the
people it was intended to serve. The dioceses, the archdeaconries and above all the parishes corresponded to the
social and geographical realities of the times. Furthermore the
resources of the Church were deployed according to the distribution of population. The clergy and the churches were in
the villages because the people were in the villages. The map
of parish boundaries was in accord with the settlement map.

Today the situation is very different. The processes of
industrialization and urbanization, coupled with transformation of the countryside resulting from the disappearance of the
self-sufficient village, have rendered the old patterns of pastoral
care obsolete. Attempts have been made to adapt and modify
the old patterns in a large number of ways. New parishes have
been created, specialized forms of ministry instituted, more
dioceses have been formed (for the present pattern see Map 10).

In recent years the Church of England has become very
concerned about its declining position within national society.
Reports have been published[26] and big changes instituted.
Unfortunately they are concerned almost exclusively with
internal reorganization. The real problem is that the Church
of England is still geared to a stable and static pre-industrial,
pre-urban society. This is reflected directly on the distribution
maps. Until this fundamental problem is tackled the Church
of England will continue to exert least influence in places like
London, Birmingham and Sheffield, and most influence in
the remoter isolated areas such as Herefordshire.

CHAPTER FIVE

The Roman Catholics

CATHOLICISM IN ENGLAND BEFORE THE 19TH CENTURY

Pre-Reformation England was staunchly Catholic, owing its allegiance to Rome. If we are to believe Maynard Smith[1] the people as a whole were devout and conscientious in the performance of their religious duties. Although they rarely had a conception of the Church in its wider aspect, they were full of enthusiasm at the parochial level. The spiritual and material sides of life were so inextricably intertwined that it was impossible to separate the two. Life was unthinkable without the Catholic Church.

The process of Reformation in England was set in motion by Henry VIII. However it took a long time for new ideas and ways to percolate to the parish level and even longer for them to gain acceptance. The average parish congregation was by nature conservative and suspicious of change. When Elizabeth I ascended the throne in 1558 the Reformation was still external to the lives of most Englishmen. Unfortunately the short reign of Mary Tudor (1553–8), when Roman Catholicism was forcibly restored and Protestants actively persecuted, had done much to discredit the Roman faith. Instead of permanently restoring the Roman variety of the Catholic faith, Mary had succeeded in laying the foundations for a more Protestant church in this country.

One of the first pieces of legislation passed by the new parliament under Elizabeth was the Act of Supremacy, which had the effect of depriving Roman Catholics of their full rights as citizens and of making them a proscribed group. During the course of Elizabeth's reign restrictions on Roman Catholics became more severe. In 1569 the Catholic North rose in revolt and although the rebellion was speedily crushed, news of its defeat was a long time in reaching Rome. Meanwhile, thinking the rebellion was successful, the Pope deposed and excommunicated Elizabeth, and released all her subjects from their allegiance. This had disastrous consequences for the Roman Catholics in England, as it was now impossible to be a faithful subject of both Pope and Queen.

The Pope's action triggered off a series of penal enactments. An Act of 1571 made it treasonable to be reconciled to Rome and a further Act of 1581 made a priest guilty of treason if he remained in England and it became a felony to shelter a priest. Roman Catholics were now technically an outlawed group. The events surrounding the Spanish Armada of 1588 and the Gunpowder Plot of 1605 were taken as further proof of the Roman Catholics' disloyalty. Thus by the end of Elizabeth's reign a Protestant Church of England was firmly rooted and legislation was in force against those who were determined to adhere to the 'old faith' and the authority of Rome.

The first attempt to estimate the number and distribution of Roman Catholics in post-Reformation England was made by Usher[2] for the year 1603. After analysing the data available he decided it was impossible to calculate accurately the number of Roman Catholic laymen in England at that time, but he hazarded a guess of between 750,000 and 1,000,000, which represented just under 20% of the total population.[3]

Of greater value to the geographer however are Usher's estimates for the various districts of England and Wales (Map 13). Roman Catholicism was still strong in the more isolated parts of the country, namely Cornwall, the Welsh Marches, Wales and the counties north of the Humber–Mersey line. By contrast the proportion of Roman Catholics in the total population base was low in the whole of south-east and south-central England, the northern Home Counties and East

Anglia. The lowest proportions were recorded in Devon and the group of counties around London.

It is difficult to obtain accurate figures for the Roman Catholic population in the 17th century. It seems their numbers declined gradually during most of the century and that the process was accelerated by the events following the Revolution of 1688 when the Catholic monarch, James II, was ousted by William of Orange. William was not as intolerant as many of his supporters and he prevented extreme measures being initiated against Roman Catholics. Nevertheless the Revolution heralded a period of eclipse for Roman Catholicism in this country, and during the following twenty-five years a series of restrictive laws were brought in which effectively banished Roman Catholics to the backwater of national life. By 1720 only about 5% of the English population was Roman Catholic.[4]

The geographical distribution of the Roman Catholics in the early 18th century can be assessed by means of a method devised by Magee.[5] He expresses the Catholic rentals for each county, given in the registrations of 1715–20, as a percentage of the Land Tax Assessment for that county. Magee admits this particular method lacks precision owing to deficiencies in the techniques used to calculate the Land Tax Assessments. However it does provide a helpful guide to the main features of Roman Catholic distribution at this time.

On average the Roman Catholic land values were 5% of the total Land Tax Assessments for this period. Magee divided England into two parts by a line drawn between the Bristol Channel and the Wash, with a bulge south to include Oxfordshire. Apart from Sussex and Hampshire, all the counties with percentages above the national average of 5% lay to the north of this line (Map 14). The average figure for all the counties south of the line was 2·7%, while to the north it was 11%.

Not only was the contrast between the northern and southern averages so great, but the line itself represented a clear divide. The counties immediately north of it (Monmouthshire, Herefordshire, Worcestershire, Warwickshire, Oxfordshire, Northamptonshire and Lincolnshire) had an average of 7·5%, while the average of those to the immediate south (Gloucestershire, Wiltshire, Berkshire, Buckinghamshire, Bedfordshire, Huntingdonshire, Cambridgeshire, and Norfolk) was only 3·1%. The abruptness of the dividing line is most evident towards the east where Bedfordshire, Huntingdonshire and Cambridgeshire, with an average of under 1%, stand in sharp contrast to their immediate neighbours, Rutland, Northamptonshire and Lincolnshire, whose average is 7%. Magee was convinced this line was no vague or arbitrary boundary, and that in 1720 it represented a definite cleavage.

Catholics were least represented in the West Country, in Wales, and the group of counties stretching south from the Wash (Cambridgeshire, Huntingdonshire, Bedfordshire and Hertfordshire). The highest percentage was in Lancashire—the chief centre of Roman Catholicism in England from the time of the Reformation to the present. Staffordshire, Durham, and Northumberland also had high percentages of Catholics. In the south only Sussex and Hampshire had percentages above the average and this was due largely to the presence of certain wealthy Roman Catholic landowning families in these two counties (both counties feature prominently in the recusancy returns for this period). The only northern county which failed to exceed the 5% average was Cheshire.

A comparison between the distribution patterns of 1603 and 1720 shows the main difference to be in the south-west where Roman Catholicism appears to have collapsed totally by 1720. The absence of wealthy aristocratic Catholic families in the south-west could have been the cause of this collapse. Roman Catholicism had also died out in Wales by 1720. In the early 18th century, as in 1603, the greatest Catholic strength lay to the north of the Humber–Mersey line.

By the mid-18th century Roman Catholicism in this country had reached its nadir. The penal legislation in the years following the Revolution of 1688 had achieved its objective and two separate counts of Roman Catholics in the late 18th century showed that they comprised barely 1% of the total population.[6] In many places congregations had completely disappeared and everywhere they had shrunk in size.

There were scarcely any Roman Catholics in the West

Country and in certain of the Midland counties by the end of the 18th century. London had the largest absolute number of Roman Catholics, but when the numbers are related to the total population, Lancashire had the highest proportion. Indeed the Protestant victory has never been complete in Lancashire. Large Catholic populations were also to be found in Staffordshire and in the northern counties of Yorkshire, Durham and Northumberland. Although absolute numbers were low, the proportion of Catholics in relation to total population was high in Cumberland and Westmorland.

Two factors go a long way towards explaining the distribution pattern of Catholics at the end of the 18th century; physical isolation and distance from London; and the influence of the gentry and nobility. The second factor is frequently dependent on the first. The northern counties of England, being a great distance from London, and containing large areas of isolated hill country, were slow to receive the ideas of the Reformation, and even slower in accepting them.

It was possible for farmers, yeomen and even townspeople to remain Catholic in the northern counties, but elsewhere the continuance of the Roman faith was dependent upon the existence of a Catholic family of squires. In most parts of late 16th-century England the feudal relationship still operated, and if an aristocratic or great landowning family was Roman Catholic, it would invariably support a priest and enable a Catholic community to centre on 'the great house'. During Elizabeth I's reign an open Catholicism was fostered by some of the great peers and peeresses, such as the Earl of Worcester, the Countess of Arundel and the Duke of Norfolk. Being peers they were not required to take the Oath of Supremacy and their estates were immune from searches. This policy of allowing recusant peers and gentry to practise their faith was continued under the Stuarts.

Under the patronage of a Catholic squire or nobleman a small pocket of Catholicism could flourish. The squire would build a chapel in his house and would support a priest without whom the administration of the sacraments and hence the practice of Catholicism would be impossible. The feudal relationship ensured that most of the squire's tenants and retainers would be Catholic and would enjoy the protection of their patron.

It was one thing to pass penal measures against the Catholics: it was another to enforce them. The government depended upon the local gentry, acting as J.P.s, to administer the laws. In the south and east where Catholics were weak and had few representatives on the local magistrates' benches, the penal laws were applied with some vigour. However where Catholicism was stronger, as in the Midlands, the Welsh Marches and the North, there was usually a sufficient number of Catholic J.P.s to ensure the penal laws had little practical effect. This process heightened the contrast between areas, as it further weakened Catholicism in places where Catholics were already in a small minority, and allowed a strengthening in areas where Catholicism was firmly established.

The dependence of Catholicism for its survival on the great landowning families had its drawbacks. If a squire abandoned the 'old faith' and became Protestant, then the chapel would be closed, the priest dismissed, and a whole Catholic community would disintegrate. During the latter half of the 17th century and throughout the 18th century many of the great Catholic families turned Protestant and others became extinct. Catholicism in England became inextricably linked with the Catholic squires and nobility. If we could plot the distribution of all the Catholic county families in 18th-century England, we would have a good distribution map of Catholicism. Thus we find the relative strength of Catholicism in 18th-century Sussex and Hampshire was due to the existence of several wealthy Catholic families in these two counties. This relationship between the Catholic Church and the landowning gentry was the hall-mark of English Catholicism up to the early years of the 19th century, and even today traces of it can still be discerned.

The first signs of the Catholic dawn in this country were the Relief Acts of 1778 and 1779. During the following fifty years the restrictions on Catholics were gradually lifted and the Emancipation Bill of 1829 finally ended all their legal disabilities. The 19th century saw two distinct strands emerge within English Catholicism; the older English Catholics; and the Irish Catholics.

THE OLDER ENGLISH CATHOLICS

In his sermon 'The Second Spring', Cardinal Newman por-
trayed the 18th-century Catholic church as follows:

> No longer the Catholic Church in the country; nay no longer, I
> may say, a catholic community—but a few adherents of the
> Old Religion, moving silently and sorrowfully about, as
> memorials of what had been.

This view of the 18th-century Catholics as a dispirited and
socially isolated group is reinforced by G. R. Cragg.[7] But were
they? In spite of the technical severity of the penal laws, the
Catholics were never confined to a 'ghetto' nor were they cut
off from social contact with their Protestant neighbours. The
respect which was paid to landed wealth and social rank was
not refused to the Catholics. Provided the Catholic gentry and
nobility had no desire to take part in public life or to enter a
military or professional career, they could still enjoy the same
quality of life as their Protestant social equals. They managed
their estates and acted as feudal lords in relation to their
tenants and families.

The Catholics were not living a shadow life and were not
socially shunned. Although out of the mainstream of national
affairs, they were still a force to be reckoned with in particular
localities. However the operation of the penal laws had made
Catholicism an exclusive religion confined to the privileged few
who had access to a private chapel or could attend one of the
London embassy chapels. From the time of the Reformation
through to the 19th century the preservation of Catholicism
in England lay in the hands of the Catholic aristocratic
families.[8]

The largest number of Catholic estates was to be found in
Northumberland, Durham, and the farming areas of Lancashire,
especially in the Fylde. There were further areas of Catholicism
in Yorkshire, particularly in the North Riding, and also in
isolated pockets throughout the Midlands. Relatively few
Catholic estates were to be found in the south, the south-west,
and in East Anglia, and even when the occupants of the 'great
house' had remained Catholic, there was rarely much loyalty

4*

on the part of the tenants and workers. The Catholic village unit had less chance of peaceful co-existence in the more hostile southern environment where the penal laws were more stringently applied.

An accelerating movement from the land to the new industrial areas took place in the 19th century and it was natural that some of these new industrial workers should have originated from the rural estates of Catholic landowners. In Lancashire there was a considerable exodus from estates in the Fylde into Preston and then southwards to Chorley and Liverpool. Similarly the new industrial ventures in Northumberland and Durham were able to draw on a long established Catholic rural population. A strong sense of group solidarity meant that whenever possible Catholic entrepreneurs would employ their co-religionists.

Historically the Catholic rural population has been small and almost entirely centred upon the estates of the Catholic landowners and aristocracy. Normally Catholics were allowed to remain unmolested provided they stepped out of national life and were content with life on their country estates. It is small wonder that by the 19th century they had become noticeably detached and unconcerned about the current political and social problems. They were well assimilated into local life, but beyond this they did not venture.

The immigration of Irish Catholics into this country in the 19th century was not welcomed by the old-established English Catholics. There was little in common between the Catholic upper class and their brethren of Irish descent, and the lack of a Catholic middle class further emphasized the gulf between the two groups.

THE IRISH CATHOLICS IN ENGLAND

By the end of the 18th century the traditional mistrust and suspicion with which the English Catholics had to contend was fast disappearing. However, just as English Roman Catholicism was beginning to be recognized *de facto*, a new element, in the form of the Irish Catholics, appeared on the scene. This had the effect of reversing the process of recognition, and again Catholicism became viewed as a threat.

The pivotal point in the history of Irish immigration into England was the potato famine of 1845–9. The origins however date back much earlier to the closing years of the 18th century with the onset of the Industrial Revolution and the resultant demand for cheap industrial labour. Already by 1841[9] there were nearly 300,000 Irish-born residents in England and Wales representing about 1·9% of the total population. The potato famine greatly accelerated a process which was already in operation. By a fortunate coincidence, at the same time as Irish economic conditions favoured emigration, the English economy was only too anxious to receive the immigrants. Unskilled labour was required in great quantity for the construction of roads, docks, railways and industrial plants, and the English were delighted to hand this work over to their Irish neighbours. Ships returning from Ireland were prepared to transport the victims of the famine to this country, as they acted as a convenient form of ballast.

The large majority of the immigrants landed at Liverpool. From here they moved in search of work into south Lancashire, Leeds and the industrial areas of the West Riding, the Potteries, the industrial parts of the North-East, and along the railway construction lines. Between 1841 and 1861 the number of Irish-born in England and Wales increased from 300,000 to 600,000, and by 1861 they accounted for 3% of the total population base.[10]

Most of the Irish immigrants, before leaving Ireland, had been engaged in agriculture and had come from rural areas. On arrival in England very few of them were able to obtain jobs on farms. They found the only work available was unskilled labouring in the great industrial cities. The skills they had learnt on the land were of no use to them in their new urban environment. Most of the Irish settled in our large urban complexes and each new arrival of immigrants made for the growing centres of industry where employment could be found. The Census of 1861 revealed that the majority of the Irish-born immigrants were in Lancashire, Cheshire, Metropolitan London, Yorkshire, Durham and Northumberland and more particularly in the big towns such as Liverpool, London, Manchester, Leeds, Bradford, Sheffield, Newcastle and Birmingham. It was the Irish immigrants who made Roman Catholicism in England an urban phenomenon.

Late 19th century Catholicism was largely an Irish affair. Writing in 1887 Cardinal Manning[11] said that he thought he had spent his life working for the Irish occupation of England. He estimated that 80% of the Catholics in England at that time were Irish, and of the remainder, the majority were in sympathy with Ireland. Even to this day there are very few Catholics in England who do not have a drop of Irish blood in them. The re-establishment of the Roman Catholic hierarchy in 1850 would hardly have been possible but for the presence of the Irish.

Unfortunately the national census of population is of only limited value in determining the total size of the Irish community in any one place. The number of Irish-*born* people is recorded but not the number of those born in England of Irish parents. It is impossible therefore to determine the number of second and third generation Irish immigrants and hence the size of the total Irish community.

Irish Catholicism in this country exhibits many of the features found in an ethnic church. Socially and culturally distinct from the older English Catholics who were found on family estates primarily in the north of England, the Irish quickly dominated and swamped English Catholicism. An ethnic church is characterized geographically by the ghetto concept. The sense of being aliens in a foreign land causes immigrants to group together, and the religious institution, transplanted from the homeland, forms a focus of community life.

When the Irish arrived in this country, they found the host community greeted them with considerable hostility. This was partly religious, the fear of a return to Roman Catholicism, and partly social, a contempt for the low social standing of the Irish. The overall effect was to convince the Irish of the need to form a self-sufficient group life. In any case the Irish population was concentrated heavily in certain areas, largely as a consequence of the type of housing available to an immigrant community.

The Irish found themselves assigned to the lowest strata within English society and clustered in the 'twilight zones' of our Coketowns.

The Catholic Church became the main cohesive agent in the Irish communities and acted as a link between them and their native Ireland. By its specific discouragement of mixed Catholic-Protestant marriages the church helped to preserve the Irish interests. It provided a focal point for national sentiment and also operated a wide variety of Irish community organizations. Most of the Irish who came over to this country were intending to stay for only a short period and so wished to remain in an Irish atmosphere. This of course greatly hindered any possibility of integration into English society.[12]

Nearly all ethnic churches have their own native priesthood. In their early formative years in this country the Irish Catholics lacked their own priests—the English bishops saw to this—and even as late as 1900 there was only a handful of Irish priests in England. Most of the Irish resented the foreign English priests who were forced on them and consequently many drifted away from the church. It was not until the early 20th century that Irish priests came over to England in large numbers, but once they settled in they helped to solidify Irish sentiment. They had suffered under English exploitation in Ireland as well and so they were gladly accepted as the guardians of the immigrant community.

The Irish in England continue to look on themselves as a distinctive group and the process of assimilation is far from complete.[13] There are still recognizable areas of Irish Catholic settlement in particular quarters of our cities, and although upward social mobility and the resultant move to the suburbs has broken their former rigidity, they still form recognizable geographical units.[14]

The first wave of Irish immigration into this country came to an end in 1880, but a second wave began in the mid-1920s and has continued ever since. The 1961 Census revealed that nearly 2% of the population of England and Wales was born in Ireland, and to this must be added the much larger percentage of second and subsequent generation Irish-born in this country. There seems to be little future prospect of this immigration tailing off, for Britain continues to provide the best alternative to unemployment at home.

The increases in the Irish-born population have been most marked in the London Metropolitan area and in the Midlands, whilst the numbers in Lancashire have only increased slightly. The six major conurbations (Greater London, West Midlands, Merseyside, South-East Lancashire, West Yorkshire, and Tyneside), account for over half the Irish-born population in this country. However not all the Irish make for the conurbations. With the diversification of industry and the spread of light industry to small centres, some of the Irish have made for these new areas. The Midlands and Greater London, rather than Lancashire, are the expanding areas of today, and it is to these that the Irish come. The majority continue to find employment in unskilled labouring, but an increasing number are entering the skilled and professional occupational groups. This increase in social status produces geographical mobility in the form of a movement out of the old Catholic 'ghetto areas'.

As long as the steady inflow of Irish immigrants continues there will be a sufficient number of newcomers into the areas of Irish Catholic settlement to more than compensate for the loss of the ones who have moved out as a result of upward social mobility.

THE 1851 CENSUS

The 1851 Census of Religious Attendance provided the first really detailed information from which an accurate picture of Roman Catholic distribution could be constructed. The Census listed attendance figures for each poor law union or registration district, but at this level appreciable errors were possible and so for most areas their use has been restricted to the county level. However in the cases of Lancashire, Cheshire, Northumberland and Durham a method has been devised which partially eliminates the errors at the registration district level so that they could be used for a more detailed study.

*Roman Catholics in Lancashire and Cheshire in
1851*

Map 15 gives the distribution of Roman Catholic attendance in
Lancashire and Cheshire for 1851. A line running north-east
from Chester separates the two counties into a Protestant east
and a Catholic west. With the one exception of the area in the
immediate neighbourhood of Manchester which many of the
Irish Catholics would have made for because of the employment opportunities, the districts of high Catholic practice all
lay to the west and north of this line. The highest proportions
of Catholics were in the three northern districts of the Fylde,
Garstang and Clitheroe—the home of an old-established
Catholic rural population based on the estates of the great
Catholic landowning families.[15]

By 1851 the growth of Catholicism in Lancashire was the
result of twin forces; the southward drift of agricultural
workers from the Catholic estates in north Lancashire to the
new areas of industrial expansion; and the fanwise movement
out from Liverpool of Irish immigrants. In the eastern part of
the county, to the north of Manchester, Catholics were very
sparse. Between here and the high incidence of Catholicism in
west Lancashire, lay an intermediate zone consisting of the
registration districts of Blackburn, Bolton and Leigh.

Compared to Lancashire the incidence of Catholicism in
Cheshire was low. Over the whole of central and south Cheshire
a small Catholic rural population registered a practice well
below the national average. Catholics were numerous on the
Wirral, an overspill area for Liverpool, and there were above
average attendances in the four districts to the south and south-
east of Manchester, and also in the industrial district of
Runcorn.

*Roman Catholics in the North-east in
1851*

A sizeable rural Catholic population was to be found in
Northumberland and Durham. The presence of Catholics in

purely rural registration districts such as Hexham, Rothbury, Teesdale and Morpeth (Map 16) attests to this. Nearly all the isolated pockets of rural Catholicism were directly dependent on the Catholic hereditary estates (e.g. Minsteracres, Felton, Hesleyside and Croxdale) for their existence.

The highest percentages of Catholic attendances however were in the urban centres of Newcastle, Gateshead and Durham, and also in the extreme south-east around the Hartlepools and Middlesbrough. These were the main industrial areas in the north-east and consequently they attracted large numbers of Irish immigrants, who were reinforced by Catholics moving from the rural estates in the region in search of better employment opportunities.

Roman Catholics in England in 1851

Map 17 shows the geographical variation in attendance by counties on Census Sunday 1851. With the exception of the London Metropolitan area, Catholics were few in number everywhere south of the Bristol to Grimsby line: that is in the West Country, the East Midlands, East Anglia, and the whole of Southern England. Two counties, Rutland and Huntingdon, were without a single Roman Catholic congregation. Lancashire stood out as the county with the largest proportion of Catholics among her population, and in all she accounted for nearly 40% of the total Catholic population in England and Wales. Two other groups of counties had significant Catholic populations: Durham, Northumberland and the North Riding in the north-east; and a belt formed by Cheshire, Staffordshire and Warwickshire. Map 18, based on the percentage of marriages taking place in Roman Catholic churches in 1851,[16] reveals the same basic distribution pattern as do the Census figures, although there are certain minor discrepancies (Middlesex and the North Riding).

The Census report also lists the attendance figures for the major towns in England. In nearly all the industrial towns of the Midlands and North the Roman Catholics registered a higher percentages of attendances than they did in the surrounding administrative counties. The predominantly urban nature of 19th-century English Catholicism was clearly reflected in the Census figures.

It is possible to draw certain comparisons and contrasts between the geographical distributions of 1851 and 1720. By 1851 Catholicism had virtually died out in the Welsh borders, in Westmorland, and along the southern limit of the 'Catholic North', that is in Oxfordshire, Northamptonshire, Rutland and Lincolnshire. Catholic influence had greatly increased in Cheshire and London by 1851, largely as a result of Irish immigration. Otherwise, the dichotomy between the Catholic North and the non-Catholic South remained intact.

ROMAN CATHOLICISM IN ENGLAND IN 1962

The Newman Demographic Survey has collected Mass attendance figures for the years 1958–62. These figures are related to the top tier local authority (either administrative county or county borough), but as the ecclesiastical and civil boundaries rarely coincided a slight margin of error has to be accepted. The statistics for Mass attendance have been expressed as a percentage of the total population for each county, and it was then possible to compile a map showing the density of the practising Catholic community in England for the year 1962 (Map 19). Four areas of high density stand out:

1. The North—Cumberland, Northumberland, Durham and the North Riding.
2. Lancashire and Cheshire.
3. Warwickshire.
4. London and Middlesex.

Intermediate densities are found in the West Riding, and in a large area to the north and south of London. Densities are lowest in Westmorland, the Welsh border counties of Hereford, Salop and Worcestershire, the West Country and a block of counties focusing on the Wash.

The distribution of the percentage of marriages[17] taking

place in Roman Catholic churches in 1962 (Map 20) broadly confirms the pattern revealed above. However there is a certain discrepancy in the London region which calls for exploration. Mass attendance is proportionally higher in East Sussex than Catholic marriages. This appears to be due to the age structure of the population in East Sussex, as most of the Catholics who are here will be retired Londoners and relatively few are likely to be young Catholics of marriageable age. The converse is true to the north of London where there are now large numbers of Catholic families who have been moved out of Inner London in overspill and redevelopment schemes. This would account in particular for the high percentage of Catholic marriages in Bedfordshire.

A direct comparison between the Index of Attendance for 1851 and the percentage of Mass attenders for 1962 is impossible owing to the different criteria of measurement used, but the overall variations in the distribution pattern can be compared. Westmorland has a small percentage of Catholics both in 1851 and in 1962. The belt of strong Catholic practice which ran from Lancashire to Warwickshire in 1851 had been broken by 1962. It seems that Catholic strength in Staffordshire had not grown at the same rate as in Cheshire and Warwickshire. The four northern counties of Cumberland, Northumberland, Durham and the North Riding have remained Catholic strongholds over the last hundred years, and Lancashire has always been in a category of its own, having the highest proportion of Catholics to total population in England.

The most significant change in the distribution pattern has been the relative growth of Catholicism in the whole area within a radius of sixty miles of the centre of London. In 1851 it was only the County of London which stood out above the general sea of low density. By 1962 this had been drastically altered. Middlesex had joined the County of London as an area of high Catholic density and a whole group of counties around London now had medium densities (Map 19).

What has caused this growth of Catholicism in the south-east? Admittedly there has been a general movement of population into the south-east, but this, in itself, would not account for the increase in the proportion of Catholics in the general population base. It is possible to discern three processes at work. The first is simply immigration from Catholic countries overseas. Secondly, in recent years the Catholic population has been increasing in wealth, leading to a greater Catholic representation in the middle classes. This upward social movement produces geographical mobility and a movement out of the Catholic 'ghetto' areas. London tends to act as a magnet to the upward spiralists. Finally Catholics have been under-represented in the London region since the Reformation, and the differential growth rate we are now witnessing can be seen in terms of a stabilizing process. The deterrents to an overt practice of Catholicism which operated from the time of the Reformation were gradually lifted during the 19th century, although the social deterrents persisted well into the 20th century. These deterrents had been enforced most stringently in the south-east of England.

THE SIZE OF THE ROMAN CATHOLIC POPULATION[18]

Unfortunately any attempts to assess the approximate size of the Roman Catholic population contain an element of conjecture. Before the 1851 Census reasonable figures are impossible to obtain. The 1851 Census recorded a total of nearly 253,000 persons at morning Mass and taking into account the various circumstances which would have prevented people from attending, the Catholic population at this time was probably in the region of 800,000–1,000,000, that is betweeen 4·5% and 5·5% of the total population. By the end of the 19th century it had risen to between 6% and 7% (2·2 million–2·5 million).

A general consensus of results points to the 1961 Catholic community accounting for about 10% of the total population. (The Newman Demographic Survey gives the slightly higher figure of 12·2%—about 5·6 million.) This rapid growth rate in the 20th century is the result of mixed marriages, immigration from Ireland, the resettlement of the Polish Army, and higher fertility rates, although this last factor is now losing its former significance. Demographically conversions have been of little importance, but they have played a large role in building up a Catholic middle class.

The centre of gravity of the Catholic population has been moving steadily south—see Table 5.[19] The drift to the south-east is even greater than the figures reveal for the Province of Southwark includes the whole of south-west England. Unfortunately a trend analysis cannot be obtained from the Mass attendance figures, as they have only been collected over a five-year period.

An analysis is possible at a county level using the Registrar General's figures for the proportion of Roman Catholic marriages over the thirty-eight-year period from 1924 to 1962.[20] Without any exceptions the proportion has increased in each county. The lowest rates of increases are in the old-established Catholic counties of the north. Conversely the highest rates of increase are in the counties which were traditionally devoid of Catholics. The trends appear to be pointing towards a gradual evening out of the Catholic distribution pattern.

URBAN CATHOLICISM

As early as the second half of the 18th century Catholicism was becoming urban in character. Berington[21] estimated that in 1780 nearly 40% of the Catholics in England were to be found in London, and a high proportion of the northern Catholics lived in the new industrial towns. The Irish Rebellion of 1798, and the consequent inflow of Irish Catholics into this country, reinforced an urban pattern that was already beginning. Thus long before the Potato Famine, English Catholicism was already established in the urban environment. However the flood of Irish which came over after the Potato Famine made English Catholicism almost entirely an urban phenomenon.

The Mass attendance figures collected by the Newman Demographic Survey distinguish between county boroughs and the surrounding administrative counties. For England as a whole in 1962 4·5% of the total population attended Mass, but this can be broken down into 6·0% for the county boroughs and

3·4% for the administrative counties. Certain key county boroughs are cited as examples in Table 6. Nearly all the county boroughs in England have a significantly higher proportion of Catholics in their population than do the administrative counties which surround them. The highest proportions are in the north-west (Table 7).[22]

The urban nature of Catholicism is also underlined by the Registrar General's marriage statistics for the six conurbations of England, which alone accounted for 55% of the Catholic marriages in 1962.[23] The figures showed that most of the Catholics in Lancashire and Cheshire were in the conurbations of South-East Lancashire and Merseyside. A similar situation was to be found in the other four conurbations.

RURAL CATHOLICISM

It is only in North Lancashire, Northumberland and Durham that there is anything approximating to a well-established rural Catholic population. Over the rest of England there are only a few pockets and these are almost invariably centred on the seats of the Catholic county families—the operation of the penal laws saw to this. Although the Irish immigrants who came over in the 19th century were almost without exception from a rural background, nearly all of them were forced to settle in the new areas of expanding industry. Very few were able to obtain employment in agriculture.

The Catholic Church is still in a very serious position in the countryside. The proportion of Catholics to general population in rural areas is low, and they are extremely scattered and have few opportunities for social contact with one another. One of the obligations which the Catholic Church imposes on its members is weekly attendance at Mass. Most villages are without Catholic churches and often the nearest Mass centre is many miles away in the county town. Naturally the people are exhorted to make the journey but the temptation to lapse is extremely great.

In recent years the Catholic Church has made significant attempts to cater for the rural Catholics, such as hiring halls and building small chapels which are manned by clergy travelling from the neighbouring market town.[24] Nevertheless it will not be economically possible to provide Mass centres in all the villages. However, unless there are Mass centres within a convenient distance, Catholics who move out into the countryside are likely to give up the practice of their religion. English Catholicism is geared essentially to an urban and not a rural environment.

CONCLUSION

The future trends in the geographical distribution of Catholicism are likely to be towards a more even spread over the country as a whole. Increasing assimilation and social mobility are in part breaking down the rigidity of the old 'ghetto' areas, and the Catholic authorities are making concerted efforts to tackle the problem of rural Catholicism. Assuming the present trends continue, the distribution pattern of Catholicism in the years to come will resemble more closely the distribution pattern of the general population.

CHAPTER SIX

The Nonconformists

The Englishman . . . likes to find his own way to heaven, and
has no scruple in leaving the beaten track with a few friends
to follow him.

W. R. Inge: Dean of St. Paul's

EARLY HISTORY

Once the powerful forces behind the Reformation in England
had broken the monolithic structure of the Roman Church,
there emerged a new period of religious experimentation. The
religious settlement reached by Queen Elizabeth and her
advisers put the stamp of approval on to the Church of England.
It was felt the Church of England was sufficiently comprehensive to satisfy the religious demands of the vast majority and by
an Act of Uniformity any further experimentation was deemed
illegal. But in the eyes of some men this was to substitute one
ecclesiastical monopoly for another. Once experiment begins it
is hard to stop, even with repressive legislation: the gradual
development of English Nonconformity[1] was witness to this.

The roots of Nonconformity go back to the beginning of the
Reformation, although it did not begin to take shape as an
organized body for a further century. From the very earliest,
Nonconformity was an umbrella title covering a wide diversity
of opinion and practice. The original followers became known

as Puritans; a designation first used in the 1560s as a term of abuse, but which quickly came to imply a failure to make allowances, over severe, over precise.

Little is known of the exact strength and distribution of these early rebels, but the records of the heretics burnt during the brief reign of the Roman Catholic queen, Mary Tudor, provide a rough guide. Out of the 273 put to death the vast majority (235) were in London and the south-east. The county figures were, Kent 59, Essex 52, London 46, East Anglia 35, Sussex 27, Middlesex 13, Hertfordshire 13, the rest of England 32, and Wales 3.[2] Already the deviant nature of Essex, Suffolk and Norfolk had begun to show.

Once Elizabeth had finalized the religious settlement and the Church of England was established as the only lawful church, the government began to turn its attention to those who had opted out of the national church. In 1593 a stringent Act was passed against Puritans and separatists; three of their leaders were executed and many others fled abroad.

However a moderate Puritanism could survive within the Church of England itself, thanks to the existence of a group of lay patrons who were in sympathy with Puritan thought and practice. Where the patron himself was a Puritan he would naturally install a Puritan incumbent, and as the local inhabitants were compelled to attend church, they would soon become soaked in Puritan ideas. It was possible for great landowners to buy the rights of presentation to particular livings solely for the purpose of creating places for Puritan ministers.

Usher[3] has listed all the known Puritan livings for 1603 (see Map 21). The greater part of the Puritan ministers held their benefices from several great landowning families, while other ministers became private chaplains to them, their relatives and their friends. The Earl of Warwick controlled a large number of livings in Warwickshire, Leicestershire, Northamptonshire, Suffolk, and Essex; similarly so did Lady Bacon and Lord Grey of Wilton in Hertfordshire and Buckinghamshire; Sir Richard Knightly, Sir Edward Monague, and Sir Francis Hastings in Northamptonshire; and Sir Robert Jermyn, Sir Drew Drury, and Sir Robert Wroth in Norfolk, Suffolk, and Essex. This sponsoring work was reinforced by several Puritan-dominated town corporations[4]—in particular Boston, Ipswich, Lincoln, Coventry and Northampton. After a careful investigation of all the records Usher was convinced that, while a few ministers would have become Puritan after their appointment, and a few more appointed by minor Puritan patrons, the vast majority owed their places to the enthusiastic sponsoring work of these few influential gentlemen.[5]

From Map 21 it is apparent that late 16th-century Nonconformity was confined to the Midlands and the eastern counties, with two small pockets in south-east Lancashire and along the Sussex coast. Elsewhere Puritan ministers were few and far between.

It was during the decades leading up to the Civil War that Puritanism became a force to be reckoned with in this country. The precise reasons for its rapid growth are complex and still disputed, but nearly all historians accept that there is a close link between the rise of Puritanism and the rise of capitalism.[6] The Church of England was a great political and economic institution, and there were many reasons apart from religious ones why men wished to overthrow it in 1640. The economic considerations appealed particularly to the rising class of industrialists and traders, both great and small, and in later years it was this group which was to form the backbone of Nonconformity.

Already it has been seen how the concentration of patronage assisted the growth of Puritanism in the Midlands and East Anglia. A further effect was to increase the number of absentee patrons. A powerful lord, administering a large number of patronages, could not hope to keep in contact with all the congregations in his charge, and inevitably many of these congregations began to relish their new-found independence. Similarly patronages exercised by town corporations tended to produce self-controlling congregations. In numerous cases the effective selection of new ministers was made by the congregations themselves, thereby creating a *de facto* voluntary system.

The Civil War in England was not primarily a war of religion, but undoubtedly religious issues were involved. Oliver Cromwell was an Independent by conviction and was prepared to allow great latitude in religious belief and practice.

It is small wonder therefore that much of his support came from Puritan East Anglia and from London. Those who were opposed to the Established Church saw Cromwell as their Protector and sided with Parliament against the Royalists. Once the Crown had been defeated and the Church of England disbanded, Cromwell was faced with the task of putting in an alternative religious system. This was difficult, believing as he did in religious *laissez-faire*, and apart from a half hearted attempt to introduce Presbyterianism,[7] he allowed men to worship more or less as they liked. The result was that the many diverse groups were barely organized and quite incapable of preventing the return of religious uniformity under Charles II. Nevertheless the principle of toleration had been established and it was impossible to return to a pre-1640 situation. The Civil War had ensured that English Nonconformity was to be a permanent feature within the national life, despite later attempts at suppression.

The unsettling years of the Commonwealth and Protectorate were finally ended in 1660 with the restoration of the monarchy. Henceforth religious experimentation was to be illegal and by an Act of Uniformity in 1662 only the Church of England was granted recognition. Many of the Puritan incumbents were unable to accept this and so were driven out of their livings (the so-called Great Ejection.) Three years later the Five Mile Act prevented the ejected ministers from living within five miles of any town—a form of banishment. An unexpected result of this Act was that a century later towns like Birmingham, which had been mere villages in the 17th century, grew up with their trade and wealth already in the hands of the Nonconformists.

During the reign of Charles II a series of penal laws, known as the Clarendon Code, was enacted against the Nonconformists. However the legislation failed to wipe out the Nonconformists from the towns because they were too well represented among the natural ruling classes there. Why was this? Largely because in urban areas most parishes had ceased to be communities and so the Church of England was not able to exercise effective supervision over all the inhabitants. By contrast, in the old geographical communities of rural England, with their hierarchical subordination, their traditional ceremonies, and their succession of popular seasonal festivals, the power of the Anglican Church was rarely challenged.

In 1672 Charles II issued a Declaration of Indulgence under which a certain degree of freedom was permitted to the Nonconformists. Under the provisions of this Declaration licences were issued and from the records kept it can be seen that Nonconformists were strong in the south-west, in London, the home counties, and the eastern counties, but weak in all the northern counties. The last years of the 17th century witnessed a period of steady growth and consolidation for Nonconformity, particularly after the Toleration Act was passed in 1689. But this was short lived.

As the century turned, so Nonconformity began to lose some of its members and influence. The next fifty years was to be an inauspicious age for the Dissenters. The decline can be traced both in the histories of individual churches and congregations, and in the reports of Church leaders and assemblies. Not only numerically, but also socially and economically the Dissenters were on the decline. Although the Toleration Act permitted the legal existence of Dissent, it was still far from acceptable socially and carried with it many practical disadvantages. Consequently its aristocratic and wealthy supporters began to move back to the Established Church, particularly as in the muted Age of Reason religious enthusiasm was no longer fashionable.

Where were the Dissenters at this time? In those parts of England which rallied to Cromwell in the Civil War, Dissenting congregations were to be found in both town and country among the business and farming communities. They were most numerous in the east of England. Elsewhere Dissent survived only in the towns where it was strong among those who formed the local leadership. Rural Dissent was never widespread prior to the Evangelical Revival.

In 1715 two attempts were made to estimate the strength of Dissent on a county basis—the Evans List and the Neal List.[8] Sixty years later a Baptist minister, Josiah Thompson, made a series of returns on lines similar to Evans—the Thompson List of 1773:[9] A comparison between the two dates is feasible, although it has to be remembered that whilst the total number of congregations had not declined very greatly, the population had risen from 5·9 millions to 7·1 millions. The considerable number of references in Thompson's manuscripts to declines within individual congregations points to the likelihood of a noticeable drop in the average size of a Dissenting congregation since 1715. The reports relating to the counties south of a line from London to Bristol, but excluding Wiltshire, and to Cheshire, Salop and Derbyshire all suggest that Dissent was in a bad condition (see Map 22). On the other hand Dissent appeared to be improving in a line of counties running from Wiltshire through the Midlands into Lancashire, Yorkshire and the north-east.

GROWTH OF INFLUENCE FROM THE END OF THE 18TH CENTURY

The latter half of the 18th century represents a clear break in the history of the non-episcopal churches in this country. By the mid-18th century older Dissent was virtually exhausted and could see no way of reviving itself. It was fighting a losing battle against stagnation and decay. Just at this time a new impetus was given by the work of John Wesley and the Evangelical Revival. This event heralded the beginning of a process of development which was to lead directly into modern Nonconformity. By the end of the 18th century not only was Methodism established as a force in the land, but the older Dissenting groups had taken on a new lease of life, their sagging spirits revived by the enthusiasm generated by Wesley.

At first the Methodists looked upon themselves as a reforming group within the Church of England and would have little to do with the Dissenters. However once the formal separation between the Methodists and the Church of England had been made, there was little to distinguish them in the common mind from the other Dissenters and they quickly became part of 19th-century Nonconformity. They all shared the same civil disabilities, and were all treated with the same disdain by the Church of England.

The main concern of the Nonconformists during the early

years of the new century was the removal of their disabilities. After much campaigning they secured the repeal of the Test Act in 1828 and were now able to enter parliament and hold other public offices. But this was only stage one. They were still compelled to pay church rates, they could not be married in their own chapels or buried without the rites of the Church of England, and the ancient universities remained closed to them. It was not until 1868 that the last of the major grievances, the compulsory payment of church rates, was finally removed.[10]

The total effect of the disabilities and the fight to have them removed was to produce a certain solidarity among the Nonconformists and also to ensure that most of their members were drawn from the middle class and below. The more ambitious and prosperous sections of the community realized it was wiser to belong to the Church of England and throughout the century there was a steady trickle of those who had struggled and succeeded, from the Nonconformist chapel, to the parish church. To announce that you were joining the Church of England was often regarded as a proclamation of success. Conversely a person of high social standing would hardly ever throw in his lot with the chapel folk—to do so would incur loss of status.

A significant result of this upper limit on the social scale, above which Nonconformists were found but rarely, was to restrict the geographical distribution of their chapels. In the areas of extreme wealth and affluence, Nonconformist presence was minimal.

Less widely appreciated was the lower social limit of Nonconformity. Nearly all chapels had to be self-supporting financially, relying on the generosity of their congregations. Among people with an extremely low income, such a system had little appeal. Few of those who had to go without some of the basic necessities of life could be enticed to support such a luxury as religion. Apart from mission chapels endowed by wealthy suburban congregations, Nonconformists were sparse in the poorest parts of the downtown inner cores of our industrial cities.

THE 1851 CENSUS

By the middle of the 19th century Nonconformity had climbed right out of its earlier doldrums, although it had still to reach the height of its influence. But the pattern revealed in the Religious Census of 1851 was to remain for the rest of the century.

The general results showed that the Church of England and the Nonconformists[11] were about equal in terms of attendances[12] and finally dispelled the lingering myth that the Church of England was the church of the vast majority. When the Nonconformist attendances were related to the general population totals on a county basis, the strength of the chapels appeared to be greatest in a group of counties to the south of the Wash and in the West Country, followed by a belt running northwards from Essex and Hertfordshire to the North Riding (see Map 23). Nonconformity was least represented in the south-east, the west Midlands, the north-west and the north-east.

However this is but one aspect of the distribution. Turning to the absolute totals, and also to the numbers relative to those attending church at all, it is found that Nonconformity was primarily a phenomenon of the Midlands and North, and it was urban rather than rural. K. S. Inglis examined all the twenty-nine towns designated in the Census report as 'chief manu-facturing districts'. He found that in fifteen of the towns, Nonconformists accounted for over 50% of the total atten-dances, but in only three cases did the Anglicans exceed 50%. Inglis concluded that it was a group of towns comprising the coal towns of Sunderland, Tynemouth and South Shields, the coal and iron town of Wolverhampton, the iron town of Dudley, the woollen towns of Bradford and Leeds, and the cotton towns of Ashton and Rochdale, which best supported the view that Nonconformity took Christianity into the great industrial towns of the nineteenth century.[13]

However urban Nonconformity met with only partial suc-cess. In the largest provincial towns, nearly all the cotton towns of Lancashire, the two great hardware towns and several iron and coal towns, both Anglican and Nonconformist attendances were at their lowest. It was in these towns that the majority of the 'submerged tenth' were to be located—the so-called class below the working class. Nevertheless in the great cities of the Midlands and the North, Nonconformist influence was greater than the numbers suggest. With the lack of a strong lead from the Church of England the Nonconformist chapels assumed the responsibility of governing social life and presenting Christianity to their urban contemporaries.

BIRMINGHAM AND MANCHESTER

Two great centres of Nonconformity emerged during the 19th century—Birmingham and Manchester. Birmingham had always lacked a strong Anglican presence and in the 17th century it was little bigger than a village. Its population increased during the 18th century but the Church of England, failing to realize the significance of what was happening, remained passive. During this whole period the Nonconformists were active. The towns which were out of bounds to the Nonconformists under the provisions of the Five Mile Act were those of the late 17th century. Working on the assumption of a stable population pattern, the legislators had not bothered to provide a mechanism for adding new towns to the list. Hence after the Five Mile Act the Nonconformists were forced to concentrate on the larger villages such as Birmingham and their work was allowed to continue unhindered through into the 19th century. By this time Birmingham had become a great industrial city and it was the old Dissenting families which formed the social elite.

There was great scope for Nonconformists in Birmingham owing to a lack of a viable Roman Catholic or Church of England alternative. The majority of the city's most influential families gave their prestige and money to the Nonconformist cause. The temptation for businessmen to move over to the Church of England or to opt out altogether had not yet arisen in any serious way and they generously supported both the work and the finances of the chapels.[14]

Birmingham Nonconformists in the 19th century operated through local politics and they were the first to proclaim the

'Civic Gospel', urging a sense of adventure and responsibility in Local Government. They were led by some of the greatest ministers of the century, men such as R. W. Dale at Carrs Lane Congregational Church, H. W. Crosskey at the Unitarian Church of the Messiah, and the Baptist minister George Dawson.[15] Dale once described Birmingham as a great family in which the decisions were taken by a small group of all powerful Nonconformist families. By the end of the 19th century Birmingham had become the great Mecca of Nonconformity.

Further north lay Manchester which was also to become a focal point for Dissenters. Manchester's history however was somewhat different: it could hardly fail to be distinctive lying as it does within the religious battlefield of Lancashire. As soon as the Reformation had got under way, the religious forces in Lancashire polarized into a strong and determined Roman Catholic party, and at the other end, a powerful and zealous Puritan party.[16] Between the two there was little room for the Church of England.

This polarization of religious allegiance manifested itself spatially, for it was in the south-east of Lancashire that the Reformation met with success. The merchants of 'Salfordshire' had already established commercial links with Germany and Holland and through these contacts had become acquainted with radical ideas. They were better educated than their rustic neighbours and frequently knew more than their priests. They prided themselves on their sturdy independence and they quickly became enthusiastic advocates of the Reformation.

During the succeeding centuries Manchester was regarded as the headquarters of the Nonconformist cause in the north-west. When the country was hit by the economic depression of the late 1830s and early 1840s, Manchester became the centre of the Anti-Corn Law League which was supported wholeheartedly by the local Unitarians, Baptists and Congregationalists. This further enhanced the city's reputation for determined opposition. It was not until 1847 that a separate Anglican diocese was created for Manchester (previously it was part of the Chester diocese) and in the minds of many Anglican clergy to work here was tantamount to entering the mission field. The life of the city was in the hands of the Chapel, not of the Church.[17]

19TH CENTURY RURAL NONCONFORMITY

In England the Victorian chapel is usually pictured within the setting of the smoky gloom of 'Coketown'. But this is not the complete story, for where the social conditions were favourable, the Nonconformists also penetrated into the countryside. Their success or otherwise depended largely upon the type of settlement pattern and agricultural system.[18] Where the village was of the closed integrated type, the squire and parson would wield a patriarchal influence ensuring the stranglehold of the Church of England. In these 'miniature welfare states' there was little possibility of chapel life developing. If the village was of the open type with no dominant landlord, independent thought and action was more possible and chapels could be easily established. However, they ran into frequent financial difficulty, for most of these villages were economically poorer and their inhabitants could barely afford a voluntary system. Similarly on poor agricultural land where settlement was scattered, the Church of England was unable to prevent chapels being built, although the independent-minded farmers were often hard put to raise enough money for their continuing existence. In general an arable economy, with its nucleated settlement favoured the Church of England, while a pastoral economy with its scattered settlement favoured the Nonconformists.

A further factor which influenced the distribution of rural Nonconformity was the battle over tithes and enclosures.[19] The large landowners in the region of open field country stretching from the south Midlands to Lincolnshire and Yorkshire realized the only way they could put into effect the improvements necessary to capture the new markets was by enclosure. Before enclosure was possible, the tithes had to be commuted, mostly in return for land. This resulted in many of the clergy becoming great landowners, and although the commutation of tithes helped to reduce the parson/landowner friction, it alienated most of the small tenant farmers and agricultural

5

labourers from the Church of England. These social changes heralded in a period of success for Nonconformity, with the Methodists taking the lead in Lincolnshire and Yorkshire, and the older Dissenters in Huntingdonshire, Bedfordshire and some of the other south Midland counties (see Map 24).

Why did Nonconformity fail to make any real headway in the south-east of England? Certainly up to the beginning of the 19th century these counties were firmly under the wing of the Church of England. It was only on high ground out of the reach of the squires and parsons of the settled farmlands that chapel life was at all possible (especially in the Chilterns and the Weald). In 1814 agricultural prices broke, and again in 1820. The counties worst affected were in the south-east and these contained most of the property still tithed in kind (Map 24). Inevitably this resulted in violent attacks on the Church of England which was seen as the root cause of the economic ills. In 1830 the Labourers Revolt broke out in Kent and swept westward as far as Dorset. With the Church of England being so obviously out of favour this might have appeared a good opportunity for the Nonconformists. In fact they achieved very little. The farmers and farm labourers of the 1830s were in no mood to increase their bills by adding the expense of voluntaryism to that of tithes.

THE HIGH NOON OF NONCONFORMITY

In the three decades leading up to the great Liberal victory of 1906 Nonconformity reached the peak of its strength and influence. The pattern of behaviour and code of conduct it imposed on late Victorian England was to become the hallmark of that era. It was typified by the so called 'Nonconformist Conscience'.[20] The culmination was the shortlived Liberal success in 1906, when, for a few months, the government of the nation was in the hands of the party so intimately associated with the Chapel way of life, D. W. Brogan writes

> It is probable that Nonconformity reached its height of political power, was most representative of the temper of the English people round the beginning of this century . . . But in

the generation that has passed since the great Liberal landslide of 1906, one of the greatest changes in the English religious and social landscape has been the decline of Nonconformity.[21]

THE DECLINE OF THE CHAPEL IN THE 20TH CENTURY

In 1906 Nonconformity was at the apex of its influence and even before the First World War began eight years later, the first signs of a period of stagnation and decline could be detected. Indeed these signs can be traced back statistically into the late 19th century when the church building programme had slowed down and apparent increases in membership totals were negated by the more rapid increase in population. However the full effects of the decline did not become obvious until the 1920s.

Over the last sixty years all the main indices of Nonconformist strength have been dropping steadily. Whereas in Victorian times membership was reserved for the hardcore faithful and many of the Sunday by Sunday congregation would consist of regular adherents, today the status of adherent has gone completely. Anyone who attended regularly would pressingly be offered membership. Despite the relaxation in membership requirements the numbers have been falling relentlessly and those who remain are predominantly in the over-forty age category. Similarly the number of children registered at Free Church Sunday Schools in England and Wales has fallen from 3 million in 1910 to 8–900,000 in 1962.[22]

In most parts of England today the Free Church picture is a bleak one. Not only have the numbers declined, but the social composition of those remaining and the influence they are able to exert has fallen dramatically.

To visit those parts of the country where the chapels are most deeply embedded in the landscape and local history, to live in Methodist Yorkshire, or Baptist Wales, or Independent East Anglia, or Unitarian Lancashire is to recognize the real plight of Nonconformity in the sixties. Anyone can point to shining exceptions in particular places, but over large tracts of country

... behind the peeling façades and plaintive wayside pulpits, there is nothing left but a faithful ingrown remnant, whiling away its Pleasant Sunday Afternoons and its Women's Bright Hours in dingy rooms from which whole generations and classes and intelligence levels have long since fled.[23]

Passing through the streets of most of our older industrial towns the traveller is conscious of many derelict or converted chapels. Once these were the centres for thriving Nonconformist communities: now they are garages, storehouses or workshops. Sometimes their abandonment has been the result of an outward population drift, but more usually it has been simply a decline of interest on the part of the local inhabitants.

Throughout most of the Midlands and the north of England the situation is particularly bad. It was in the industrial towns of these areas that chapels were built in profusion during the 19th century. Most of the buildings were in the middle-class zones of the towns which in recent years have suffered social decline. The former inhabitants are now living in the new suburbs several miles away. The Victorian bricks and mortar remain, but the human element of the chapel is only a shadow of its former self.

So too in the countryside the Nonconformists are fighting a rearguard action. Up to the coming of John Wesley most of rural England was staunchly Anglican. There was little room in a patriarchal village for a dissenting chapel even if enough villagers could be found to finance such a smack in the eye for the local squire. The circuit system adopted by the Methodists provided them with an organizational structure capable of penetrating the countryside. Even so they only evangelized certain areas and were unable to secure a complete coverage. Recent years have witnessed a retrenchment policy, largely dictated by force of necessity, and many rural chapels have been closed.

Many villages in rural England have never been divided seriously on matters of religion and the shepherd role of the Church of England has never been effectively challenged. In his study of the Lakeland parish of Gosforth, Williams[24] found that the village was almost exclusively Anglican. This was typical of the area and it was only in the larger towns that Nonconformity had an effective hold. Any villagers who were determined to stand out against the Church of England had to accept a long journey to their nearest chapel.

Similarly Pons[25] found that in the rural farming parish of Little Munden in Hertfordshire, the Anglican Church was the only place of worship. Among the villagers only a handful were Nonconformists and a few of these attended regularly at the parish church. Of the remainder who attended chapel in a neighbouring village, nearly all would go to the parish church on special occasions (indicative of the power of occasional conformity in the countryside). This absence of religious strife was not exceptional to Little Munden but was the norm in many of the other Hertfordshire parishes.

Unfortunately detailed assessments of particular localities are few and as yet there is not nearly enough accurate information on the role of religious divisions in rural communities. Undoubtedly the Anglican monopoly operates in many of them. Where there is a Nonconformist alternative it is most likely to be in the form of a Methodist chapel, although in certain parts of England the older Dissenting denominations would be represented.

FUTURE GROWTH POINTS

The future promise for the English Free Churches lies in the prosperous and successful areas of suburban England, 'the Cyprus Sherry and Morris 1100' belts. Particularly where the suburbs have been developed recently and the sense of 'neighbourhood belonging' is at a minimum, the Free Church denominations are in an excellent position to provide a so-called 'community church'—rather on the American pattern.[26] The church becomes a focus and reflector of the prevailing suburban norms and provides the local residents with an anchor point and a place to which they feel they can belong. The Anglican Church can act in this way, but one of the Free Churches, stripped of its more gaudy denominational clothing, fulfils the function much better. A stranger, walking into a modern church building on one of the new suburban estates, usually has difficulty in discovering its denomination. Were he to stay for a service it is unlikely he would be much wiser. The community church is essentially non-denominational, irrespective of whatever official label is attached to it.

In recent years the Free Churches have been gaining considerable ground in the south-east of England. This area was by-passed in the heyday of Nonconformist Victoriana and so the 19th century ethos which pervades much of northern Nonconformity is largely absent here. Lacking this negative image, the Free Churches are ideally suited for running the neighbourhood integrating churches of southern suburbia.

THE COMPLEMENTARY DISTRIBUTION PATTERNS OF METHODISM AND OLDER DISSENT

Writing in 1932, Tillyard[27] was the first to draw attention to how the work of the Methodist Church appeared to complement that of the other three main Nonconformist denominations. His method was to calculate for each county the number of total population per full-time minister and he believed this would give a rough and ready indication of the strength of each group. However the presence or otherwise of a minister is not a particularly successful way of assessing strength, especially in the case of the Methodists who make so much use of lay preachers.

Tillyard's thesis can be checked however against the patterns of distribution revealed by the membership figures (Maps 28, 34, 36 and 45). Methodism is at its most influential in Cornwall, Lincolnshire, the East Riding, the North Riding, Cumberland and Westmorland (Map 45), and it is precisely in these counties that older Dissent has always been weak (with the partial exception of Presbyterians in Cumberland and Westmorland). Conversely in the northern home counties, in East Anglia, apart from Norfolk, and in the south-east it is the Baptists, the Congregationalists and the Presbyterians who provide the main Nonconformist presence. Such a pattern is hardly surprising. Where the Church of England was being counterbalanced successfully by one of the older Dissenting groups there was little need or scope for Wesleyanism; but in Cornwall, the east coast from Norfolk northwards, and the north, old Dissent had made little headway and the religious climate was ready for the voice of Wesley.

While it is useful to talk in general terms of the Nonconformists, or to use their 20th-century designation, the Free Churches, there is a danger that a sense of false uniformity is conveyed. In fact the four main constituent denominations, the Baptists, the Congregationalists, the Methodists and the Presbyterians, each have a distinctive history and distribution pattern of their own. The internal diversity within Nonconformity is great.

CHAPTER SEVEN

The Baptists, the Presbyterians and the Congregationalists

THE BAPTISTS

Development of Baptist influence

Baptist ideas were first introduced into England in the 1530s by groups of Dutch immigrants who had been driven out of Holland during the religious persecutions there.[1] However nearly a century was to pass before the English Baptists began to emerge as an organized movement. Their institutional origins date from the time J. Smyth broke away from the Brownists[2] and left for Holland where he founded the first English Baptist church. He returned to England in 1612 with a small group of followers and established a number of local Baptist churches. Smyth and his followers came to be known as the General Baptists, for they rejected the Calvinist doctrine of predestination[3] and the more radical organization and methods of the early continental Baptists. They were essentially moderates.

A second group, known as the Particular Baptists, began to take shape from 1633 onwards and they adhered to the stricter Calvinist theology. On the eve of the English Civil War the Baptist movement was still small in numbers but no longer was it insignificant. The intolerant tone of many of Laud's ecclesiastical policies had driven a considerable number of intelligent and noted people into the ranks of the Baptists. There were now seven congregations in London and a further 40–50 scattered around the rest of the country.[4] Until this decade all the Baptists had followed the traditional method of baptism, but in 1641 the Particular Baptists officially adopted the rite of immersion[5]—from which the Baptists get their name.

Under the more liberal ecclesiastical policies adopted by Oliver Cromwell's regime which followed the Civil War many small Baptist congregations were founded and began to flourish. Although Cromwell was himself an Independent he was prepared to allow other Reformed congregations to practise their faith. It was this period which established the Baptists as a permanent fixture on the English religious landscape.

The Restoration of the monarchy in 1660 marked the end of the period of religious tolerance and from henceforth the life of the Dissenter was made increasingly difficult. One of the great Baptist leaders, John Bunyan, was incarcerated in Bedford gaol for twelve years from 1660–72 and many other Baptists suffered similar persecutions.

Where were the Baptists to be located in the 17th century? In 1672 Charles II issued a Declaration of Indulgence whereby Dissenting congregations and ministers might be licensed and from the records kept of the licences issued it appears that Baptists were strongest in Kent, Lincolnshire, Somerset and Wiltshire.[6] This general picture is confirmed by two further sources of information which are available for the late 17th century. From the minutes of the Association of the General Baptists we learn that the General Baptists' stronghold was in Kent, and that they were also numerous in Buckinghamshire, Leicestershire, Lincolnshire, and Sussex—these five counties possessed two-thirds of the total number of the General Baptist churches. The Particular Baptist position can be ascertained from the Rippon Register[7] of 1689. They were most numerous in the group of counties formed by Devon, Somerset, Gloucestershire, Wiltshire and Berkshire, and also in London. Elsewhere congregations were few and far between. The two main elements of the late 17th century Baptist Church are

5*

shown on Map 25. There was very little Baptist influence in East Anglia and in all the counties north of a line from the Severn to the Humber.

The first half of the 18th century saw the Baptists enter a period of decline. They were greatly weakened by the increasingly strict application of civil penalties which were in force against all Dissenters, and also by their own internal divisions. Most of the General Baptist congregations, which had originated during the Commonwealth and before, gradually moved over towards a Unitarian theology.

By the end of the 18th century Baptists were on the increase again, but this expansion was due almost entirely to the Particular Baptists and for a picture of their distribution in 1798 we turn once more to the Rippon Register. Whereas in the 17th century they were restricted almost exclusively to the West Country and London, during the next hundred years they became established in new areas (see Map 26). A large development took place in Lancashire and Yorkshire and many new congregations were founded in East Anglia and in the northern home counties. The already sizeable London and West Country followings grew, and the Particular Baptists took over from the declining General Baptists in Kent and Sussex. However they were still virtually absent in the four northern counties of Durham, Northumberland, Cumberland and Westmorland, and also in Cornwall, and there were very few in the belt extending from Cheshire and Shropshire eastwards to Lincolnshire.

In 1770 a new group was formed, called the General Baptists of the New Connexion, and in the following years they preserved the orthodox Arminian faith of the Baptists, walking the tightrope between the slide into Unitarianism on the one hand and strict Calvinism on the other. Thus by the end of the 18th century there were three main groups of Baptists; the Particular Baptists who represented the vast majority; the declining General Baptists, many of whom had become Unitarians; and the newly-created General Baptists of the New Connexion. There was also a large number of small autonomous congregations who refused to be associated with any of the major groups.

The 19th century marked a period of coming together among Baptists and as early as 1813 a Baptist Union was created to provide a common meeting ground for Particular and General Baptists. However the General Baptists were only lukewarm about the scheme and by 1830 the Union had achieved very little. More time was needed in order to ease out many of the rank and file Baptists from the firmly entrenched theological positions taken up during the 18th century. Gradually the high Calvinist views held by the Particular Baptists began to fall into disfavour, opinions no longer differed so greatly on the question of predestination, and the majority of the Particular Baptists were prepared to accept 'open' communion.[8] A minority still clung on to the old Calvinist views, and desiring 'closed' communion they split off and created associations of Strict and Particular Baptists.

By 1870 it looked as if a fusion between the General and the Particular Baptists was a possibility, and in 1891 such an amalgamation was in fact achieved. Those who felt the Union failed to preserve the essentials of Calvinistic theology joined or created Associations of Strict Baptists, and yet others remained completely independent and refused to join any larger organization.[9]

As a result of the impetus provided by the Evangelical Revival, the Baptists began to grow rapidly in numbers during the 19th century. Between 1800 and 1850 they quadrupled both their membership figures and the number of their chapels, this increase being particularly marked in the industrial areas.

The Baptist position in 1851

The first really accurate overall assessment of the geographical distribution of Baptists is provided by the 1851 Census (Map 27). The Baptists' main strength lay in a block of counties stretching from the East Midlands to the coast of East Anglia— i.e. Leicestershire, Rutland, Northamptonshire, Bedfordshire, Huntingdonshire, Buckinghamshire, Cambridgeshire, Hertfordshire, Suffolk and Essex. It was in this area above all others that the Baptists had gained in numbers since the 17th century. The old West Country stronghold of the Particular Baptists is still visible on the map, especially in Gloucestershire and Wiltshire. Except in Dorset and Methodist Cornwall, Baptists had increased in all the southern counties of England. By contrast there were few Baptists in the northern counties apart from the West Riding, neither were there many in Shropshire, Staffordshire and Cheshire. The main features of this distribution pattern are confirmed by an analysis on a county basis of the percentage of the population which could be accommodated in Baptist churches.

When the attendance figures were broken down into their component groups an interesting pattern emerged. The General Baptists of the New Connexion found that the overwhelming proportion of their attendances were recorded in counties north of the Severn–Wash line. Their heartland was composed of four counties, Lincolnshire, Leicestershire, Nottinghamshire and Derbyshire, with certain extensions into the West Riding and Warwickshire. In these six counties the Particular Baptists had very little influence. To the south however the position was somewhat different and the Particular Baptists were the majority Baptist group. There were still a few General Baptist congregations in Kent and Buckinghamshire (those which had survived from the end of the 17th century— see Map 25) but elsewhere they were few and far between. The Particular Baptists account for most of the Baptist attendances in the south.

The Baptists in the 20th century

Baptist membership figures, both in absolute terms and in relation to total population, continued to increase during the second half of the 19th century and reached a peak in the first decade of the 20th century. This picture is reinforced by a comparison between *The British Weekly* Census[10] of 1886 and Mudie Smith's Census[11] of 1903. Since 1906 however membership totals have been fast declining and in the fifty-four-year period from 1911 to 1965 the proportion of Baptist members to total population has almost halved. Even more drastic has been the drop in the numbers of Sunday School scholars (1901 —131 per 10,000 total population: 1961—40 per 10,000 total population) and it was no comfort to learn that most of the church members graduated from the Sunday Schools.

A clear indication of the contemporary pattern of Baptist allegiance is provided by the map of Baptist membership as related to total population on a county basis (Map 28). The main area of Baptist strength runs from Leicestershire to Suffolk and includes the counties of Northamptonshire, Buckinghamshire, Bedfordshire, Hertfordshire and Cambridgeshire. A second area of strong Baptist influence is centred round the Bristol Channel in the counties of Herefordshire, Gloucestershire and Somerset. Baptists are to be found in considerable numbers through southern and south-east England, with the one exception of Cornwall. By contrast Baptists are fewest in the whole of northern England, the West Midlands and Lincolnshire.

The figures relating to the proportion of marriages with religious ceremonies which take place in Baptist chapels are not the most reliable indicators of Baptist allegiance, but they do provide confirmation of the general pattern as outlined above. Using the Registrar General's Marriage Statistics it was possible to carry out a trend analysis for the period 1924–62. No great accuracy could be imputed to most of the results, but it did appear conclusive that a considerable increase in Baptist marriages had occurred in London and Middlesex. This could be explained by the relative weakness of the other Free Churches in the London area. Slight proportional increases had also occurred in Essex, Sussex and Surrey, while Somerset registered a great decline and Northamptonshire a reasonable decline.

Since 1851 there have been several significant changes in the Baptist distribution pattern. Relative increases have been registered in most of the southern and south-east counties, and also in the counties round the Bristol Channel. There has also been a southward shrinkage of Baptist influence and they appear to have made little impact in Cornwall or Norfolk. The Baptists belong to the south rather than to the north of the country.

THE PRESBYTERIANS

Early history

The origins of the system of church organization which became known as Presbyterianism can be traced back to John Calvin, the 16th-century ecclesiastical legislator for Geneva. Calvin attempted to develop a mode of church government founded upon New Testament teaching and the resultant code of laws became recognized as the basis of Presbyterianism. The two distinguishing characteristics which differentiated the Presbyterians from the other Dissenting groups were firstly, the one order of ordained ministry within which all were counted equal,[12] and secondly, the power of these ministers, assembled with a certain proportion of laity in local and general synods, to decide all questions of church discipline and polity. The theological position adopted by Calvin was rigorous and strict (it quickly became known as Calvinism) and a strong emphasis was placed on the doctrine of predestination.

John Knox was the first to introduce Presbyterianism into Scotland from the continent in 1560, and its influence quickly percolated across the border into Elizabethan England. The newly-established Protestant Church of England was still highly susceptible to modifying forces, and in the twenty years from 1570 small groups of English Presbyterians made concerted efforts to graft the Presbyterian system of church government on to the Church of England. Unlike other groups such as the Baptists and the Brownists, the Presbyterians wished to capture the Church of England from within, rather than to separate from her and form churches of their own, but these efforts were doomed to failure.

After their defeat in the 1590s, relatively little was heard of the English Presbyterians for the next twenty years. There were a few organized Presbyterian congregations, largely in Warwickshire, Northamptonshire, in the area around Cambridge, and in London, but elsewhere there was little evidence of their activity. However, as the Civil War drew nearer, Presbyterian activity began to increase very rapidly. The lead was taken by groups of country gentry, city merchants and Common lawyers, most of whom had become increasingly exasperated with the intolerance shown by Archbishop Laud. These centres of resistance were located above all in the Midlands, in Yorkshire, and in the south-east.[13] During this period, despite the original impetus coming from Scotland, Presbyterianism in this country took on a definite English character—its Scottish ethos was of a later date.

It was the Civil War which brought about the brief moment of glory for the English Presbyterians. The worsening of the war situation in 1643 compelled Parliament to turn to the Scots for help. The Solemn League and Covenant was signed, and in return for the assistance of the Scottish Army, Parliament accepted a religious league based on Presbyterianism. In 1645, on the orders of the Westminster Assembly, Presbyterianism was established over the whole country and each parish church was required to elect a number of elders. By 1646 this ecclesiastical polity was working in theory, although in practice it worked only in London, Lancashire and certain other scattered areas, and not very efficiently at that. Presbyterianism remained the national church right up to the Restoration, but it only maintained its status on account of the presence of the Scottish Army, and it failed to win any popular support. The English Army under Oliver Cromwell was Independent in its leadership, and tended to doubt the amount of religious diversity which the Presbyterians would tolerate. Indeed the Presbyterians had no desire to see a multiplicity of religious groups springing up and wished for a national and compulsory church—only Presbyterian not Anglican. This produced the famous saying of Milton, 'New Presbyter is but Old Priest writ large.'[14]

Presbyterians as a whole became increasingly dissatisfied with Cromwell's *laissez-faire* religious policy, and began to work for the return of Charles II in the belief that the resultant national church would be comprehensive enough to include within it the main features of Presbyterianism. After his restoration to the throne, Charles II hesitated for some while and then finally dashed the Presbyterian hopes in a series of Acts which branded them as Dissenters, beginning with the Act of Uniformity in 1662.

The only reliable information relating to the distribution of late 17th-century Presbyterianism is provided by the records[15] of the licences issued under the 1672 Declaration of Indulgence. Of the total 923 Presbyterian ministers licensed, the largest single number were to be found in Devon (89), followed by London. There also appeared to be considerable numbers in the rest of the West Country (apart from in Cornwall), in Lancashire and in Yorkshire. Relatively few were to be found along the east coast stretching from the Scottish border as far south as Suffolk (with the one exception of Yorkshire).

A doctrinal dispute which broke out early in the 18th century set the seal on the break-up of the old English Presbyterianism. The dispute centred round the doctrine of the Trinity, and at a special conference convened at Salters Hall in 1719 all the ministers were asked to subscribe to a formula couched in traditional Calvinist terms. This split the English Presbyterians down the middle, for while the majority refused to subscribe, a sizeable minority held on to their Calvinism, and Presbyterianism as an organized church system silently disappeared in England.

What had taken place within the ranks of Presbyterianism over the last sixty years to enable a clear division to occur? A considerable number of Presbyterians had become prosperous, particularly the rising class of gentry and merchants, and finding the Calvinist theology rather too strict and uncompromising, they began to adopt the more optimistic Arminian views which were to become an integral part of the Age of Reason. The keyword was moderation in all things. However once the slide away from Calvinism was started, there was no holding it, and many Presbyterian congregations veered through Arianism to outright Unitarianism. The majority of these congregations were to be found in the larger towns, particularly in the West Country. There are still about a hundred Unitarian congregations surviving today which can trace back their origins to 18th-century Presbyterianism.

Those who wished to retain the orthodox Calvinist theology gradually separated themselves from their more liberal brethren and in most cases formed Independent congregations. They were particularly strong in parts of Lancashire and Yorkshire where they fought the Unitarian drift with grim determination. The majority of the Independent chapels which had Presbyterian origins were to be located in rural areas, and as time passed, although they held on to their Calvinist theology, they quietly dropped the remnants of their Presbyterian polity.

Unitarianism and Independency between them absorbed the vast majority of the 18th-century Presbyterians. A few congregations joined up with the Methodists, although the Evangelical Revival initiated by John Wesley hardly touched the Presbyterians as a whole. The residue of the pre-Salters Hall Presbyterianism consisted of a few orthodox congregations and classes who tenaciously clung on to the Presbyterian polity, and by the end of the 18th century they were the only group who could legitimately claim the title of Presbyterians.

Early 19th century Presbyterianism

The Presbyterianism which was to re-emerge in the 19th century was very different in flavour from that of the 17th and early 18th centuries: it was essentially orientated towards Scotland. The few congregations which had survived the vicissitudes of the 18th century looked northwards to Scotland for help, but at first the Church of Scotland was reluctant to lend encouragement. It did not wish to justify episcopal dissent in Scotland by aiding Presbyterian dissent in England. However the 19th century witnessed a steady Scottish immigration into this country and these exiles, for so they regarded themselves, naturally demanded a Presbyterian church polity and form of worship. The growth of English Presbyterianism during the course of the 19th century was due almost entirely to this immigration.

For the most of the 19th century the Presbyterians were disunited. The Scottish immigrants viewed with suspicion the few surviving congregations of the old English Presbyterian church which in varying degrees had sheltered under the wing of Independency. Presbyterian congregations were organized wherever a sufficient number of Scotsmen had settled, but most of these looked upon themselves as churches for the Scots in England—they were essentially ethnic in concept. Most of these congregations were grouped together into Presbyteries which in turn formed part of one or other of the main divisions of 19th-century Scottish Presbyterianism.[16] Although union plans for one English Presbyterian Church were first mooted in the 1820s it took most of the congregations a further fifty years to reconcile themselves to being part of an indigenous English church. Finally in 1876 the United Presbyterian Church, the Presbyterian Church *in* England, and the older English Presbyterian congregations surviving from the 18th century, joined together to create the Presbyterian Church *of* England.[17]

The 1851 Census

The results of the 1851 Census provide the first accurate overall assessment of Presbyterian distribution in England. However a certain caution has to be applied in the interpretation of the Census results, for in 1851 Presbyterianism was still fragmented and many of the older English Presbyterian congregations which had survived from the 18th century and earlier would have been listed as Independents or Isolated Congregations. It was not until the Union of 1876 that these congregations began to call themselves Presbyterians once again. Therefore the distribution pattern of Presbyterianism as revealed by the 1851 Census (Map 29) is almost entirely a reflection of Scottish immigration into England.

Half the total number of Presbyterian attendances on Census Sunday were recorded in the three northern counties of Northumberland, Durham and Cumberland, and these three counties also had the highest proportions of Presbyterians to total population. While the I.A. for England as a whole was 0·48, in Northumberland it was 9·5, in Cumberland 2·1, and in Durham 1·6. Lancashire and Metropolitan London each accounted for about 20% of the total attendances and the remaining 10% was made up of isolated congregations in Westmorland, Yorkshire, Cheshire, Staffordshire, Warwickshire and Worcestershire. In all the other Midland and southern counties of England Presbyterianism was either absent, or represented by congregations which failed to acknowledge their allegiance to their titles.

By 1851 the United Presbyterian Church and the Presbyterian Church in England had begun to make certain concessions to their English environment and were becoming less rigidly ethnic in their outlook and approach. Not so a number of Church of Scotland congregations in London, Lancashire and Northumberland which looked on themselves as Scottish ethnic churches for exiled Scotsmen. Taken altogether these Church of Scotland groups had surprisingly large followings and accounted for nearly 12,000 attendances on Census Sunday.

In order to establish clearly the close relationship between the Scottish border and mid-19th-century Presbyterianism in England, the attendance figures for the four northernmost counties were analysed at the registration district level. Only three churches in all failed to complete the attendance returns and satisfactory estimates could be made for these. Map 30 shows beyond doubt that Presbyterianism had seeped across the border from Scotland into the northern extremity of England, and the greater the distance south from the border, the less the influence of Presbyterianism. Northumberland possessed a total of sixty-eight Presbyterian churches, and the I.A.s were at their highest in the border districts of Berwick, Belford and Glendale, followed by inland Bellingham. Presbyterian influence gradually declined southwards and was at its weakest in the southern inland districts of Hexham, Castle Ward and Haltwhistle. In the north-west the only two registration districts with moderate I.A.s were the Lake District area of Cockermouth, and Longtown on the Scottish border. Westmorland had only one congregation and that was at Kendal. Organized Presbyterianism was absent in seven out of the Durham registration districts, and apart from South Shields and Sunderland which between them housed nine out of the fourteen Presbyterian churches in the county, all the registration districts had I.A.s of under 4. There was no Presbyterian polity at all in the inland parts of Durham.

The stronghold of mid-19th-century Presbyterianism lay to the north of a line drawn from the Solway Firth to Blyth on the north-east coast, with an extension south to include Newcastle and Tyneside. It was in this area that Scottish influences were most potent.

Late 19th-century Presbyterianism

In 1877, the year after the various branches of Presbyterianism had joined together, the Statistical Committee[18] of the newly-formed Presbyterian Church of England attempted to estimate the number of communicants in each county. Out of a total of 259 congregations, all but thirty completed the returns. As in 1851 the statistics were dominated by the northern counties of Durham, Northumberland and Cumberland which together accounted for 45% of the total number of communicants and these three counties also had the highest proportions of Presbyterians within their total populations (see Map 31). Metropolitan London with 20% of the total communicants, and Lancashire and Cheshire with 27% each had a strong Presbyterian presence as well.

In the twenty-six years following the 1851 Census, Presbyterianism had spread over large tracts of central and southern England, primarily as a result of two factors. Scottish immigration had been increasing rapidly and the new immigrants were beginning to settle over the whole of the country and not just along the narrow strip adjacent to Scotland. Wherever a sufficient nucleus of Scotsmen formed, a Presbyterian church would be established: this largely accounts for the complaint in the 1877 Report of the Statistical Committee that a great number of congregations had extremely few members. In the second place the Union of 1876 brought back into Presbyterianism a considerable number of old surviving English Presbyterian congregations which until this time had operated under the wing of Congregationalism, or had remained as completely isolated congregations. This would account for the emergence of a Presbyterian polity in Devon, Gloucestershire, in certain of the southern and eastern counties,[19] and in the north Midlands (see Map 31). There were still no signs of organized Presbyterianism in a solid block of counties to the south-west of the Wash, nor in the four West Country counties of Wiltshire, Dorset, Devon and Cornwall.

In 1882 the Statistical Committee again examined the membership figures and although a considerable increase was recorded, nearly all of it was the result of membership transfers from Scottish churches. Although technically an indigenous English church, the Presbyterians still drew most of their membership from among the Scots—so far they had failed to make any real impact on the English.

Modern Presbyterianism

The present pattern of Presbyterian distribution in England is of recent origin. The *Presbyterian Handbook* gives information concerning the dates of foundation and erection of church buildings for all the congregations which are still in existence today, and this information can be used to provide an index of the continuity of Presbyterian presence in any one area.

Map 32 shows those congregations which can trace back their date of foundation to the end of the 18th century or earlier. Of these only nine are located in the Midlands and the south whereas fifty-two are found in Lancashire, Yorkshire and the four northern counties of Cumberland, Westmorland, Northumberland and Durham. More particularly the vast majority lie to the north of a line from the Solway Firth to Sunderland.

Naturally enough when we take the congregations which can trace back their origins to 1850, the number is larger. Nevertheless their relative distribution is basically the same. Only seventeen out of the total eighty-nine are south of the Humber–Mersey divide, and nearly half the total are in Northumberland alone. It is here in the extreme north-east that Presbyterianism has been established for longest and its roots most deeply embedded in the local environment. To this day a good part of rural Northumberland is Presbyterian and something like a Presbyterian parish system prevails.[20]

Over most of England few congregations can trace their origins back further than the mid-19th century. Well over two-thirds of the congregations in existence today were founded after 1851: modern Presbyterianism was essentially a creation of the second half of the 19th century. If we were to omit the statistics for the congregations in the north-east corner of England, the figures for the rest of the country would emphasize this recent origin.

In attempting to analyse the contemporary distribution pattern, one approach has been to look at the distribution of church buildings, for presumably a congregation of any size and vitality would possess some premises for the institutional practice of their beliefs. On Map 33, four main areas of concentration stand out:

1. A triangle formed by the Scottish border, the north-east coast, and a line from Sunderland to the Solway Firth
2. Merseyside
3. South-east Lancashire
4. The Greater London area

The tremendous Presbyterian strength in Northumberland is reflected by the fact that England is divided into thirteen Presbyteries of which two and most of a third are located in Northumberland. There is also a cluster of churches in the heart of the Black Country, a series of churches in the popular south coast resorts within easy reach of London, and four churches in Hull—a port with strong seafaring connections with Scotland. Churches are virtually absent from the West Country, from large areas of Yorkshire and North Lancashire, and from the whole of central England running from the Welsh border to the east coast.

Little use can be made of the Registrar General's marriage statistics for detailed analysis, as the absolute numbers involved are too small. However they do confirm that the main areas of Presbyterianism influence are in Northumberland, parts of Durham, Cumberland, Lancashire, Cheshire and London.

Membership figures are published annually for each congregation and these have been grouped into their relative geographical counties and then expressed as a percentage of total population (see Map 34). The two northernmost counties stand in a category of their own, with Northumberland having 159 Presbyterian members per 10,000 total population, and Cumberland having 73 per 10,000. They are followed by Westmorland, Durham, Cheshire and rather surprisingly, East Sussex. The pattern in the north could have been predicted, with the greatest Presbyterian influence being found in the Scottish border counties and then extending down the west coast to Cheshire and down the east coast into North Lincolnshire. Similarly the relative absence of Presbyterianism in central England and in the West Country is to be expected. However a recent and startling expansion of the Presbyterian polity has occurred in the area to the north and south of London.

Why should there have been such a great development of Presbyterianism in the south-east in recent years? Undoubtedly it is due in part to the settlement of Scottish immigrants who have naturally wanted their own brand of religion. More significantly however, Presbyterianism has become a provider of 'community churches' in the south-east. It is well suited for this task being traditionally a high prestige denomination which has kept itself aloof from the levelling influences of the Evangelical Revival. The high quality of its ministerial education has further added to its status.

Two similar development cycles can be observed within the history of Presbyterianism in England. Originating in Scotland, Presbyterianism percolated into England as a Scottish religion and although it gradually acquired an English character, the Scottish flavour was boosted during the Civil War by the presence of the Scottish Army. By the beginning of the 18th century however Presbyterianism had been virtually assimilated into the English way of life and had lost its Scottish distinctiveness. The second cycle began in the early 19th century when Presbyterianism was re-introduced into England by the increasing influx of immigrants from Scotland. In recent years we can again see a process of assimilation taking place, with increasing emphasis placed on Presbyterianism as an English church for Englishmen and not just a haven for homesick Scots. Its new role in the south-east is indicative of this. Should the proposed merger with the Congregational Church eventually take place, the movement away from its Scottish origins will be virtually complete. It appears that Calvinistic theology is not readily in accord with the English temperament, for in both of the development cycles the Presbyterian form of church polity has been retained, but the Calvinistic theology discarded.

THE CONGREGATIONALISTS

Early history

The very *raison d'être* of Congregationalism meant there was often little in common between one group and another. Nevertheless certain distinguishable characteristics can be isolated which typify most of the groups which have come together under the umbrella of Congregationalism. Every individual church was held to be a complete unit within itself, consisting of a congregation of true believers bound together in a covenant relationship—this concept of covenant was fundamental to Congregationalism. All authority was vested in the congregation itself, expressed through the agency of the Church Meeting, and none was given absolutely to any of its officers, ministers included. Their total freedom from outside control earned them the name of 'Independents': the later variation of 'Congregationalist' expressed the idea that every member of the fellowship participated in its administration. These features of classic Congregationalism are not altogether suited to an age of economic efficiency and ecumenical dialogue and have been modified in recent years.

The founder fathers emerged from the left wing of the Puritan Party in Elizabethan England. Although initially hoping to reform the Church of England from within, they were gradually driven into separatism by the increasingly suppressive religious policies adopted by Elizabeth and her advisers. By 1567, if not earlier, there existed a few groups who found Church of England worship intolerable and so began illegal and secret meetings of their own. The Leaders were often suspended Anglican clergy and the concept of a covenant relationship was already being formulated.

The first formal organization of Congregationalists is traditionally traced back to the separated congregation gathered together in Norwich by Robert Browne in 1581. It was Browne who first spelt out the general principles which were later to become basic to Congregationalism. However the prevailing atmosphere was hostile to such groups and the Norwich congregation quickly broke up. After the execution of three separatist leaders in 1593 most of the leading lights left for Holland, which was one of the two great centres of Reformed theology.

During the early years of the 17th century Congregationalism was subdued but quietly gaining in prestige and numerical strength. The exiled leaders in Holland were doing their best to establish and build up clandestine congregations in this country and it is small wonder therefore that East Anglia became the centre of early Congregationalism. The link between Holland and East Anglia had always been a close one, due primarily to the easy sea crossing and the common concern over flood control, drainage and land reclamation. Calvinist theology and dedicated men could be shipped unnoticed across the Channel.[21] On the home front the intolerant and bigoted policies of Archbishop Laud and his ecclesiastical courts drove many moderate members of the Church of England into separatism. Furthermore certain failures in the system of patronage encouraged congregational self-government. Where the patron was absent and took no interest in the affairs of the parish, the congregation would acquire a *de facto* independence, choosing its own ministers and controlling the purse strings: such was the case among many of the London congregations. Once the Civil War removed the hierarchical framework, congregational independence was revealed as already in existence.

Congregationalism, along with Presbyterianism and a whole galaxy of sects, greatly benefited from the Civil War. Oliver Cromwell was an East Anglian steeped in the philosophy of religious independence. Naturally enough the upper reaches of the army command were of a similar outlook, along with the majority of the other officers and the rank and file. However it is hard to create a religious system out of men of such independent spirit. Once Cromwell had defeated the Royalists and theoretically dismantled Anglicanism he was faced with the task of putting in an alternative religious system, and a watered-down version of Presbyterianism was adopted. Although much of Cromwell's work was undone at the Restoration he had laid the foundations for the principle of religious toleration. The Civil War had established Congregationalism as a permanent feature, and at this time its main strength lay in London, East Anglia, and the towns of the south-west.

The Restoration was inevitably accompanied by a return to established Anglicanism. On St. Bartholomew's Day 1662 all clergy who refused to subscribe to the Act of Uniformity were ejected from their parishes. The vast majority were Presbyterian but some were Congregationalists. However the subsequent persecution of the Dissenters encouraged them to organize themselves into self-contained congregations rather than attempt to run a centralized Presbyterian system. Ten years later Charles II issued a Declaration of Indulgence, and from the licences given, Congregationalism seems to have been strongest in Norfolk, Suffolk, Gloucester, Bedfordshire and London. A closer examination revealed that it had a particular hold in the towns.[22] Further evidence from a Religious Census of Essex, 1676,[23] suggests that Essex was also a great centre of Congregationalism. The quiet Independency of Dorset and Somerset was suddenly thrust into the limelight in 1686 when many of its members led by the Duke of Monmouth joined in the abortive attempt to overthrow James II. The consequent bloody reprisals taken by the infamous Judge Jeffreys gave the West Country Dissenters their own local martyrs—valuable assets for holding and recruiting more of the local population.

After the passing of the Toleration Act in 1689, Congregationalism settled into a period which was mediocre and nondescript. The Act removed the worst excesses of the punitive Clarendon Code, but enough disincentives remained to make the life of a Dissenter unattractive. Deprived of the chance of any further martyrdoms, Congregationalism adapted itself to the 18th-century Age of Reason—a grey and uneventful era.

The pattern of distribution which emerged during the Civil War was carried through into the 18th century, with the south-west, London, and East Anglia being the strongholds. In these regions congregations were found both in town and country, with the business and farming communities most strongly represented. Elsewhere the chapels tended to be located in urban centres, apart from the group of rural chapels which the Congregationalists inherited after the break-up of the old Presbyterian denomination. The only significant growth point was in Lancashire and the West Riding, and began after 1750 with the industrialization of these two counties. Particularly in Lancashire, many of the new entrepreneurs built Congregational chapels to cater for the religious needs of their mill workers. These chapels were greatly appreciated by the large numbers of Scottish weavers and traders coming into the manufacturing areas of Lancashire: being Scottish Presbyterians they preferred independency to the unfamiliar ways of the Church of England and the chapels of the English Presbyterians.

At the end of the 18th century Congregationalism began to emerge once again as a potent religious force in the nation. The causes of this, while hard to delineate accurately, were undoubtedly linked with the Evangelical Revival and with the upsurge in urban population accompanying the Industrial Revolution. Whilst the Evangelical Revival was primarily a Methodist affair, the Congregationalists were caught up in its wake and given a new impetus. The first visible sign of this occurred in 1795 with the formation of the London Missionary Society to promote the evangelization of overseas lands.

As Congregationalism began to expand, the old independent structure was no longer adequate. Co-operation between one group and another became increasingly necessary. Associations of ministers were formed to discuss the evangelization of their areas and many wished these County Associations to be federated into a national union. There were good economic reasons behind the desire for a union, as it was only through such an agency that the weaker chapels could be supported. The lead was taken by the London ministers who, as early as 1727, had formed themselves into the London Board of Ministers. This was hardly surprising, for living in the capital they lacked the narrow provincialism and village mentality of most of their fellow ministers.

By no means everyone was happy at the prospect of a union. There were many who felt it was Independency's peculiar glory not to be a denomination at all. But the movement for federation was too strong and finally in 1832 union was achieved. The resultant Congregational Union of England and Wales consisted of several diverse strands. There were chapels which could trace back direct links to the Independency of Oliver Cromwell; a further group were former Wesleyan or Presbyterian chapels; others had been Anglican proprietary chapels and still retained the liturgy of the prayer book; and there was also a miscellaneous collection of congregations[24] which had begun an independent existence during the Revivals. It took a further two decades before they were welded together into something like a denomination.

The 1851 Census

The 1851 Census revealed the same basic pattern as was operative at the end of the 17th century. Congregationalism attained the highest I.A.s in a line of counties stretching eastwards from Devon to Essex and Suffolk (see Map 35). I.A.s were lowest in the West Midlands and Staffordshire; Cornwall; the northern counties of Northumberland, Durham, Cumberland, Westmorland and the North Riding; and the three counties focusing on the Wash (Norfolk, Lincolnshire and Leicestershire).[25] The Census figures for all the large manufacturing districts showed that whatever hold the Dissenters had in these largest urban complexes was due predominantly to the work of the Wesleyans: the one exception was in London where the leading role was taken by the Congregationalists.

London had been a centre of Congregationalism since the time in the early 17th century when the failures of the patronage system had made many of the London parishes for all practical purposes independent. But not all of mid-19th-century London was conducive to Congregationalism. There were few congregations in Kensington, Chelsea and Bayswater where the influence of the Establishment reigned supreme. The East End also proved to be poor soil and apart from a number of missions supported by wealthy suburban congregations there were hardly any Congregational chapels. In the ordinary lower middle class suburbs, particularly to the south of the Thames, the field was left clear for the Baptists and the Methodists.[26] It was in the prosperous and successful suburbs of the mid-Victorian era that Congregationalism reached its zenith— suburbs such as Hampstead, Brixton, Highbury, and Clapham.

By the 1850s Congregationalism in London[27] was the most thriving of the Nonconformist groups. Nearly all its chapels were well filled and in some it was difficult to find a vacant seat.

Late 19th-century Congregationalism

The clue to the distribution pattern of late 19th-century Congregationalism lies in its organizational structure. Each church was in theory self-contained and depended entirely on its own membership for financial support. It was the local congregation which paid its own minister and so this gave the church members a tremendous control over the policy decisions. In practice a small caucus of very wealthy people usually provided the effective leadership. Because of this need for economic self sufficiency most chapels were firmly tied to a mid- to upper-middle class environment—the wealthy suburbs.

The Congregational system appealed particularly to the new class of traders and industrialists. Having made their fortunes, many of them found it more satisfying to be king of a prosperous Congregational church than to fight an unrewarding battle with the local gentry for a footing in the Establishment. Industrialists such as Lever were quick to realize that a Congregational church could readily be used as an agency for maintaining a paternal watch and control over their workers' social activities. The minister knew where his salary came from and it took a brave man to stand up to his benefactor. Chapels built in poorer areas, particularly in the cotton towns of Lancashire, were nearly always financed and controlled by the local industrialist.

The late Victorian Congregationalists were successful and this spirit of achievement had to be expressed visually. The older humble meeting places were pulled down and replaced by 800–1,200-seater Gothic cathedrals. Some of these were filled Sunday by Sunday; others were built on the pious hope that some day a large congregation might be developed; and yet others were simply colossal monuments to Victorian prosperity with no chance of them ever being filled. Especially in the north of England these cathedrals have now become a constant source of embarrassment to their dwindling congregations.

By the last decade of the 19th century the high noon of Congregationalism in England had been reached. The rate of chapel building began to slacken off and with the closure of many mission halls supported by wealthy suburban churches they retreated from the downtown areas. Yet there was still one further success. The Liberal victory in 1906 gave to the Nonconformists in general, and to the Congregationalists in particular, an influence in the affairs of the nation they had not experienced since the time of Cromwell. But the 1914 War eclipsed all this.

The Congregationalists in the 20th century

During the course of the 20th century Congregationalism has progressively rationalized its organizational system to meet the requirements of the age. Increasingly small independent units have become economically unviable, and with the onset of ecumenical discussions and negotiations, the need for a central mouthpiece was recognized. The logical conclusion was the formation in 1966 of the Congregational Church of England and Wales. Not all the congregations in the old Union have joined and these will be given a breathing space to make up their minds before they are finally severed from the new parent body.

Where are the Congregational strongholds today? From the map[28] of membership density (Map 36) the counties with the highest densities are those with a long-established tradition of Independency, namely Essex and Suffolk, Northamptonshire, and a group consisting of the three West Country counties of Gloucestershire, Wiltshire and Dorset, plus Hampshire. The one exception is the high density in Sussex, a feature of the 20th century. Lancashire and Cheshire, and a belt of counties running from the Wash south through London to Surrey, all have intermediate densities.

A comparison between the maps of 1851 and 1964 reveals there has been little change in the pattern over the last hundred years. Apart from a slight growth in Lancashire and Cheshire relative to the other northern counties the only major difference is in Surrey and Sussex. Why should Congregationalism have blossomed so suddenly in these two counties? Part of the reason is undoubtedly the outward movement of members from the fashionable churches of Victorian London. But then Congregationalism is particularly unsuccessful at transferring its members from one church to another (this is an inherent drawback in any loosely federated system which places the emphasis on the local unit). In the ordinary course of events many of these people, once they settled in their new areas, would have made for the local Anglican church[29] or ceased church attendance altogether. However many of the Congregational churches in the south-east have adopted a new image. They have become community churches with the implicit role of achieving the social integration of the local inhabitants.

Congregational churches are well suited for this new role. Already anchored firmly in the middle class they possess the right social status qualifications and their essential autonomy enables them to adapt to and be moulded by their new environment without too much fear of outside interference. The only effective control which the central body can exert is through finance and as most of these new community churches are in affluent areas, they are invariably self supporting, and so, independent.

Rural Congregationalism has never been strong. Few villages could muster enough financial support to maintain a chapel, let alone a minister. Where chapels had been built, congregations felt obliged to make heroic efforts to keep them functioning.[30] In 1929 the moderators of the Congregational Union suggested grouping rural congregations, thereby enabling several to share one minister, and where practicable, to close some of their chapels. This scheme would have allowed Congregationalism to continue effective operation in many rural areas, but at the time it was felt to be negating the essential principle of independency and hence was rejected. As the years have gone by most of these rural congregations have got progressively weaker and some have disbanded while others struggle to retain a nominal presence.

In downtown working class areas too, Congregationalism has failed to make any impact. People who found it hard to raise money for food were not the best material for supporting a voluntary chapel. There had been downtown mission chapels financed by wealthy suburban congregations but most of these were discontinued in the 20th century. The only exceptions were in some of the Lancashire and Yorkshire mill towns and in a few market towns in the Midlands and West Country where 19th-century Congregationalists had founded factories or mills or academies—in these places the chapels were handsomely endowed and so able to continue irrespective of the financial condition of their congregations.

Where the downtown area has spread to engulf some of the prosperous Victorian suburbs and their Congregational chapels, it is usual to find the chapels remaining but the congregations coming in by car or bus from the new suburbs some distance away. These eclectic congregations are frequently the first and second generation descendents of the late 19th-century 'chapel-fathers' and people who spent their formative years under the influence of the chapel, but in later years moved further out geographically. They feel an obligation to stoically support the chapel despite their falling numbers and the crippling financial burden of the piece of Victoriana inherited from their ancestors. Slowly but surely many of these chapels are becoming redundant. In some instances the high market value of the site encourages the congregation to move out and a new office block replaces the familiar Gothic landmark. But the proceeds are used to build a modern community church in one of the nearby expanding suburbs.

The natural habitat of the present-day Congregationalist is the prosperous residential suburbs of our towns and cities. Essentially from the middle of the middle class, the typical Congregationalist is 'the man who lives in his own house in Mill Hill or Winchmore Hill or Bromley or Purley or, for that matter, in Hale, or Sutton Coldfield or Redland Park, or who has retired from any of those places to Bournemouth or Westcliff or St. Anne's, the man who owns a large shop or a small factory, who is an accountant or a bank manager or a secondary school master or a senior official in local government . . .'[31] This is almost inevitable, as these are the people who are best able to carry the financial burden of a voluntary system. Despite recent changes in the organizational structure at the top, the basic principle of congregational autonomy is unlikely to be sacrificed. New churches will continue to spring up in the smart suburbs and rarely elsewhere.

The density of Congregational membership (Map 36) is highest in the counties with a long-established tradition of independency. Devon, Dorset, Gloucestershire, Somerset, Hampshire, London, Essex, Suffolk, and Northamptonshire[32] have a considerable number of chapels which can trace back a continuous existence to the 17th century and it is in these that classic Congregationalism is firmest. Many are unable to support themselves financially, but the 'Robin Hood' policy of the federation ensures that money from affluent suburbia is available for struggling congregations. Chapels in these counties are well distributed in the large villages and the market towns. Here, and in the declining Victorian suburbs of industrial England, Congregational chapels and their members will continue to maintain a presence. But the future vitality will be in the community churches of the new suburbs.

6

CHAPTER EIGHT

The Methodists

The spread of Methodism as a popular movement was decidedly uneven, and its geographical density was deeply conditioned by various social and economic factors which affected men's receptivity to its message.

J. D. Walsh[1]

ORIGINS

Methodism can trace its origins back to John Wesley's conversion experience in 1738. From this time onwards until his death in 1791 Wesley travelled the length and breadth of the country preaching his gospel of 'scriptural holiness'. The first ten years of the Revival, from 1740–50, were the most crucial and it was during this period that Wesley formulated the main principles of the Methodist organizational system which was to become the vital factor in the future success of Methodism.

There was no element in Wesley's teaching which of necessity separated him from the Church of England. Wesley was an ordained member of the Church of England and throughout his long active life he insisted he was always loyal to his ordination charge and denied he had any intention of forming a separate denomination. However the methods used by Wesley in conveying his message were so different from those used by the Established Church that an eventual split was inevitable. Enthusiasm and popular appeal to the masses were at total variance with 18th-century Anglican practice, and even worse, Wesley refused to be bound by the inherent restrictions of the parish system—'I look upon all the world as my parish.'[2]

Wesley always regarded himself as a loyal Anglican, but many of his followers were unable to share his love for what they regarded as a corrupt and incapable church. By the closing years of the 18th century the majority of the Methodists were ready to form a separate denomination and four events precipitated the final separation. In 1784 a Deed of Declaration was drawn up giving Methodism a formal constitution and thereby ensuring the existence of Methodism after Wesley's death. The same year saw the first two of what were to become a series of Methodist ordinations. In 1787 all Methodist chapels and preachers had to be licensed under the provisions of the Toleration Act and so Methodists now became legally classed as Dissenters. The final step was taken in 1795 when Methodist preachers began to administer the sacraments. Thus by the end of the 18th century Methodism had become a denomination in its own right.

FACTORS AFFECTING THE GEOGRAPHICAL
EXPANSION OF METHODISM

The distribution pattern of Methodism which emerged in the 19th century was largely determined by the geographical variations in the Church of England's ability to maintain a proper pastoral oversight of the people in the 18th century. As a faithful member of the Church of England John Wesley saw his own work as complementing and reinforcing the work of the Established Church in areas where the Church was weak. Where the Church was running efficiently and catering for the needs of the local community, Wesley left well alone.

The effectiveness of the parochial system differed greatly from place to place. By and large at the beginning of the 18th century the Church of England was able to exercise an effective pastoral control over the majority of the people. Most of its parishes and most of its clergy were in the south, but then this is where the majority of the people were to be located. In the north parishes covered extremely large geographical areas, and as they were invariably poorly endowed they were held in plurality and frequently suffered from absentee incumbents. At the time however this was of little consequence for only a minority of the English population lived in these counties.

As the 18th century progressed, perspectives were to alter dramatically. From 1740 onwards population totals began to rise steadily. The discovery of the industrial uses of waterpower, coal and iron gradually provided the north with a new impetus. The mill, the terraced house and the factory chimney were soon to appear on the landscape. The critical period for the spread of Methodism was from the time of its institution in 1740 right through the 18th century to the early years of the 19th century. It is a strange coincidence that John Wesley began his work just as the population graph started its upward climb and just as industrialization began in earnest.

Throughout the expanding industrial north and the Black Country the Church of England's parochial machinery was unable to cater for the needs of the mushrooming population. Churches were too small, too few, badly endowed, badly staffed and unrealistically sited. Nobody could remember when changes had last been made. The inherited structures were hallowed by time and protected by legal safeguards. The essential quality of flexibility had been lost and so the Church of England was completely unable to adapt itself to the changed conditions. To insist on the population of a booming industrial town making a journey of several miles to its parish church was ludicrous in the extreme.

Greaves[3] has suggested that there is a direct (although not a complete) relationship between the success of Methodism and the inadequacy of church accommodation provided by the Church of England in the West Riding. This same direct relationship also applies to the other northern counties. It was to these new industrial towns, where the traditional ministrations of the Church of England were lacking, that John Wesley brought the message and organization of Methodism.

The initial response of the Anglican Church to the new

situation was to ignore its existence. New parishes were eventually created after long delays but it was then decades too late and Methodism was already firmly rooted in most of the new population centres. Even when new parishes were formed, the Church of England found its success was strictly limited, for the parochial system, developed in a rural environment, was ill-suited to the urban way of life. By contrast the organizational system of circuits and classes created by Wesley, which placed the emphasis on loyalty to a particular group of people rather than to a geographical area, was more in keeping with the changed circumstances. The Methodist practice of building new chapels as soon as there was a demand for them, and then allowing them to draw members from the natural catchment area, was far better fitted to the urban environment than the static system of territorial parishes. The flexibility[4] of Wesley's organizational method provides the key to understanding the success of Methodism.

It was the newly industrialized settlements which became the natural habitat for Methodist work and influence. Here the Church of England was at its weakest and Methodism came in to fill the vacuum. Greaves has shown that all the townships in the triangle formed by Leeds, Halifax and Sheffield which needed a new Anglican church in the period 1821-7 had become strongholds of Methodism.

Even in many of the northern rural areas which had been left untouched by the Industrial Revolution, Methodist success was widespread. Once agricultural improvements were initiated, tithes became a greatly increased source of friction and led to violent hostility against the Anglican clergy—a state of affairs profitably exploited by the Methodists. Where the tithes were commuted then the source of friction was largely removed and Methodist advance was held up. If the parishes were small and possessed adequate church accommodation and endowments, Methodism made little headway. This was especially true in the head townships which had a strong manor-parsonage link. Where the parishes were large and contained several townships, and were neglected by non-resident or pluralist incumbents, Methodist activity and influence was at its greatest.

Methodism was to become most influential in the areas where

the Church of England had failed to provide for the pastoral needs of the people—in Cornwall, the Black Country, the north-east coast and the new industrial areas in Lancashire and Yorkshire.

THE DIVISIONS WITHIN METHODISM (Table 8)

As soon as John Wesley died, divisions began to appear within mainstream Methodism. The first half of the 19th century saw Methodism splitting internally in such a way as to mirror the main socio-economic divisions of Victorian society. The precise causes of the divisions were extremely complex but the under-lying motive in each case was an attempt to recover the flexible and democratic spirit of early Methodism which was fast fading in the increasingly conservative main body of Methodism.[5] One group however was to break away during the lifetime of Wesley: it was the Calvinistic Methodists.

The Calvinistic Methodists

George Whitefield (1714–70) was a close associate of Wesley in the early years of the Evangelical Revival, but the two soon parted company. Whitefield subscribed to a Calvinistic theology of predestination in which only the elect few were to be saved. While this approach won him much support from the older Dissenters, it separated him from his Arminian co-revivalist, J. Wesley, and led to a basic division within the Methodist camp.

In 1746 by a fortunate chance Whitefield was able to interest Selina, Countess of Huntingdon, in his message and for the next forty-five years she acted as his patron. Through her good offices Whitefield and other selected Methodist preachers of Calvinist persuasion, had the opportunity to preach to Selina's aristocratic friends and she often built chapels to help this mission. Although her variety of Methodism looked sus-piciously like a polite diversion for the rich, without her active support Methodism would have left the upper classes completely untouched.

After a controversy with the Wesleyans in 1770 the Calvinistic Methodists finally split off and formed 'Lady Huntingdon's Connexion'. The 19th century saw the progressive decline of predestinarian doctrine and the Connexion eventually broke up, the individual churches either rejoining mainstream Methodism or becoming disconnected congregational churches. In Wales Calvinism had a much stronger appeal and towards the end of the 18th century the Calvinistic Methodist Church was formed, which changed its title in this century to the Presbyterian Church of Wales.

Map 37 reveals the two main features of the distribution of Calvinistic Methodists in the mid-19th century. A distinct concentration is to be observed in the west, extending from Somerset northwards along the line of the Welsh Marchland counties into Lancashire. This clearly reflects the power of the Calvinist doctrine in Wales itself. The other concentration is an expression of the Countess's own sphere of influence and extends in a belt from Cambridgeshire and Hertfordshire, south through London into Kent and Sussex. It was here that the Countess's aristocratic friends were most numerous and one of her largest chapels was built at Brighton.

Today the Calvinistic influence has waned in the south-east of England, but it is still kept alive in the Marchland counties and in Merseyside where the number of Welshmen is considerable.

The Methodist New Connexion

It was inevitable that a group should form within Methodism which thought the final separation from the Church of England was taking far too long. This group united under Alexander Kilham and put forward a proposed plan which would give wide powers to the local chapel trustees and congregations. When Methodism finally organized itself into a separate denomination in 1797, Kilham refused to sign the Plan of Pacification and started the breakaway Methodist New Connexion, with an initial membership of around 5,000.

In all but the power given to the laity, the New Connexion was virtually identical to the parent body, although it continued as a distinct Connexion right through the 19th century and it was not until 1906 that it joined with the Bible Christians and the United Free Methodist Church to establish the United Methodist Church.

The New Connexion drew its membership almost exclusively from north of the Severn–Wash line (Map 38). There were only nine churches to the south of this line in 1851—five in Metropolitan London, three in Cornwall and one in Norfolk. Its main strength lay in the complex of counties formed by Worcestershire, Staffordshire, Cheshire, Nottinghamshire and the West Riding, and in the north-east. The New Connexion was essentially a phenomenon of the Midlands and the north.

The Primitive Methodists

Primitive Methodism arose as a counter to the increasing rigidity and the stifling of enthusiasm which were taking place within the main body of Methodism. It originated in the area around Burslem and Tunstall in Staffordshire and can be dated specifically at 1810 when the Society of Primitive Methodists was instituted. The underlying causes which gave rise to Primitive Methodism have not yet been properly assessed, but the immediate cause was undoubtedly the decision of the Wesley Methodist Conference to forbid outdoor revivalist 'Camp Meetings'. The two men who were to lead the Primitive Methodists, Hugh Bourne and William Clowes, felt the Conference was unduly restricting their freedom to evangelize and so they formed their own movement.

The Primitive Methodists grew steadily in numbers and geographical coverage during the first half of the 19th century. From their original home in Staffordshire they spread along the line of the lower Trent Valley, and encountered their greatest success in the East Riding. Moving out again from the East Riding they evangelized their way northwards into Durham and south through Lincolnshire into Norfolk.

By the time of the 1851 Religious Census they were established as a denomination in their own right. They accounted for over 20% of the Methodist attendances on Census Sunday and this made them the second largest Methodist group (Table 9).

Davies has estimated there were about 110,000 Primitive Methodist members in 1852.[6] In addition to the members there would have been a large number of adherents and the Census records show there were 223,000 people at evening service alone.

The geographical distribution of the Primitive Methodists in 1851 is shown on Map 39. Their main strength lay along the east coast from Durham to Norfolk with two arms penetrating south-westwards; one through Nottinghamshire and Derbyshire into Staffordshire and Salop; and the other through Cambridgeshire, Bedfordshire, Buckinghamshire and Berkshire, into Wiltshire. On reaching the Bible Christian strongholds in south-west and south-east England Primitive Methodism lost its impetus.

In the mid-19th century Primitive Methodism was largely rural in character and with the two exceptions of Durham and the Potteries its main strength was in the predominantly agricultural counties of England. We find the Connexion was weak in Lancashire, the Black Country, Northumberland and London. To a considerable extent Primitive Methodism was used by the 19th-century agricultural worker as a medium to fight his battle for recognition as a human being. The countless country chapels erected by the Primitive Methodists provided the rural worker with his symbol of independence and defiance of the established social order under which he suffered. It was under a Primitive Methodist Leader, a certain Joseph Arch, that the struggle to create an Agricultural Trade Union was taken up and successfully accomplished in the 1870s.

However the Primitive Methodists were not entirely a rural Connexion even in their early years. Their success among the Durham miners goes right back to the beginning of the 19th century, and it was the Primitive Methodists who formed and fostered the coalfield Trade Unions from the time unions were legalized in 1825 right through to the end of the 19th century. In East Anglia large numbers of fishermen were members of the Connexion, and its success in Berkshire and Wiltshire was due to converts made among the railway workers of Swindon and Didcot.

In the closing three decades of the 19th century Primitive Methodism became more specifically urban in character. Its

6*

appeal was almost exclusively to the artisan class, and it is as a result of the work of the Primitive Methodists that there is any truth in the assertion that Methodism had a certain hold on the working classes. However, they were able to reach only a small proportion of the urban workers, and their impact on the poor as a whole was very marginal. There is certainly no evidence to justify the belief that Methodism Christianized the artisan class.

By the end of the 19th century the economic and social impetus which had sustained the expansion of Primitive Methodism had begun to wane. Most of the chief grievances of the agricultural workers had been met, and the leadership of the Trade Union and Labour Movements had passed out of the hands of the Primitive Methodists. By 1932 the social and economic *raison d'être* of the Primitive Methodists had vanished and so there were no external pressures stopping them from joining the Union of Methodist churches. Although Primitive Methodism officially disappeared in 1932, its ethos still lingers in the Primitive chapels of the villages, the Durham coalfield and the industrial cities.

The Bible Christians

The Bible Christians[7] were essentially a product of the West Country. The movement began on the Devon–Cornwall border under the charismatic leadership of a certain William O'Bryan. Unlike the other branches of Methodism, the Bible Christians were not a breakaway group, but an independent body which had adopted features very similar to Methodism. In fact they applied for membership of the Wesley Methodist Church but, on account of the uncompromisingly independent character of O'Bryan, their application was rejected.

The beginning of the Bible Christians as an institutional group can be traced to the opening of their first chapel at Shebbear in North Devon in 1815, and four years later they held their first Connexional Conference. During the course of the 19th century Bible Christian influence spread gradually over Devon and Cornwall, so that by 1900 they could claim 17,000 members in these two counties.

Naturally the leaders of the movement wished to spread their particular brand of Christianity over the whole country. In the early 1820s a mission was sent out to Kent and from here they moved into London. They gladly accepted an invitation to take their cause to Somerset. A successful mission went to the Isle of Wight in 1823 and from here they spread into Southampton and Portsmouth. As early as 1824 the Kent mission had established a thriving branch in Brighton. By the mid-19th century there were small groups of Bible Christians all along the south coast from Cornwall to Kent (Map 40).

However the geographical expansion of the Bible Christians was very limited. The mission sent to London met with little success and an attempt to establish branches in Westmorland between 1859 and 1861 was a complete failure. A determined effort was made to evangelize other parts of England between 1851 and 1894 and small groups of Bible Christians were organized in some of the northern towns in the 1870s and 1880s.

The leaders of the Bible Christians were puzzled by their relative failure over most parts of England. Apart from their successes along the south coast in Kent, the Bible Christians were restricted to the West Country. Even where Bible Christian congregations were established in the North of England, in nearly all cases the members were found to be migrants from Devon and Cornwall.

Why did Bible Christianity have such a hold in the West Country? The appeal of the Bible Christians was largely to the rural inhabitants—the farmers and farm labourers. Its form of government, in contrast to the Wesley Methodists', was extremely democratic, and its religious appeal was simple and of a highly emotional nature. The farmers hated the tithe system and the power wielded by the clergy and the gentry. Bible Christianity provided a religious front from which the farmers could attack the economic system, symbolized by the Church of England, which they so hated. Thus the causes which gave Bible Christianity its distinctive characteristics were largely economic and dependent on a rural environment.[8] It is no surprise therefore that the Bible Christians found the industrial towns difficult to evangelize.

Rural resentment against tithes, the Church of England and the gentry was not limited to the West Country and the south coast, and yet Bible Christianity made little headway in the rural districts of central and north England. For the explanation of this we must turn to the part played by the Primitive Methodists. The Bible Christians and the Primitive Methodists were very similar. Both groups arose in response to the need to fill the religious vacuum left by the Church of England among the rural workers. Both provided the farmers and the rural labourer with a medium for self expression with a religious focal point from which to attack the economic and social system which had kept them in constant subjection.

The similarities between the Bible Christians and the Primitive Methodists made it unlikely that both groups would flourish in the same locality. This is confirmed by a comparison of the distribution of Bible Christians (Map 40) and Primitive Methodists (Map 39) in 1851. Only in Hampshire and Cornwall did they overlap to any extent, and the environment of Cornwall was such that it could safely contain any number of Methodist variants. The south and westward spread of Primitive Methodism halted when it reached the Bible Christian strongholds and conversely the Bible Christians found it almost impossible to establish footholds in Primitive Methodist territory in north and central England.

Bible Christianity was a feature of the West Country and only extended out in a narrow belt along the south coast to Kent. It finally gave up its separate institutional expression in 1907 when it merged into the newly-created United Methodist Church. However its influence still lives on in the many rural chapels in the villages of the south coast and the West Country.

The Wesley Methodist Association

The origins of the Association go back to a dispute in 1827 over the installation of an organ in a chapel in Leeds. The results of the dispute convinced many Methodists that the Wesleyan Connexion was not only moving towards an artificial form of worship, but that the Methodist Conference was assuming almost dictatorial powers, and so they broke away to form the

Protestant Methodists. This in turn united with the followers of Samuel Warren to make the Wesley Methodist Association.

The distribution of its adherents in 1851 is seen from Map 41. With the exception of a strong following in Cornwall, the Association was weak everywhere south of the Severn–Wash line. The main concentrations were in the north-western counties of Cheshire, Lancashire, Westmorland and Cumberland, with eastern extensions into Durham and the West Riding, and then south from the West Riding into Nottinghamshire and Leicestershire. The Association made little headway in the strong revivalist counties to the east—Norfolk, Lincolnshire, the North Riding and the East Riding.

The Wesley Methodist Reformers

The Reformers had a short history spanning only eight years and their formation was the result of a personal quarrel between James Everett and the leader of the Wesleyan Methodists, Dr. Bunting. Everett was expelled in 1849 and created his own group, the Reformers.

At the time of the 1851 Religious Census the Reformers were barely organized, but Map 42 reveals the main regional variations in their distribution. To a large extent the Reformers were complementary to the Association (Map 41). We find there were few Reformers in the north-west and Cornwall: their main allegiance being in Somerset and Gloucester; Northumberland; and a belt of counties running south from Yorkshire to Buckinghamshire and Norfolk.

The Reformers and the Association joined together in 1857 to become the United Free Methodist Church with an initial membership of around 40,000, and this body had a distinct existence for nearly fifty years. Its main strength lay in the West Country and the north, with pockets of allegiance in the east and south Midlands, and in Norfolk.

METHODIST UNITY

In spite of all the various splinter groups which formed during the first half of the 19th century, the parent body of Methodism (called either the Wesleyan Methodists or the Original Connexion) was still able to claim 60% of the total Methodist attendances in 1851 (see Map 43). There were no further serious divisions within Methodism after 1857, although the Salvation Army was created by ex-Methodists and drew a great deal of support from Methodists who were against the late 19th century respectability of their own church.

The question of Methodist union became a live issue from 1880 onwards.[9] In the 1860s and 1870s Methodism achieved its greatest successes and reached the peak of its building programme, and from then onwards a gradual decline set in. The First World War accelerated the movement away from the churches, and although Methodism experienced a slight resurgence in the 1920s, this was short lived. The population drift to the south meant many Methodists were entering this 'chapel-less' region and the three major Methodist churches of the early 20th century had their resources strained to the limits in attempting to build the necessary chapels. The three branches of Methodism saw the need to pool their resources to cope with the population drift, and many hoped a united church would reverse the fall off in membership.

Accordingly the United Methodists, the Primitive Methodists and the Wesleyan Methodists united in 1932 to form the Methodist Church. The high initial hopes of Union were not fulfilled and Methodism divided appears to have been more successful than Methodism united.[10]

METHODISM IN SOUTH-EAST ENGLAND

The south-eastern counties of Sussex, Surrey, Hampshire and large parts of Wiltshire and Berkshire were almost devoid of Methodists in the mid-19th century (Map 44). This region became known as 'the Methodist Desert' and no sustained attempt was made to introduce Methodism here until 1865. It has been argued that Methodism was weak in the south-east precisely because John Wesley failed to devote much of his time to preaching in its towns and villages.

Why did Wesley ignore the south-east? We know his policy was to concentrate on areas where the Church of England was weak and failing in its task, and on areas which he thought would readily receive his message. Wesley obviously realized the south-east was potentially unresponsive. The Church of England was already firmly established and almost every settlement had its own parish church. This was a wealthy part of England and endowments were large, so most parishes could be sure of having their own parish priest. In contrast to parts of the north, the population of the south had not increased too rapidly since the basic layout of the parochial system was established in the 12th century, and so most parishes were of a manageable composition, both in area and number of parishioners. There was no wholesale breakdown of the parochial system such as had occurred in the north.

The effects of the Industrial Revolution were less acutely felt in the south-east than elsewhere and so the rural population in the south-eastern villages was relatively static. The Church of England was still an entrenched part of the social scene and the parsonage-manor link remained strong. Although the revolt over tithes alienated many of the rural workers from the Church of England, they were in no mood to substitute a voluntary payment to a Nonconformist body for the payment of tithes. Wesley must have realized the environment of the south-east was not congenial to the spread of Methodism and consequently he left well alone.

The causes of the relative failure of Methodism to catch on in London itself await careful investigation. Wesley appears to have neglected London, and the Bible Christian mission met with little success. Part of the failure can be attributed to the influx of people into the Metropolis from the surrounding countryside where Methodism was virtually absent. Pocock[11] advances the view that the gradual growth of Methodism in London was due to the gravitation of people from the great Methodist regions of the north during the latter half of the 19th century.

Methodist influence is still weak in the 'Methodist Desert' counties (see Map 45), although it is no weaker now than in the counties to the immediate north of London. It appears a 'balancing out' process is taking place, for the counties of Hampshire, Sussex, and Surrey have been gaining Methodists both in absolute terms (Map 46) and relative to population over the age of fifteen (Map 47). As population mobility increases it is possible to expect an even larger number of Methodists moving into the south-east.

METHODISM ON THE ISLE OF WIGHT

The environment of the Isle of Wight appears to have been peculiarly well suited to the message of Methodism. Although little impact was made in the 18th century, in the early years of the 19th century Methodism spread like wildfire and by the middle of the century there was hardly a settlement on the Isle of Wight which had not been touched by the Revival. A successful Bible Christian mission was sent to the Island in 1823 and along with the main body of Wesleyanism it was responsible for evangelizing the population (see Maps 40 and 43).

The success of Methodism on the Isle of Wight stood in sharp contrast to its relative failure in the adjacent counties of Hampshire, Surrey and Sussex. Did the inhabitants of the Isle of Wight possess any peculiar character traits which made them psychologically susceptible to the Methodist approach? It seems not. Writing in 1865 J. B. Dyson says:

> The native islanders are not so excitable and impulsive as the Cornish, nor do they possess the same energy and decision of character as the Yorkshire Methodists. They are more even, but possess less fire and originality.[12]

The root cause of the Methodist success was the existence of a religious vacuum on the Island in the 18th century. The Church of England retained the allegiance of only a small part of the Island's population. Most of the livings were poorly endowed and served by pluralists and absentee clergy, and consequently the majority of the parishes were neglected. Not only had the Church of England lost its hold, but Dissent had failed to make any substantial contribution and was almost unknown in the rural districts. The religious life of the Island was at such a low ebb at the end of the 18th century that any new popular approach was assured of success. Methodism stepped in to fill the vacuum.

The Isle of Wight stands out as a stronghold of Methodism even today (Map 45). She has a higher percentage of Methodists in her population base than even the celebrated Methodist county of Yorkshire. The Registrar General's marriage statistics confirm this picture (Map 49). In 1952 and 1957 the Isle of Wight came second only to Cornwall in the percentage of 'religious ceremony' marriages which were conducted in Methodist chapels. Unfortunately there are no Church of England membership figures available for the Isle of Wight, but the map of religious marriages (Map 48) suggests that the Church of England has still not regained its lost ground.

During the period 1951–61, the Methodist Church on the Island had been losing membership, both in absolute terms (Map 46), and in relation to total population over 15 (Map 47). By contrast, the adjacent counties of Hampshire, Sussex and Surrey had been gaining membership—a levelling out process. The historical factors which made the Island a stronghold of Methodism in the 19th century seem to have lost their momentum.

CORNISH METHODISM

Over much of England the success of Wesleyanism varied in an inverse proportion to the strength and vitality of the Church of England in any particular locality. Nowhere was this more true than in Cornwall. It would be impossible to understand the spread of Methodism in Cornwall without detailed reference to the position of the Church of England.

The earliest Christian buildings in Cornwall were those erected by the Irish missionary saints who brought Christianity to their Celtic neighbours. With the passage of time the sites of these original churches, due to their saintly associations, became holy and venerated. The building of a hermitage on the site would help perpetuate the tradition and it was normal to find a holy well or spring near the hermitage.[13]

These sites acquired an aura of sanctity in the popular imagination and it was almost inevitable that the first parish churches should be built on them. By this means the new parish church would take over the local religious patriotism already in existence, even if the sites were far away from the nearest settlements. Thus from the very beginning many of the parish churches were physically isolated from the communities they were supposed to serve.[14] Ordnance Survey maps of Cornwall provide many examples of settlements named after Celtic saints which have parish churches some distance from the settlements. However not all the isolated parish churches grew up in this way. Some were the result of the dispersed settlement pattern which necessitated siting the church in a central position for the parish as a whole.

Not only were the 18th-century parish churches physically distant from the settlements, but also the number of churches was small both in relation to the physical area and to the size of population. Cornwall was economically poor and many of its communities were not able to raise the big endowments necessary to establish a parish church. Eighteenth-century Cornish parishes were usually very large and many of the inhabitants had to travel great distances to get to their church. The livings themselves were poor and so parishes were often held in plurality or had absentee incumbents.

By the mid-18th century, the time when John Wesley first appeared on the scene, the combined effect of large parishes, remote churches, pluralism and absentee clergy had produced a virtually heathen population in Cornwall. Life was very basic and primitive and a considerable section of the population was engaged in smuggling and wrecking.

The economic structure of Cornwall changed in the late 18th century. Extensive flooding had previously forced most of the Cornish low-grade copper mines to close down, but the development of the steam pump enabled them to be reopened. Thus a large mining population was brought together in Cornwall to exploit these minerals just at the time when the Church of England was at a low ebb.

John Wesley's arrival in Cornwall in 1743 marked the beginning of a new era. He regarded his work as being complementary to that of the Church of England and so in Cornwall, where the Church of England was virtually dormant, he had tremendous scope. His message of personal salvation and his revivalist technique had a powerful effect on the Cornish miners. The Cornish revivals harmonized remarkably with the Cornish temperament. The call to personal salvation struck the right note with the independent spirit of the Cornish miner; the new hymns appealed to his Cornish love of music; and the formation of the class and circuit system with its great emphasis on lay control, gave the miner a sense of responsibility and developed his latent powers of leadership. The success of Methodism in Cornwall was due in a large measure to the receptive nature of the Cornish miner.[15]

Methodism completely transformed Cornwall. The lawlessness and chaos of its early 18th-century life came to an end and by the beginning of the 19th century Methodism had become virtually the established religion of Cornwall. Small and simple chapels, so characteristic of the Cornish rural landscape, were built in large numbers and most of them are still there today in the villages and hamlets. In the expanding towns however, the original simple structures had to be rebuilt to cater for the growing population, and the new buildings were invariably products of the Gothic Revival.

When the 1851 Census was conducted, Methodist influence had reached its height in Cornwall and all the various divisions of Methodism were represented (Maps 37 to 43). During the latter half of the 19th century the revivals gradually died out, due primarily to the decline in mining and the consequent outward flow of population, coupled with the emergence of the Church of England as a new power in the area under the impetus of the Oxford Movement. The miners who moved out of Cornwall took their Methodism with them and were responsible for establishing pockets of Methodism in the new areas they settled—especially in Cumberland and Westmorland.

Methodism did not seize hold of people at the same rate over the whole county. It developed far more slowly in the east of the county, which was estimated to be forty years behind the west.[16] Wesley paid frequent visits to Devon[17] but Methodism never caught on to the same extent as in Cornwall and it was not until 1850 that Methodists had any substantial success in Devon. The strong position of Dissent in Devon prior to Wesley helps to explain this. On the other hand, in Cornwall Dissenting churches were few.

It is still meaningful to speak of Methodism as being the established religion of Cornwall, and the Church of England has never regained the ground it lost to Methodism. No other counties of England even come half-way to matching the strength of Cornish Methodism (Maps 45 and 49), and the growth rates for the period 1951–61 (see Maps 46 and 47) show that Methodism is still holding its own in relation to the total population of the county. Cornwall and Methodism are still inextricably linked.

RURAL METHODISM

Over large tracts of rural England Methodism has provided the only Nonconformist counterbalance to the Anglican Church. Although the occasional Roman Catholic recusant and Puritan Dissenter upset the rural scene from the 16th century onwards, English country life was not divided on matters of religion until the coming of John Wesley in the latter half of the 18th century (the only exception being the Dissenting influence in Essex, Hertfordshire and the south Midlands). The Methodist village chapel is now an integral part of the English rural landscape.[18]

The spread of rural Methodism cannot be discussed without reference to the late 18th century agricultural situation. The great landowners in the belt of open field country which stretched from the south Midlands to Yorkshire realized the only way they could improve their yields was by enclosure. In order to do this the tithes had to be commuted, usually for land. Social position at this time was normally measured in terms of acreage and it was noticed by all that the clergy were climbing rapidly up the social ladder as a result of tithe commutation. Furthermore this was largely at the expense of the small peasant proprietor.

Enclosure battles were fiercest in Lincolnshire and Yorkshire and so in these counties the rural population was least sympathetic to the Church of England. It was here that Methodism achieved its greatest success. Village Methodism inevitably took on a class-conscious form and the chapel became a symbol of revolt against the squire and the vicar, and a centre where the agricultural labourer could gain his self-respect and his independence.

The circuit system was an organizational model developed by Wesley. A number of chapels would be grouped together into a circuit and the circuit would be assigned a number of ministers. These ministers would be responsible for the overall pastoral work and control, although class leaders and lay preachers would do much of the local work. The Methodists were very fortunate in that the circuit system was singularly well suited to the rural environment. It enabled them to maintain chapels in all the villages and in some of the small hamlets as well. The refusal of the Methodists to adopt the traditional principle of one minister for each congregation meant they were able to populate the English countryside with their chapels.[19]

The Methodists experienced great difficulty in establishing themselves in townships where the ancient village communities were least altered, even in the famous revivalist territories of Yorkshire and Lincolnshire. Where the parishes had adequate endowments and enthusiastic clergy, then Methodism was stoutly resisted. This was especially true in the head township with the strong link between the manor and the parsonage.

Eighteen-seventy marked the beginning of the break-up of the self-contained agricultural community and from this time onwards village Methodism gradually became a financial burden to the various branches of Methodism. Rural depopulation removed countless members from the chapels, and as the prestige and influence of the Church of England began to decline, so the need for a Nonconformist opposition faded. The recent trend for villages to become middle class dormitory areas has done little to boost village Methodism: the chapel is essentially part of the village into which the commuters are rarely integrated.

A sizeable section of the Methodist membership is still to be located in the countryside. A commission reporting in 1958[20] estimated between 33% and 50% of all Methodists lived in rural circuits. The Union of 1932 created the problem of surplus village chapels and countless villages had three chapels (one for each of the three main branches of Methodism prior to 1932) each with a dwindling congregation. The problem has now been eradicated and in 1958 only 4% of the Methodist village chapels were redundant.

Methodism today still forms a vital element in the English village and its small chapels are an integral part of the rural landscape.

THE DISTRIBUTION OF METHODISTS

It is impossible, on the information available, to draw an accurate distribution map of Methodism before the mid-19th century. Edwards[21] has attempted to analyse the distribution pattern in 1815 but he failed to produce the evidence on which his conclusions was based. His prime concern was to show that Methodism was strongest in the industrial and manufacturing counties (particularly Staffordshire, Durham, Northumberland, Lancashire, Yorkshire and Middlesex), in order to support his thesis that Methodism was the church of the Industrial Revolution.

Methodism in 1851 (Map 44)

The Religious Census of 1851 provides the first reliable picture of Methodist regional variations. Taken as a whole Methodism accounted for nearly a quarter of the total number of attendances at all places of worship on Census Sunday (see Table 9).

Methodism was most dominant in the belt of open arable country stretching from the south Midlands through Lincolnshire into Yorkshire, and in Cornwall and the Isle of Wight. The influence of Methodism was least felt in three regions:

1. Everywhere south-east of a line from Great Yarmouth to Bournemouth. It was here that Methodist attendances related to population were at their lowest.

2. The three northern counties of Westmorland, Northumberland and Cumberland.

3. The counties bordering the Bristol Channel (Devon, Somerset and Gloucestershire) and extending north into Herefordshire, Worcestershire and Warwickshire.

The variation in the amount of accommodation available in Methodist chapels throughout the country is shown on Map 50. In general the distribution pattern closely resembles that of Map 44, but with one important exception. In the south Midlands chapel building did not appear to have kept pace with the rise in Methodist membership.

Mid-20th century Methodism

The percentage of Methodists in the total population base in 1961[22] has been calculated for each county (see Map 45). Methodists (i.e. professed members) account for about 1·5% of the total population of England, or nearly 2% of the total population aged 15 years and over. The distribution pattern of Methodist members in 1961 is largely confirmed by the variation in the proportion of marriages taking place in Methodist chapels (Map 49) and the two combined give a clear picture of the strength of Methodist influence and allegiance in a particular area. Apart from Devon, Cornwall and the Isle of Wight the main strength of Methodism lies in the northern half of the country—north of a line from Worcester to the Wash.

The main features of the distribution pattern over the last 110 years have remained constant. Cornwall continues to stand out as the 'granite rock of Methodism' and Methodist influence is still powerful in Yorkshire, Lincolnshire and the Isle of Wight. At the other extreme the south-east remains a Methodist desert. However there have been two distinct alterations over the last century. The four northernmost counties of Cumberland, Westmorland, Durham and Northumberland have all become centres of Methodism since the time of the 1851 Census. Similarly Methodist influence from Cornwall gradually seeped across the border into Devon.

Distribution trends in Methodism

Over the period 1924-62 it has been possible to analyse the

significant variations in the proportion of marriages taking place in Methodist chapels.[23] This is a positive indicator of the vitality of Methodism in a particular area. In the three Methodist strongholds of Cornwall, the North Riding and the West Riding there has been a gradual decline throughout the period. This has been counterbalanced by large post-war increases in Northumberland and in the south-eastern counties of Hertfordshire, London, Middlesex and Surrey. Methodism appears to be holding its own in Durham, Cumberland, East Riding, Derbyshire and Staffordshire—all counties with large Methodist followings.

Variations in membership have been assessed on a county basis over the period 1951–61. The change in absolute membership over this period (Map 46) varied greatly from county to county, although over England as a whole there was a decline of over 2%. The largest absolute increases were in the northern Home Counties and in the whole of south-east England (except for the County of London) extending as far west as Hampshire. Smaller increases were also recorded in the Black Country, Derbyshire and Westmorland. Membership figures dropped in a line of counties stretching from East Anglia and Bedfordshire, north-westwards through Lincolnshire into Lancashire, Yorkshire and Durham. Large numbers of Methodists also moved out of the County of London.

From the Methodist Church's viewpoint, changes in absolute membership are of greatest significance. Where a county loses members there will be fewer to pay for the existing plant and ministers. As in the south-east, where membership has been growing rapidly, finding the money for new churches becomes a great burden.

Although absolute numbers are of prime importance organizationally, when we examine the relative strength of Methodism within each county, membership figures have to be related to total population (see Map 47). The population under fifteen years was not included, as the Methodists will not admit to membership under that age. The position revealed in this map is more depressing. Over England as a whole Methodist membership in relation to total population has declined by nearly 6%. In all but a few areas population increase has negated the apparent growth of Methodism. The exceptions are Westmorland, Cornwall and above all a small group of counties in the south-east (Middlesex, Surrey, Sussex and Hampshire). Methodism is maintaining its position relative to population changes in Cumberland and Northumberland; the East Riding; Dorset; and a group of counties radiating round Staffordshire, namely Cheshire, Derbyshire, Warwickshire, Worcestershire and Salop. Everywhere else Methodism is on the decline.

The effects of population movement on the distribution pattern of Methodism have been widespread. It was the Cornish miners who took Methodism to the new mines in Cumberland. The large-scale movement of people from the Methodist counties of the north into the south-east has brought many Methodists into this previously untouched part of England. However not all Methodists, when they leave their home chapels, continue to be faithful to their denomination. Geographical mobility normally goes hand in hand with social mobility and, on moving away from his old chapel-orientated home, the staunch Methodist will frequently change denominational allegiance and patronize the socially higher Anglican church in his new place of residence. As population mobility increases, the effectiveness of traditional norms and controls will lessen and fewer people will be conditioned to be Methodists. The balancing out process between different areas is likely to continue and eventually a monochrome distribution pattern may be the result. Methodism would no longer add a special distinctiveness to certain parts of the English landscape. Such a process would be speeded up if the proposed Anglican-Methodist Union is ever achieved.

CHAPTER NINE

The Smaller Christian Groups[1]

THE EUROPEAN ETHNIC CHURCHES

The role played by institutional religion in linking immigrants with their countries of origin has been well documented in the U.S.A.[2] To the immigrants who flooded into the States in the 19th century the church or synagogue back home had been, for most of them, the real centre of community existence. Once they arrived in the New World they immediately set about re-establishing it. The church became the visible link between the old and the new ways of life.

In England today we find the ethnic churches fulfilling a similar function. The intensity of commitment on the part of the congregations is greatest among the exiled Lutheran and Orthodox groups from Communist-controlled countries. They have little hope of ever returning and so they cling on very tenaciously to the former ways. However this intensity will die with them, for the second and third generations have no reason to maintain these links: their roots are already planted firmly in this country.

In addition to the exiled churches are a number of other Lutheran, Reformed and Orthodox churches which cater for temporary and permanent (voluntary) residents from continental Europe. Apart from some of the Lutheran and Orthodox groups, their sphere of operation is almost entirely limited to London. Elsewhere the numbers are too small to support a permanent religious community, although very occasional services may be held in a few of the largest provincial centres. Thus the Swiss Reformed Church has two regular congregations in London and their pastors hold annual services in Plymouth, Liverpool and Leeds. The Dutch and French Reformed Churches also have thriving London congregations.

The Orthodox churches

By far the largest branch of the Orthodox Communion in England is the Greek Orthodox Church. Unfortunately there are no statistics available either for local parishes or for the size of the total community in England and the Archbishop's secretariat is unable to supply any estimate.[3] However from the information in their 1969 *Handbook* a general picture of their distribution can be obtained.

Over England as a whole they maintain thirty-seven parishes in addition to the Cathedral in west London. Twelve of these parishes are to be found in London, and more specifically in north and west London: there is only one parish south of the Thames in Camberwell. Twenty-five other parishes are located in the provinces, of which eight are in the large urban centres to the north of the Bristol Channel–Wash line (Manchester, Liverpool, Leeds, Bradford, Newcastle, Hull, Coventry and Birmingham). The distribution of the remaining seventeen suggest they are composed primarily of people who have moved out of the London communities. In particular the parishes of Torquay, Brighton, Eastbourne, Hastings, Margate and Southend would cater for the more prosperous members who, on retiring from their London jobs, would move down to these established resort-town parishes.

The Orthodox communion presents a diverse face and most congregations are closed communities of a single national or ethnic group. Apart from the Greek Orthodox Church there has been a big influx into England of immigrants from various East European countries, each bringing its own national Orthodox Church. The variety is bewildering—the Armenian, Serbian, Polish, Ukrainian, Bulgarian, Estonian, Latvian and

Russian (two brands) Orthodox Churches are all represented. They all maintain thriving communities in London and some have several outposts in the provinces. Reliable statistics of membership, attendance and commitment are impossible to obtain and estimates are futile. The general impression given is that the few provincial communities are very small and struggling, while the real vitality is found in London. Most of the East European churches are in exile and so this provides an additional cohesive element.

The Lutheran churches

While at the Reformation an ecclesiastical system known subsequently as Lutheranism was established over much of north and west Europe, in England the resultant church settlement was neither Lutheran nor Calvinist. Lutheranism was considered too foreign to be accepted by the English, but from the very beginning of the Reformation it was represented in this country by Protestant refugees from continental Europe. In 1550 Edward VI allowed these foreigners to set up their own 'Strangers Church' at Austin Friars, London. Apart from a brief period of persecution during the reign of Mary Tudor, the congregation was free to worship as it pleased right through to the end of the Commonwealth and Protectorate. This was a liberty not granted to Englishmen.

By the 1660s there were already many other Lutherans in London apart from the religious exiles—people such as tradesmen, students, diplomats and craftsmen. Trade with the New World had made the Port of London a centre of world commerce and sharp-witted merchants from north Europe were quick to establish themselves in the Steelyard. This wealthy trade colony now numbered well over 4,000, most of whom were Lutherans. Some joined the congregation at Austin Friars, but most became members of the Anglican parish of Allhallows the Great, a few hundreds yards from the Steelyard. This church was destroyed in the Fire of London in 1666, but in 1673 the first exclusively Lutheran church was consecrated in the centre of the newly-built City.

The last forty years of the 17th century were not renowned

for religious toleration, yet by a Royal Charter of 1669 the Lutheran congregation was exempt from interference by any secular or religious authority—an expedient Charter from the viewpoint of foreign policy. The Toleration Act of 1689 regularized the position of the Lutheran Church and put it on the same footing as the other Dissenting groups, and this Act also enabled other Lutheran congregations to be formed. By the end of the 18th century seven new Lutheran congregations were in existence and so each Lutheran country now had its own religious base in London.

Contemporary Lutheranism in England is composed of three distinct strands. First come the Scandinavian Seamen's Missions which can trace back their origin to the work of the Norwegian Seamen's Mission in the 1870s. This example was quickly followed by the Danes, the Swedes and the Finns. Today full-time seamen's pastorates are maintained in London, Liverpool, Hull, Middlesbrough and Tyneside by one or more of the Scandinavian countries, and in addition Norway has welfare stations in several of the other ports which have sea connections with Norway.[4] Sweden and Denmark also maintain full-time pastorates in London catering for the sizeable communities of resident expatriates. Only a very few of the people attending any of these pastorates are permanently resident in England: the vast majority have their roots planted firmly in Scandinavia. Therefore these pastorates are essentially ethnic in their orientation and form little islands of alien culture and language.

The Lutheran Church is well established in the U.S.A. and it is from here that the second strand of Lutheranism in this country originated. Earlier in this century a missionary effort was mounted by the Missouri Synod and this resulted in the Evangelical Lutheran Church of England. Its members are theologically conservative, believing in the verbal inspiration of the Bible, and the links between them and the other Lutheran groups in England are rather tenuous. While they emphasize their 'English' nature, their American origin is still influential. Twelve churches are maintained, five in Greater London, and the other seven in Harlow, Cambridge, Sunderland, Plymouth, Coventry, Liverpool and Sheffield.[5]

Just as the original Lutheran congregation was formed by Protestant refugees, so the third strand of Lutheranism is composed of Second World War refugees settling in England. Between 1946 and 1949 over 100,000 European Volunteer Workers were admitted into Great Britain, of which about a third were Lutherans from Latvia, Estonia and Germany. Together with some of the ex-soldiers from General Anders's Polish Army and Hungarian refugees from the 1956 rebellion, they form the basis of the present Lutheran population in this country.

The English churches made gallant attempts to provide a home of worship for these refugees, but most of them longed to worship in their own language and according to their own customs. The Lutheran congregations already established (mainly Scandinavian and Evangelical Lutheran Church of England) had neither the resources nor the strength to come to the rescue, and so in 1948, with American financial aid, the Lutheran Council of Great Britain was established. This Council organized the Lutheran refugees into congregations and synods on an ethnic basis and provided pastors, most of whom were themselves exiles.

In 1966 the Lutheran Council published the results of a sociological self-study carried out in 1965.[6] Although it was restricted to the Latvian, Estonian, Hungarian, German and United Synods, and despite the fact that only 51% of these congregations provided all the required statistics, it does give an unusually clear and factual picture of Lutheranism in England.

Between 1946 and 1950 about 14,000 Latvians, of whom about 80% were Lutherans, arrived in Britain from displaced persons camps in Germany. Many of them, particularly from the younger generation, have subsequently emigrated to Canada, but there are still over 3,000 who are enrolled as members of Lutheran congregations in England. Sizeable congregations are based on London, Corby, Bradford, Leicester, Leeds and Coventry and preaching stations maintained in many of the other towns.

The present Estonian community in England has a similiar history and has congregations in the same towns as the six main

Latvian congregations. The only distinction is in size—the Estonian Lutheran synod has 1,300 members, just over one-third of the Latvian total. In the years to come both synods will have to fight for survival, for the Latvian and the Estonian communities have a top-heavy age structure. It was found in 1965 that 50% of the Estonians and 45% of the Latvians were over 50. As members reach retirement and are forced to live on a limited pension, it becomes increasingly difficult for them to supply the church with financial support. There is little chance of their children playing an active role: most of them have been brought up and educated in England and can see little point in perpetuating the old ways.

The Polish Lutheran Synod ministers to approximately 1,800 members most of whom were connected with General Anders's army. The synod has four permanent congregations in London,[7] Leeds, Birmingham, and Cambridge, and also maintains preaching stations in twenty-four other towns. However the overwhelming majority of Poles entering England belonged to the Roman Catholic Church.

The Hungarian Lutheran community, most of whom arrived in England as refugees from the 1956 revolution, is estimated at only 500. Of these about 350 belong to congregations in London, Manchester and Bradford.

The history of the German Lutheran Synod goes right back to the foundation of the first Lutheran Church in London in 1669—the church being associated with the merchants of Hamburg. Before the Second World War there were already a number of small congregations in the larger towns, but they were not linked together in any way. Various attempts had been made to bring the congregations into some sort of corporate grouping, but no results were achieved until 1955, when a synod was formed. Even today some congregations are unwilling to join.

The Lutheran Council estimates there are about 200,000 people of German origin in Great Britain[8] today. A large number of them have been settled in England for many years and feel little need for a link with their homeland through the church. Consequently membership of the synod is only 3,500,[9] although it is still the largest national Lutheran synod in

England. Of great significance is the fact that over three-quarters of the present membership arrived in England after the Second World War—these are the people who at the moment are least assimilated into English life and have the greatest need for cultural/religious links with their home environment. Congregations are to be found in most of the large towns and the steady influx into this country of German girls (especially 'au pairs') marrying English men ensures there is likely to be a continuing demand for German Lutheran churches in the major cities.

In 1961 a group of Lutheran ministers and laymen formed the United Lutheran Synod in an attempt to give organizational expression to the growing English language ministry of the Lutheran Church. The eventual hope is that all the ethnic synods will come in with them to constitute a United Lutheran Church. So far the synod has only 700 members, with congregations in London, Leeds, Birmingham, Corby and Leicester. Whether they will succeed in catching the imagination of the second-generation immigrants who are being increasingly assimilated into English life remains to be seen. Unless they succeed in establishing a fully indigenous Lutheran Church, drawing in large numbers of English converts, the outlook for English Lutheranism is likely to be bleak. It is difficult to visualize any new large-scale influxes of Lutheran immigrants. With the passage of time the hard core traditionalists who insist on the retention of their church's ethnic identity will dwindle away, and with them a large section of contemporary Lutheranism.

The Scandinavian churches in London and the German synod are assured of a steady trickle of expatriates to keep them buoyant. The Evangelical Lutheran Church of England, being more akin to some of the evangelical sects than to mainstream Lutheranism, is likely to share in the general future of evangelical Christianity. The long-term fortunes of English Lutheranism lie in the ability or otherwise of the present ethnic congregations to turn progressively into indigenous ones drawing on the native population. This is the assignment which the United Synod has allotted itself.

Welsh and Scottish churches in England

In addition to the other ethnic churches, there are congregations which cater almost exclusively for expatriate Welshmen and Scots. The Scottish influence within the Presbyterian Church of England has been analysed already, but for some Scotsmen this influence is not considered strong enough. For them the Church of Scotland operates its own English presbytery which is linked directly to the General Assembly in Edinburgh. The presbytery has a total communicant membership of about 6,000,[10] of which the three London churches account for 3,600 (the fashionable St. Columba's Church in Knightsbridge being the largest—2,600 members). The other congregations are at Gillingham (242 members), Liverpool (164), Newcastle (188), Berwick-on-Tweed (454), and Corby (1,846). The inclusion of Corby calls for explanation. In fact it is due entirely to the presence of the big steel works (Stewart & Lloyd) which moved down to Corby from Scotland in the 1930s. The company brought with it a large number of Scottish employees who naturally wished to have their own Scottish form of Presbyterianism and not the watered-down English version.[11]

The need for Welsh language churches is felt most keenly in the Border Marches, in the Bristol region and on Merseyside. A number of chapels provided by the Presbyterian Church of Wales and the Union of Welsh Independents cater for the Welsh expatriate in these regions who desires the comfort and security of a familiar service in his own tongue. Inevitably London also has a number of Welsh churches.

MISCELLANEOUS CHRISTIAN GROUPS

The Moravian church

The Moravian church goes back to the martyrdom of the Bohemian Protestant patriot, John Huss, who was burnt at Constance in 1415. The Church of the Bohemian Brethren, as it was then called, reached its greatest extent at the beginning of the 17th century when over a third of the population of

7

Bohemia and Moravia belonged to it, along with small groups in Poland. After the Battle of the White Mountain in 1620 the church was utterly suppressed, although a few of the Polish branches survived.[12]

In 1722 some families from Moravia, who had kept alive the traditions of the old church, found refuge on the estates of Count Zinzendorf in Saxony and here they built the village of Herrnhut. Like the primitive Christians they believed in living together in perfect peace and love as a real community. A group came over to England and built a settlement at Fulneck, just outside Bradford, in 1746. They aimed at providing a self-sufficient economic community and to this end they created for themselves a clothing business, a worsted and glove factory, a farm, a tailor's shop and a shoemaker's.

Count Zinzendorf died in 1760 and his successor clung rigidly to the community ideal—a policy which effectively prevented any real expansion. Centres had already been established in Manchester (Fairfield), Bradford (Fulneck), Ockbrook near Derby for the Midlands, Bedford for the south Midlands and Tytherton in Wiltshire for the west of England.[13] From these places a number of preaching stations were maintained in the surrounding areas and had these been allowed to grow into proper congregations, then the Moravian Church could easily have rivalled the other main Nonconformist groups. However all full members had to sign a 'Brotherly Agreement' not to take members from other denominations, to do everything in their power to help the Church of England,[14] and to submit themselves to the full discipline of the communities.

Present membership of the Moravian Church in England is about 2,500.[15] The two main centres are around the original communities of Fulneck and Fairfield. To the south and southeast of Bradford (Fulneck) there are now six congregations with a total membership of 680, and in the Manchester (Fairfield) area are five congregations with 610 followers—the two centres accounting for over half the total membership. Other sizeable congregations (membership over 100) are found close to Leeds and Derby, and in London, Bath, Bristol, and Bedford. Small churches at Crook, Co. Durham, two near to Rugby, three in Wiltshire, and one at Leominster complete the picture.

While the Moravian Church itself has never achieved fame in England, its influence has been of great importance. John Wesley was very attracted by his experience of the Moravian community spirit and some of its ideals were incorporated into Methodism.[16] Of even more significance was the effect of the Moravian example on the planners and designers. When J. M. Morgan, the real founder of the Christian Socialists, put forward his scheme for self-supporting villages, he was using the Moravian communities as a model. One of his pupils, J. S. Buckingham, produced the first draft scheme for a garden city, which in its turn was to lead to Letchworth (1903) and Welwyn Garden City (1919).

Today it is the norm to place great emphasis on the social considerations of physical planning, but two hundred years ago the reverse was true. The Moravian communities of the 18th century were heroic social gestures well ahead of their time and their community ideal had a visible affect on the physical landscape. Although the contemporary Moravian Church is but small, its influence still lives on through the garden cities and the ideal of self-supporting and harmonious communities.

The Evangelical sects

The English religious landscape exhibits a great variety of small religious sects and groupings. Most have only a small following and may well be completely independent of any other congregations. There are however four large bodies which each operate a type of 'federal' organization for the many small congregation of believers which shelter under their wings. These are the Assemblies of God, the Plymouth Brethren, the Elim Church, and the Disciples of Christ. Together they claim a membership of around 150,000[17]—a sizeable following.

The evangelical sects present a problem to the geographer. Their great emphasis on the individual local congregation has meant that the larger federal structure is but loosely organized and is unable to furnish any accurate statistical information. Furthermore their stress on quality of belief rather than on quantity of members makes them extremely suspicious of numerical analysis. Short of undertaking a full-scale survey of each of the groups concerned (each one would be long-term and costly) only comments of a general nature are possible.

Most of the evangelical sects display certain common characteristics.[18] Their members are normally alienated from the dominant ethos of middle class life—the underprivileged, the social inadequates. The sect promises them order out of chaos and assures the outsider that he is really an insider because of his religious identity—he is one of the chosen few who will enjoy the fruits of salvation. The best recruiting grounds are the poorer areas of our towns and cities where the density of social casualties is at its highest.[19] The sects thrive in an urban environment. In rural areas the strong pressures of social conformity tend to keep people away from groups which are socially unacceptable. This distinction is not completely clear cut, for wherever a handful of zealous believers can be assembled, a sectarian branch can be established. Whatever their aesthetic drawbacks may be, the 'tin tabernacles' are cheap to build and maintain. Nevertheless the most conducive habitat for sectarian religion is in the towns and cities.

The Society of Friends (Quakers)

The religious confusion of the Civil War in England provided a unique opportunity for the growth of little groups of every kind. Out of this bizarre collection, all were ephemeral apart from one—the Seekers, who were later to be called the Society of Friends. The organizing genius behind the Seekers was George Fox (1624–91). He was able to stabilize the Quakers into an organized and structured movement without letting go of the doctrine of the indwelling light and the unsacramental quietism which were their reasons for existence.

The big expansion of the Society took place in the 18th century and they were numerically strongest in the north (Lancashire, Yorkshire and Westmorland), in the south-west, and in London, Bristol and Norwich.[20] Most Quakers came from the rural and urban *petite bourgeoisie*: very few members were drawn from the upper classes or from the proletariat. Quaker businessmen were particularly active in the textile trade and so the leading centres of cloth manufacturing, Manchester and East Anglia, were also centres of strong Quaker influence.

Businesses run by Quakers would normally flourish, as economic success proved to be a by-product of their strict conscience. Profits were not to be spent on easy living and so could be ploughed back into the business. Men would deal with a Quaker firm because it could be trusted. They also had an excellent reputation in the field of labour relations and where possible Quaker would employ Quaker. Even where this did not happen, the Quaker reputation enabled the firm to cream off the labour force in that locality.[21] The great success of Fry's and Cadbury's established Bristol as an important Quaker centre and other thriving Quaker businesses would also act as nuclei for Quaker communities.[22]

The present distribution of Quakers can be assessed from information provided in the yearbook of the Society.[23] Membership figures are carefully revised each year by people who are in a position to know whether a person is active or not. Over 40% of the total Quaker membership is to be found in London, Lancashire, Yorkshire and Warwickshire. The actual percentages are given in Table 10.

The other main feature of contemporary Quakerism is the growth of the movement in certain of the southern counties, in particular Sussex, Hampshire, Hertfordshire, Surrey, Essex and London itself.[24] Attempts to account for this are difficult. It may be that the rational calm appeal of the Quaker approach to religion is of increasing attraction to the growing middle class 'thinker' in the south. Certainly in these days of impersonal big business there is little chance of Quaker influence again being radiated by benevolent entrepreneurs.

The Free Methodists

When the three main strands of Methodism united in 1932 it was inevitable there would be some members who felt the united church was a betrayal of Methodist principles and that it was their duty to remain outside. The majority of these people belong to one of two groups.

The Independent Methodist churches

This is essentially a 'connexion' joining together in a loose federation a whole medley of independent congregations who for one reason or another refused to join the united church in 1932. In all, 140 congregations are affiliated to the connexion which could muster a total membership of 6,800 in 1966.[25] For some years now the connexion has been numerically on the decline and a number of churches are likely to close in the near future. This is the result of older members dying off and a failure to attract the young, which is hardly surprising as the whole *raison d'être* of the connexion is rooted in past Methodist squabbles and is unlikely to appeal to future generations.

The main strength of the connexion is in Lancashire and north-east Cheshire, and these churches account for nearly 75% of the total connexional membership. A further 15% is made up from the members of chapels in the mining villages of Durham and the remaining 10% from isolated congregations in Yorkshire, Nottinghamshire, Staffordshire and Bristol.

The Wesleyan Reform Union

The history of the Reformers goes back to the events of 1849 when three ministers were expelled by the Wesleyan Conference. Whereas most of the Reformers eventually rejoined mainstream Methodism, some have continued to keep alive the old issues of contention and have maintained an independent existence. In 1961 they had a membership of 6,000,[26] but like the Independent Methodists they are on the decline. The reasons for their separate existence have little power to attract new blood.

Nearly half their total membership is in Yorkshire, and Sheffield is their Union headquarters. Otherwise their chapels are scattered widely over the rest of England, apart from in Lancashire and Cheshire where they have left the field clear for the Independent Methodist Churches. The two groups are essentially complementary in their distribution patterns. However the future for both is not at all bright. Their failure to attract a regular trickle of new members can have but one result.

The Unitarians

Before the 19th century Unitarianism was lacking in organized shape and expression, but it can trace its roots right back to the left wing of the Reformation.[27] From the very earliest upheavals within Catholic Europe there had been a few small groups of Christians who began to question the divinity of Christ and the doctrine of the Trinity. This movement was given impetus during the late 17th century by a large section within the English Presbyterian church who gradually adopted Arian views and veered away from orthodox Trinitarian teaching. Throughout the 19th century, and particularly after the Salters Hall Conference of 1719, Unitarian beliefs spread steadily and won the allegiance of the old Presbyterian and Independent congregations. They were particularly prevalent in Devon, Gloucestershire, Somerset, Kent, south Lancashire, and south Yorkshire.

Unitarianism, as a formal institutional movement, flowered in the 19th century. With the establishment of the Unitarian Book Society[28] in 1791, Unitarians in different parts of the country gradually began to meet and get to know one another. Nevertheless Unitarianism only met with partial success in attempting to weld its members together into a united body. The British and Foreign Unitarian Association, set up in 1825 to stimulate united action, failed to achieve its objective and was finally disbanded in 1867: at no time did more than 40% of the 200 congregations belong.

The rational beliefs of the Unitarians are intimately associated with Victorian England and it was in the second half of the 19th century that the movement reached the zenith of its influence. Although the religion of only a small group, Unitarianism played a role out of all proportion to its numbers and occupied a strategic position within civic life. Particularly in the great Midland and Northern cities, the Unitarians provided mayors[29] and officials and encouraged a whole variety of social reform projects. The great Unitarian families of

Birmingham, Manchester, and Liverpool wielded a tremendous power, and the Unitarian chapel in Birmingham became not just the meeting place for a small sect, but the intellectual and cultural centre for the whole of Birmingham society.

Although the prestige and influence of Unitarianism was immense, the movement was never able to claim a large membership. It appealed essentially to the educated, the rational and the prosperous, whilst to the village and urban poor it was altogether too cold and remote. The 1851 Census recorded only 27,612 attendances in the morning, 8,610 in the afternoon, and 12,406 in the evening. Map 51 gives the I.A., for each county and provides the first clear indication of 19th-century Unitarian distribution. Significant I.A.s were recorded in the Black Country, Lancashire and Cheshire, the West Country and the south coast. However the total numbers involved were small and so it is equally necessary to look at the distribution of absolute numbers (see Table 11). Nearly 40% of all the Unitarian attendances were in the West Riding, Lancashire and Cheshire—the home of 19th-century Unitarianism.

Something of the early 19th-century development of Unitarianism can be traced from information supplied in the 1851 Census concerning the dates when new churches were built. Unitarian influence had already reached its saturation point in East Anglia by the beginning of the 19th century and no new chapels were built. There was a continuing gradual expansion in the West Country, along the south coast, and around London, but the real development took place in Lancashire, Cheshire, the West Riding and Derbyshire, particularly in the immediate hinterland of Manchester.

It is difficult to follow the changes in the relative distribution of Unitarianism since 1851 as the necessary statistical information[30] is almost entirely absent. However two guidelines are available. Firstly the *Unitarian Handbook*[31] gives details of all the chapels which are used by Unitarian congregations and although there is no way of assessing their size and relative vitality, the overall picture given by their spatial distribution is a clear reflector of present-day Unitarianism. By far the greatest concentration of chapels is to be found in the area comprising south Lancashire, north-east Cheshire, south Yorkshire and north Derbyshire (see Map 52). Much smaller concentrations occur in London, Merseyside and the Black Country, and there are also a reasonable number along the south coast, and the West Country (apart from Cornwall). By contrast Unitarianism is virtually absent from the Welsh borders, East Anglia, south-central England and the northern Home Counties, Lincolnshire and all the area to the north of a line from the Humber to Morecambe Bay.

The second guideline is provided by the Registrar General's Marriage Statistics for 1952—the first and last time that Unitarian marriages were separately tabulated (see Table 11). Although marriage figures only give a rough indication of denominational support, Table 11 leaves no doubt about the overwhelming dominance of Lancashire, Cheshire and the West Riding within Unitarianism.

Since the time of the 1851 Census the distribution of Unitarianism has undergone a significant change and it is possible to analyse this by making a comparison between the Census attendance figures and the 1952 marriage figures as set out in Table 11. In each case the figures are expressed as a percentage of the national total, thus making it feasible to compare two different sets of criteria. The trend over the last 100 years has been towards a decline in the minor centres of Unitarianism, i.e. Worcestershire and Warwickshire, the south coast and West Country counties, and in the London area. This has been coupled with a proportional increase in the Unitarian heartland centring round the Manchester region. It appears that Unitarianism is gradually retreating back into its heartland, having failed to catch the popular imagination and establish itself as the denomination for progressive liberals. This is in strange contrast with the situation in the U.S.A., where the Unitarians and their associates have a big following. Perhaps English Unitarianism is too intimately associated in people's minds with its Victorian heyday.

The British Israel Movement

The aim of this movement[32] is to show that the British people are the chosen race of God and that the Anglo-Saxons are literally descended from the ancient House of Israel. The theory first gained supporters over a century ago, but it was not until the 1920s and 1930s that the movement made any rapid headway, when under the dynamic leadership of H. Garrison the membership of the World Federation of British Israelites rose to over 10,000. It was particularly successful in attracting a considerable number of the aristocracy. This is hardly surprising for the movement looks upon itself as the guardian of the national conscience and has a strong reverence for tradition and authority especially as symbolized in the monarchy and the aristocracy. Its whole philosophy is one of reaction to change.

Membership figures are unobtainable, but it is most unlikely that active participants number more than two or three thousand. More may well support it in a nominal or financial capacity. The movement maintains local branches in most of the large cities as well as in some of the smaller towns.[33] The geographical spread is wide and fairly even, and although all branches are encouraged to have premises of their own, only two succeed in doing this (Bedford and Bristol)—the rest meet in hired halls or in private houses. Most of the members are old and are usually retired. This is reflected directly in the location of branches for a significant proportion are in towns with a large retired community—towns such as Southend, Tunbridge Wells, Scarborough, Southport, Deal, Folkestone, Hastings, Bath and Bournemouth. The movement is essentially middle to upper-middle class both in its membership and in its geographical location.

CHAPTER TEN

Quasi-Christian Groups and Eastern Religions

QUASI-CHRISTIAN GROUPS OF AMERICAN ORIGIN

During the course of the 19th century a number of religious movements grew up in the U.S.A., which claimed to be either adjuncts to or replacements of the historic Christian Churches. The Christian Scientists and the Spiritualists both claim to add a new dimension to the Christian faith as traditionally understood. In the case of the Scientists it is spiritual healing while the Spiritualists profess to establish direct contacts with the spiritual world.

A second group is composed of those who believe they have superseded the old Christian churches and that from henceforth they are the only true and valid church. The Mormons, the Jehovah's Witnesses, and the Seventh Day Adventists all come into this category. Unfortunately, while the Jehovah's Witnesses supply excellent publicity material on the number of hours broadcasting they put on throughout the world, the number of man-hours worked by their ministers and so on,[1] there are no available statistics for England, let alone for particular towns or regions, whereby a geographical assessment could be undertaken. However the other four organizations have provided sufficient source material to make analysis possible.

The Christian Scientists

The origin of the movement which became known as Christian Science dates from the revelation to Mrs. Mary Baker Eddy in 1866 in which she believed she was given the secret of Jesus' healing method. It first took on an institutional form in 1879 when the First Church of Christ, Scientist, was founded in Boston, U.S.A. Until 1897 Christian Science remained an American phenomenon, but in that year Mrs. Julia King brought the movement to England.

In its early years in this country Christian Science was primarily an upper class movement. Today it draws the bulk of its members from the middle and upper-middle classes although it retains much of its former genteel and aristocratic ethos. Working class Christian Scientists are rare—a strong contrast with Mrs. Eddy's original pupils who came from a humble and uneducated background.

Christian Scientists in England are not a proselytizing group, unlike their American counterparts. Their only form of approach is through their reading rooms, their Sunday services and the occasional advertisement. Most of their new recruits come as a result of witnessing a successful healing. They wait for potential members to come to them as enquirers—a typically English approach.

Their theology is rationalistic rather than emotional with great emphasis placed on thought and self-examination. Education is held in high esteem and is reflected in the large numbers of teachers in their membership. If their numbers drop they look for the causes of decline in themselves rather than indulging in evangelistic fervour. Naturally such an ethos rarely appeals to people in the lower socio-economic groups, and in this respect Christian Science has much in common with Unitarianism.

Church by-laws prevent them from publishing any membership or attendance figures, but information is available concerning their meeting places.[2] Organizationally they distinguish between a society and a church. A society needs a nucleus of 10–12 members of the Mother Church[3] before it can be formed, and it will normally be able to recruit a number of local members in addition. Before a local group can form a church it needs a complement of twenty-five members of the Mother Church. Neither a society nor a church is required to possess its own buildings, although in fact most do have permanent premises. The national distribution of churches and societies can be seen from Map 53.

Although Christian Science has no clergy, it does have a category of people who work full-time for the church: the practitioners and teachers. They are fully trained and vetted by the church's lecturers and then have their names entered in *The Christian Science Journal*. As there is no proper system to distribute the practitioners it means their distribution tends to reflect directly the actual distribution of Christian Scientists— the open market arrangement ensures that practitioners gravitate to their patients. The pattern of the distribution of church buildings (Map 53) confirms this.

Christian Science in England is essentially an urban phenomenon. The limited size of its following makes it impossible to establish small rural societies. Those members who do live a distance from an urban centre are forced to travel many miles to their nearest society or church. Although our large cities can support a number of Christian Science practitioners, they are not the ideal habitat. In a detailed study of Christian Science, Wilson concludes that although Christian Science is an urban phenomenon, it is often successful in quite small places where sufferers and hypochondriacs are concentrated, whereas in very large urban areas with working class populations it encounters no response.[4]

From the lists of practitioners for 1967[5] the total number in each of the resort and spa towns was calculated (Table 12). These seventeen towns accounted for only 2·6% of the nation's population but they possessed 13·4% of all the practitioners. It is here that Christian Science exerts its greatest influence. The statistical study of all the towns in England and Wales with 1951 populations of over 50,000 undertaken by Moser and Scott[6] provides detailed information on the social composition of the larger resort towns and spas. All of them are characterized by a top-heavy age structure with a high percentage in the over sixty-five age bracket, and most have a larger proportion of women than men (particularly among the over 65s). A few of the resorts such as Blackpool, Bournemouth, Torquay and Eastbourne have over 10% of their population living in institutional households, such as hotels and old people's homes.

This group of towns, by virtue of the large element of retired and elderly in their population bases, have the lowest percentages of residents in full-time employment. Of those who are employed, the emphasis is on the service industries, especially catering and the retail trade, which serve the large elderly and retired middle class community. These towns also rank high in terms of social class and are predominantly Conservative in politics. Small wonder therefore that Christian Science should find the resort and spa towns a most responsive environment. Nowhere else is there such a concentration of well-to-do elderly people, most of whom will be ailing, and some will have a morbid preoccupation with their health—a preoccupation on which Christian Science thrives.

London presents a difficult case, for it is impossible to relate geographically the practitioners to their likely catchment areas for patients. Practitioners based in London could easily travel considerable distances to see patients. Nevertheless, from an examination of their addresses, they are found concentrated in the prosperous and better class areas (postmarks such as W.1 and S.W.1 abound) whereas they are conspicuous by their absence in working class districts. Of the 125 practitioners based in London, not one resides in the East End (1967).

An analysis on a county basis would be of little value for a small organization like Christian Science, for the areas involved are so large that local variations in areal distribution would tend to be levelled out. However one county, Sussex, with 8·8% of the total practitioners for only 2·6% of the overall population, illustrates just how committed to the elderly middle and upper-middle class section of the community Christian Science actually is.[7] The beliefs of Christian Science are reflected in the composition of the membership it attracts, which in turn is reflected in the areal distribution of churches and practitioners. Thus a direct link can be traced between its theology and its geographical distribution.

The Spiritualists

Spiritualism is the belief that the spirits of those who have died are actually able to communicate with the living. It has been described as a refined form of primitive ancestor worship[8] and as such its lineage can be traced right back to the earliest times. The present movement began in Hydeville, New York, in 1847, and it was brought over to England in 1852 where it established itself in two main centres—London and Keighley. During the 1850s its influence spread out from Keighley to a series of towns in the West Riding and Lancashire. By the end of the 1870s the movement had grown considerably, but geographically it was still very limited—confined essentially to Lancashire, the West Riding, the north-east focusing on Newcastle, the west Midlands, and London. Statistical information collected by J. Morse for presentation to the Conference of Spiritualists in 1880 showed just how heavy was the concentration of societies in the northern industrial towns.

Since the 1880s the movement had grown but slowly.[9] The only time it really flourished was immediately after the First World War when it attracted nearly 500,000 supporters. After the Second World War the expansion was much more subdued. From its first establishment in England, Spiritualism has been an essentially urban phenomenon. The industrial towns of the north-east, Lancashire, Yorkshire and London where Spiritualism took root in the 1850s, were those to which rural workers were flocking in. These workers, cut off from their former way of life and having to adjust to a completely new set of conditions, often became victims of 'anomie'—a state of mind on which Spiritualism thrives.

It was only in the 1920s and 1930s that Spiritualism began to spread beyond the industrial cities of the north, the Midlands and London. Even as late as 1908 there were only three societies in the Home Counties (excluding London) whereas there were sixty-two in Yorkshire and eighty-eight in Lancashire. Unfortunately there is a lack of complete statistics for any later period, but Nelson[10] concludes that in recent years the centre of interest and activity has moved away from the north to London and the south-east. As the inflow of migrants into the northern industrial towns began to slow down and people adjusted to urban life, the demand for Spiritualism started to wane. This was accompanied by a growth of influence in the resorts along the south coast which are occupied by a high percentage of old people. Both Spiritualism and Christian Science flourish in the same type of southern environment.

The Seventh Day Adventists

Seventh Day Adventism is essentially a millennarian movement and claims it is the only true Church because it alone keeps the proper Sabbath, the seventh day of the week, and not Sunday, the first day of the new week, as in the rest of Christendom. On account of this its members argue that from their ranks alone will be drawn the 144,000 who will attain everlasting salvation. The movement began in the 1840s in America and was founded by Mrs. Ellen White who claimed she was taken up into Heaven in 1844 to witness the cleansing of the heavenly sanctuary by the Lord.

A missionary venture was mounted in England in 1878 and since then the numbers of converts have grown slowly but steadily to reach a 1965 total of 9,241 in full membership.[11] There are about 100 properly organized churches throughout the country, most having a membership of well under ninety. In addition there are thirty-three companies, each with a handful of members who meet in rented halls or private houses.

The church has attained a good geographical coverage of the country and has groups in most of the large towns and some of the smaller centres also. Inevitably the largest number of members is to be found in London. Central London has 1,660 members and several of the suburban churches each have over 100 members (Wimbledon, Croydon, Watford and Walthamstow). Next in numerical strength come Birmingham with nearly 600 members and then Manchester with nearly 300. Churches of over 100 members are also found in Bristol, Bournemouth, Ipswich, Leeds, Leicester, Wolverhampton, Nottingham and Sheffield.

The theological emphasis on the exclusive character of the

elect few predisposes them to favour a large number of small groups rather than a few large anonymous congregations. The outreach of the American-backed missionary venture seems to ensure a continuing increase in the number of members in the years to come and this is likely to result in an ever wider geographical spread. When a handful of Adventists are available in an area they have no hesitation in forming themselves into a company.

The Mormons (The Church of Jesus Christ of Latter Day Saints[12])

The history of the Mormon Church began in the U.S.A. in the early 1820s when the founder of the movement, a certain Joseph Smith, claimed to have had two visions and a call to be 'a prophet of the Most High God'. He was told by the angel Moroni in 1822 that he would find a precious religious volume hidden in a hill. This volume would be written on gold plates and would contain the fullest account of the Gospel as delivered by Christ to the ancient inhabitants of North America. Four years later Joseph Smith was led to the hill, found the gold plates, and translated the inscribed hieroglyphics using two special crystals. The resultant work became known as the Book of Mormon.

During the following twenty years the Mormon Church grew in numbers and strength, despite encountering severe opposition and persecution. Its original Zion was at Nauvoo, Illinois, and it was here that Joseph Smith was murdered in 1844. This had the effect of turning Smith into a martyr and thus new vigour was added to the movement. Brigham Young became the new leader and under his guidance the Mormons moved from Nauvoo to Salt Lake City, Utah, in the early months of 1846.

The Mormons first appeared on the English religious kaleidoscope in 1837 when seven Mormon missionaries landed at Liverpool. From here they made their way north to Preston where they received an enthusiastic welcome and baptized their first converts in the waters of the Ribble. A second mission was sent to this country in 1840, this time headed by the leader himself, Brigham Young. Again it was based on Liverpool and missionaries were sent out round the country and often they were asked to preach in small independent chapels, being mistaken for itinerant Christian evangelists. They met with early successes in Herefordshire and this was quickly repeated in Gloucestershire, Worcestershire, and the West of England.

The missionaries preached that the Kingdom of Christ was shortly to appear at Nauvoo and that it was the duty of all true Christians to go there. As Nauvoo was also built up to sound like a contemporary Garden of Eden, it is small wonder that many of the English converts to Mormonism, most of whom were poor, gladly responded to the call. Furthermore the Mormons organized a very efficient emigration system out of Liverpool. The first two winters of 1841–2 and 1842–3 saw nearly 3,000 emigrants leaving Liverpool for Nauvoo, but after that numbers tailed off a little. All emigration was suspended in 1846 and 1847, the period of the move from Nauvoo to Salt Lake City, but in December 1847 the leadership issued a new appeal urging emigration to Zion (this time located at Salt Lake City). According to Mormon statistics,[13] nearly 17,000 English converts had emigrated by 1850, most sailing from Liverpool but some also from Southampton, Bristol and Plymouth.

The Mormons in 1851. By the time of the 1851 Religious Census, Mormon activity had spread over large parts of England. It is fortunate that the date of the Census coincides with the period of the greatest Mormon influence in England prior to the 1960s.

There was a total of about 35,000 attendances at Mormon places of worship on Census Sunday. However as some members would attend more than one service a day it is unlikely that the 35,000 attendances would represent 35,000 actual persons. An estimate of between 25,000 and 30,000 people attending Mormon services on Census Sunday is hazarded.

Absolute numbers tell us very little: they need to be related to the total population base. This has been achieved by expressing the number of Mormon attendances per thousand total population on a county basis. Over England as a whole the

Mormon attendances were two per 1,000 total population, and the regional variations are shown on Map 54.

The Mormons in England looked to the New World as the source of their religious faith and also for a supply of Mormon missionaries. Many of the English converts emigrated to their new Promised Land. It was inevitable therefore that those English ports which maintained regular services to and from the eastern seaboard of America should become centres of Mormon activity. Liverpool, Southampton and Bristol became focal points linking the English Mormons with their prophets in the United States. The high incidence of Mormonism in Gloucestershire and Hampshire is clearly seen on Map 54, although the large number of Mormons in Liverpool did not have much effect on the general total for Lancashire.

Lines of Mormon penetration can also be traced out from these three centres. From Southampton they spread over Hampshire and north-west into the surrounding counties of Dorset, Wiltshire and Somerset. Similarly from Bristol Mormon influence filtered south into these three counties, as well as travelling along a south-west/north-east axis through Gloucestershire, Warwickshire and Leicestershire into Nottinghamshire. The importance of Liverpool's link[14] with the New World is reflected in Mormon presence in Lancashire, Cheshire and the West Riding.

Of the total number of attendances, nearly 75% is made up of the following counties or groups of counties:

1. Lancashire (11·6%), Cheshire (5·2%),
   West Riding (7·2%)   24%
2. Dorset (2·2%), Somerset (2·5%),
   Wiltshire (2·8%), Hampshire (8·7%),
   Gloucestershire (7·3%)   23·5%
3. Metropolitan London   12·8%
4. Warwickshire   7·5%
5. Nottinghamshire   5·7%

However Mormonism was a relatively new phenomenon in this country in 1851, and it had not spread to the extremities of England. There were no Mormon attendances registered in Cornwall, and the five northern counties of Cumberland,

Westmorland, the North Riding, Northumberland and Durham only accounted for 1·9% of the total Mormon attendances. Similarly in the south-eastern counties of Suffolk, Essex, Surrey, Kent and Sussex attendances were low.

The 1851 map reflects the pattern of an organization very much in its infancy. It was only just beginning to spread out from the ports of arrival into their immediate hinterlands. It is interesting that Mormon missionaries had already achieved successes in Metropolitan London. This is an obvious place to begin an evangelizing campaign on account of its key position and its unique role in the country. They had been successful also in the northern Home Counties (Hertfordshire, Bedfordshire, Huntingdonshire, Cambridgeshire and Northamptonshire).

Mormonism had reached its 19th-century peak in England by 1851. In 1852 the Mormon doctrine of polygamy was officially formulated by Brigham Young, who claimed its authority rested on a special revelation from God to Joseph Smith eleven months before his death. The official organ of Mormonism in England, the *Millennial Star*, set about proclaiming the new doctrine with gusto, and very quickly the Mormons became a laughing stock. Membership figures fell drastically and for the next hundred years English Mormonism was in the doldrums.

The Mormons in 1967. Since the Second World War the Mormon Church has undergone a profound change. In many respects its organization is now modelled on lines similar to those of American big-business and its missionaries are fully trained in salesmanship technique. An air of professional competence is exuded. The average Englishman, brought up amid the historic pageantry of his religious institutions, usually finds the Mormon approach difficult to comprehend, although its very novelty appeals to many.

A picture of Mormon strength and activity in this country today can be built up by using its membership figures and also from information concerning its church buildings. Membership of the Mormon Church is conferred by the rite of baptism. Children from the age of eight upwards can be admitted, but the percentage of new members who have been 'born into the

Church' (i.e. born to parents who were already members themselves) is low. Less than 20% of the total membership of this country is estimated[15] to be birthright membership. The remainder are baptized as teenagers or adults as a result of conversion.

However not all members continue to participate in the life and activities of the church and so they delimit a further unofficial category—that of the 'active' member. He is a person who attends regularly at services and lives according to the rigorous standards of the church, namely physical cleanliness (not drinking tea, coffee, or alcohol, and not smoking) and moral cleanliness. He would also be expected to obey and uphold the church leaders and church teaching. This active membership is estimated at 25%[16] of the total, but as no statistics are kept of this category, it cannot be used for geographical analysis.

Although none of their membership figures are published, it was possible to obtain them from their various regional headquarters. Totals were given for each Mormon chapel or meeting place and these were certified as representing the exact membership on the date of enumeration. There is just one proviso: any American servicemen stationed in this country who were Mormons would be included in the English totals[17] and so would distort the indigenous pattern somewhat. Apart from this, the Mormon membership figures can be taken as indicative of actual allegiance and practice.

The distribution of Mormon members over the country (Map 55) forms a distinctive pattern. The four ports which have or had close links with the U.S.A. (Bristol, Southampton, Liverpool and Plymouth) each has a large Mormon following among its population. A further port, Hull, also has a surprisingly large Mormon congregation.

Mormon strength lies in the northern half of England. Taking two of the traditional dividing lines, we find that about 60% of the Mormon membership is to the north of the Severn–Wash line, and 45% to the north of a line between the Humber and the Dee. More specifically, a large proportion of the northern total is found in the three 'stake' areas[18] of Manchester, Leeds and Sunderland.

The Mormons have met with little success in London, the south-east and right along the south coast from Kent to Cornwall (with the exceptions of Southampton and Plymouth). Congregations are to found in these areas, but relative to the size of their total population, membership is very low. The map of Mormon church buildings (Map 56) confirms the general features of geographical distribution as outlined above. There is a Mormon Temple at Lingfield on the Surrey–Sussex border but this is not in any way indicative of Mormon activity in the south-east. The temples are set aside for rather detached spiritual purposes and are more akin to contemplative monasteries than to cathedrals.

What does the future hold for the Mormons in this country? Their missionary effectiveness is rapidly increasing and already they have a missionary force of approaching a thousand young volunteers operating in England. Their authoritarian structure has prevented any serious theological rifts from developing within the church and so they present a united front. Their membership figures have been climbing rapidly and between 1962 and 1967 they went up from 11,000 to over 45,000. It is difficult to see how the Mormons in this country can do anything but increase in numbers in the years ahead. Whether they can modify their approach in order to appeal to the southerner remains to be seen.

NON-CHRISTIAN RELIGIONS OF EASTERN ORIGIN

Since the end of the Second World War there has been a large-scale influx of immigrants from the East and they have added an entirely new dimension to the English religious scene. The average Englishman, long since used to viewing the East as 'heathen lands afar' where 'thick darkness broodeth yet',[19] is now waking up to find 'the heathen religions' in his very midst. Although estimates are difficult to make with any accuracy, Buddhists, Hindus, Sikhs and Muslims[20] probably account for about 350,000 of the English population—this is over half the total size of the Methodist Church in England.

The Muslims

The Islamic faith commands a total numerical allegiance of about 465 million people. It has a wide geographical spread with large followings in the Middle East, Indonesia, India, Pakistan, China, Afghanistan, and the northern half of Africa. In this country the majority of the immigrant Muslim population is made up of Pakistanis and Arabs, although many other nations are represented by minority groups. Unfortunately there is no accurate record of the Muslim population in England at present, but the Islamic Cultural Centre[21] makes an estimate of about 250,000 of whom about 100,000 are resident in London.

The faith of the Muslims is stern and simple. Although various schisms have occurred from time to time, they all agree that 'there is no God but Allah and Muhammad is the apostle of God'. Five times a day, wherever they may be, all Muslims are under a solemn obligation to recite the prescribed prayers and passages from the Koran. Whenever possible adult males are expected to fulfil this obligation in a mosque, where the services will be conducted by an *imam*. On the weekly holy-day, Friday, male attendance at the mosque is compulsory, although the women have to stay at home for their prayers and seldom, if ever, attend the mosque. The rigorous spiritual routine imposed on Muslims has developed a strong sense of corporate religious life and this has been a powerful integrating influence within the Muslim community.

The overwhelming majority of the English Muslims live in the big cities. When a new immigrant arrives in this country he inevitably makes for one of the existing communities where he knows he can find security. Although few of the communities have their own mosques, each has its own sacred Zoaia or prayer room which, along with the secular Muslim-run café, forms the focal point of the Muslim community.[22] As the centre of religious activity, the Zoaia leads the immigrants of several nationalities, languages and cultures into the full life of the immigrant community. By carefully maintaining their Muslim beliefs and practices, the immigrants have forged a strong link between their new settlement and their old society and culture

—a vital psychological link for them in a difficult transition period.

Not only does the Zoaia serve as a religious centre, but it also acts for the wider social interests of the community. The *imam* or sheikh is looked upon as the head of the community and advises its members on all aspects of their lives. Most Zoaias have a mutual aid society to help the new immigrant to establish himself and find a job.[23] At present the religious and the social sides of the Muslim communities are inextricably intertwined. It is small wonder that the new immigrant makes for one of these semi-ghettoes in our large urban centres, and once settled into it, finds it very difficult to leave. To settle in suburbia or the countryside would mean deserting his fellow countrymen and forsaking his Islamic faith, thereby cutting the last links with his former culture and pattern of life.

The Buddhists

The Buddhist heartland is in south-east Asia. Japan, China, Thailand and Cambodia account for approximately 235 million Buddhists and a further six million are resident in Ceylon.[24] There has been no large-scale immigration into England of people from these countries and as a result Buddhism has failed to achieve the same numerical representation as some of the other non-Christian faiths.

Attempts have been made to establish an indigenous Buddhist following and with this in mind the Buddhist Society was founded in London in 1924. Affiliated groups and societies have grown up in various parts of the country and their distribution[25] suggests that Buddhism draws most of its support from the intellectual 'thinking' classes. Several of the groups are located in university towns (Newcastle, Hull, York, Manchester, Edgbaston in Birmingham, Cambridge, Oxford, Bristol and Brighton), two more are found in south-east resort towns, and one in Mousehole catering for the 'arty set' who live there. It appears that Buddhism in England completely fails to attract the interest of the lower-middle and working classes.

There is also a second strand to English Buddhism, composed of immigrants from Buddhist countries. Although their numbers are small, there are sufficient of them in London to support several Buddhist organizations, including the Buddhapadipa Temple in East Sheen. A steady trickle of Buddhist monks from Asia and Ceylon has helped to support and extend the work of the provincial groups and the arrival of Tibetan refugee monks has further swelled the missionary potential. Eastern mysticism and meditation, having been popularized by the Beatles, is the current vogue among a section of the younger generation, and it will be interesting to see whether this will result in a future expansion of Buddhist membership in this country.

The Hindus

The complex religious system known as Hinduism is almost exclusively limited to India and is so bound up with the Indian environment and culture that it is almost impossible for it to be taken abroad. Indeed some varieties of Hinduism forbid their members to travel across the sea since this involves abandoning the rules of ritual purity.

Since the end of the Second World War there has been a considerable influx of Indians into the industrial towns of England, particularly London, Southall, Gravesend, Bradford, Coventry, Liverpool and the Birmingham conurbation. But they have left most of their religion behind in India. The elaborate rituals necessary in a temple are normally forbidden outside India. Furthermore in the Punjab and Gujarat, from where most of the immigrants come, temple worship itself is on the decline. Desai[26] points out that the Hinduism of the immigrant has a basis in village or caste in India and that it is the village-kin group rather than the total community which is concerned with the ritual observances. Frequently this group is too small to afford a temple, which is in any case inessential to the philosophical nature of Hindu religious life. The majority of the immigrants delegate their ritual obligations to relatives still in India, even to the extent of wedding and funeral rites, where the English ceremony is merely a token of the real ceremony being performed by delegation in India. Hinduism has not made any real impression on the English social landscape.

The Sikhs

Little is known about the origins of the Sikhs in England. The London Sikh Temple was already established by the end of the 19th century and so there must have been a number of Sikhs resident in London by then. Some of the early settlers were businessmen; others were pedlars from the Bhattra tribe who also told fortunes—they were originally very ignorant and poor, but now many of them are well educated. It was the partition of India in 1947 which initiated the first large-scale immigration of Sikhs into this country. This was followed by the unrest in East Africa and the eventual granting of independence to the constituent national groups, which caused many Sikhs who had been resident there to leave for England. The vast majority of the Sikhs have arrived in England over the last fifteen years, and more in the second half than in the first half of the period. Inevitably therefore their religious institutions are barely established and very poorly organized.

So far there has been no proper survey of the Sikh community and the total community size can only be estimated by guesswork: it is thought to be around 100,000.[27] No attempts have been made to guess the population size of the individual local communities. Most of the Sikhs are gathered together in the larger urban centres and so their population base is normally large enough to support a Sikh religio-cultural centre and maybe a Sikh temple in addition. Only the Maidenhead[28] community has a full-time religious leader but some others have a 'Granthi' who is employed to conduct religious services and look after the temple, although he has no spiritual authority.

The distribution pattern of the Sikhs, as reflected by the presence of their temples and other Associations,[29] reveals no surprises. In the south they are well settled in London with outlying communities in Edgware, Southall, Slough, Maidenhead, Woolwich, Gravesend and Gillingham. Southampton, Portsmouth and Bristol also have settled Sikh populations. Moving into the Midlands, communities are to be found in Leamington, Coventry, Leicester, Nottingham, Birmingham, Walsall and Wolverhampton, all centres of considerable

immigrant settlement. Further north, Manchester, Huddersfield, Bradford, Leeds, and Newcastle complete the picture.

The future for the Eastern religions in England

The future rests almost entirely with the Muslims and the
Sikhs, for the Buddhists only number several thousand and are
unlikely to receive any massive influx of new immigrant membership, while the Hindus leave their religion behind in India
and fail to give their philosophy of life any organizational
expression in this country. The constant tightening of our immigration laws renders any large-scale immigration of Muslims
and Sikhs into this country in the future most unlikely. Nevertheless the two communities will grow as a result of natural
increase and also as relatives join their families over here—
although this latter method is being restricted severely at
present.

However as the numerical size of the two communities
increases, so growing assimilation into the English culture pattern will take its toll. In both communities the main cohesive
element is the religious institution with its obligations, rules and
social system. But there is a fringe group among the Sikhs and
the Muslims who flout the traditions of their elders. They are
composed largely of second generation British-born immigrants
along with new young immigrants who quickly fall in with the
norms and values of British society. Whether the processes of
secularization will outweigh the natural increase within the
communities is as yet uncertain. Up until now the immigrant
groups have used their native religions to provide a focus of
solidarity and security. If assimilation rather than integration
takes place, then this need will disappear.

CHAPTER ELEVEN

The Jews

The proportion of Jews in the general population will presumably fall steadily while those Jews who remain will be more and more integrated into the majority group. Thus, after the passage of some time, little may be left that is distinctively Jewish in this country.

Neustatter[1]

The Jews in England account for about 1% of the total population (428,000 out of a total population of *c.* 45,000,000). This is two-thirds the size of the Methodist membership and over twice the size of the declared Congregational membership. Both on account of their size and their distinctive history the Jews form a basic component of the English religious landscape.

DEFINITION OF A JEW [2]

Who is, and who is not to be counted a Jew? The official talmudic definition of a Jew is anyone who is born of a Jewish mother. However this is not a very useful definition for the geographer, as such a person may well have severed all connection with both the religious and the social sides of Judaism. Also this definition of birthright membership raises a big question-mark over the status of converts. Although there is little if any active proselytizing, many of the less conservative and less orthodox synagogues will admit converts. At the other end of the spectrum is the definition which limits the title of 'Jew' to those who attend the synagogues, along with their immediate dependents.

Until the end of the 19th century the definition problem hardly existed. Everyone knew who the Jews were, for they then formed a distinctive group with their own religion, social life, dietary laws, observance of the Jewish Sabbath, and affiliation to a synagogue. These definitive group characteristics marked them off from the rest of English society. Today, however, liberalization within English Judaism, along with the increasing assimilation of Jews into English society, has meant that the Jews no longer form a distinctive group.

In view of the lack of a general consensus as to a clear definition of a Jew, it would seem that the best definition is one of self-identification. On being questioned, anyone who claims Jewish affiliation is to be counted as a Jew.

JEWISH STATISTICS

The question of the definition of a Jew is going to require careful examination once the techniques for collecting Jewish statistics become more sophisticated. At present however the basic statistical information is so unsatisfactory that the question of definition makes little difference.

The Jewish Yearbook publishes membership figures for each Jewish community and, on the basis of these estimates there are 428,000 Jews in England, of whom 280,000 live in Greater London.[3] How reliable are these figures? An examination of the method used to collect the figures does not inspire confidence. The *Yearbook* publishers appoint an observer for each community, usually the local rabbi, and it is his job to estimate the size of that local Jewish community. In a small compact community, where all the Jews will be known to the observer, the task is relatively easy. However as the size of the community increases, so the figures given become more and more a matter of conjecture. In large communities it is difficult enough to record all the orthodox Jewish families and it becomes virtually impossible to keep track of those families which have severed some, if not all, their connections with Judaism. Those who choose to dissociate themselves from the Jewish community and worship are unlikely to be known to the observers.

This method was of dubious enough value when the self-contained Jewish community was the norm. Now that an increasing number of Jewish families are moving into the suburbs and the countryside, it becomes of even less value, for the statistics take no account of isolated families. As the geographical dispersion of Anglo-Jewry increases, so the number of Jews not included in the *Yearbook* totals will increase. Nobody really knows just how many Jews are living outside the reach of organized Judaism. Neustatter[4] estimated they formed 15% of the total English Jewry in the early 1950s, but this is no more than an intelligent guess.

An examination of the *Yearbooks* for the last thirty-eight years reveals another problem. Often the observers send in rounded-off estimates which, once made, are returned unaltered year after year. Thus according to the *Yearbook* the Jewish population of Exeter has remained at twenty since the 1940s.

In spite of all these inadequacies however, the *Yearbook* statistics are sufficiently accurate to reveal the basic pattern of Jewish distribution. The estimates given by the observers roughly correspond to the state of affairs within their various communities. The figures given for Greater London are based primarily on the work of two people in the 1930s and could well do with revision.[5]

The Jewish Statistical Office is at present working on the question of national totals. It hopes to be able to relate the number of Jewish burials to the total number of burials and then to 'gross up' the Jewish population accordingly. This method does have drawbacks and even if the results obtained are substantially accurate, the figures will be available only for large regions and one or two of the largest communities.

Statistics of synagogue membership are of little value as a criterion of the size of the Jewish population in a particular area. Some synagogues restrict their membership to men, in others women can only become members by virtue of their husband's membership, and in yet others women are allowed to become members in their own right. Furthermore when Jews move into a new area they often retain membership of their old synagogue for sentimental reasons, as well as joining the synagogue in their new area.

The whole subject of Jewish statistics is bedevilled by memories of religious censuses in Eastern Europe during the inter-war years. Several countries included a question on religion in their national census of population and on the basis of the answers the returning officers drew up lists of religious adherence. Unfortunately the Jewish lists fell into the hands of the Nazis and were used as the criterion for deciding who was to be classified as a Jew. It is understandable, therefore, that the Jews should regard any form of statistical recording with a certain amount of suspicion and any attempt to introduce a question on religion into the British census would be violently opposed.[6]

THE HISTORY OF ANGLO-JEWRY

The history of Jewish settlement in England prior to the Conquest is shrouded in obscurity. Legend has it that St. Paul first brought Christianity to England and such a visit by St. Paul would have presupposed a settled Jewish community with a synagogue.[7] There were probably a few Jewish families in England during Roman and Anglo-Saxon times but we have no record of any properly organized Jewish communities.

Soon after the Conquest Jewish immigrants began to arrive in England and settled in London in an area which is still known as Old Jewry. From here they gradually spread out into many of the old medieval provincial centres, such as Lincoln, Exeter, Norwich, Bedford and Bristol. The Jews, in their capacity as moneylenders, were needed by the English Crown, for the Christian Church forbade its members to engage in usury. However, despite their function, the position of the Jews in medieval England was by no means secure. Many were massacred in 1190 and by 1290 the situation had deteriorated so much that Edward I expelled them from England,[8] after which time only secret adherents and converts to Christianity remained.

The mid-17th century saw the readmission of Jews into this country and a Portuguese and Spanish congregation was established in London in 1656. For some time however the numbers remained small and by 1684 Roth[9] estimates there were only 414 Jews in the whole of Great Britain. The first real growth of the Jewish community in England began with the establishment of the Ashkenazi (European) community at the end of the 17th century.

The London communities soon experienced difficulty in absorbing all the new immigrants into their ranks and so a policy was initiated which led to the growth of provincial Jewry. As immigrants arrived in London they were furnished with supplies by the London Jews and sent out into the provinces as pedlars. The early pedlars led extremely isolated lives and only returned to London or the nearest large Jewish centre for the major Jewish festivals. It was during the mid-18th century that the first provincial communities were founded and by 1800 there were about twenty such communities in the more important market towns and seaports. It appears that none of the provincial communities were properly organized before 1740 despite the presence of Jews in the provinces from the beginning of the 18th century onwards.

These 'first wave' provincial centres were composed of the original pedlars sent out from London, who in time had became prosperous. In turn they equipped the latest arrivals with goods and sent them out into the inland towns and villages to earn a livelihood. Eventually this 'second wave' of pedlars settled down in the inland centres and by this means the foundation of provincial Jewry was laid. The beginning of the 19th century saw provincial Jewry firmly established, with Plymouth, Portsmouth, Liverpool and Birmingham as the four most important Jewish centres outside London.

Provincial Jewry and London Jewry have formed two quite distinctive strands within Anglo-Jewry from the time Jews were readmitted into England and so separate assessments of each are required.

PROVINCIAL JEWRY

It was still possible in 1900 to observe traces of the 18th century and 19th century geographical distribution pattern of English Jewry. Many of the seaports at which the immigrant Jews arrived had large Jewish communities, as well as certain of the industrial centres of provincial England. By 1920 a redistribution had taken place in which many of the smaller communities had disappeared to the benefit of the largest Jewish centres. The lure of the big communities was fatal.

The period immediately before and after the Second World War witnessed a new dispersal from the major centres of Jewish population but this was not a movement back to the towns deserted a couple of generations previously. The new communities were established in seaside resorts and in small towns near to the largest Jewish centres. This outward movement which began in the 1930s was given a big impetus as a result of wartime evacuation, and continued through into the post-war period. The pattern is still for new settlement to take place in the suburbs, rural areas and seaside resorts.

Map 57 shows the new Jewish communities which have been established since 1935. All the new communities catering for London Jewry are situated to the north and west of London— an outward extension of the sector occupied by the Jews in Metropolitan London. However these communities are still small in size and it is difficult to know whether they will be capable of surviving.

The largest Jewish provincial community is to be found in the Manchester–Salford district.[10] Before its industrialization the attractions of Manchester did not differ from those of other small inland towns. After the Industrial Revolution, however, Manchester became a major focus for immigrant Jews and numbers increased rapidly, especially from 1883–1905, the period of the greatest intensity of the persecution of Jews in Russia.

Although Manchester (Table 13) has the highest absolute number of Jews in provincial England, Leeds can claim to have the highest proportion of Jews (4% of her total population). There were Jews in Leeds from the 18th century onwards, but

8

the first real growth of the community did not take place until the time of the Russian persecution at the end of the 19th century. Leeds had the obvious attraction of its clothing industry which acted as a magnet to the Jews. Liverpool possessed a Jewish community as early as 1750 but this failed and had to be restarted in 1780. Its subsequent growth was due in part to the number of intending immigrants for the U.S.A. and the West Indies who decided against the voyage at the last minute and remained in Liverpool.

Apart from Brighton and Southend, the only other Jewish community of 3,000 is in Birmingham. Dating from 1730 at the latest, Birmingham is one of the oldest Jewish communities in the provinces. Jewish settlers were attracted by the light industries and it quickly became a regional centre for Jewry.

Several other towns have Jewish populations of between 1,000 and 3,000 (see Map 58). Apart from the resorts of Bournemouth, Southport and Blackpool, they are Newcastle, Sunderland, Hull, Luton and Dunstable, Sheffield, Nottingham and Leicester. In the early 19th century Hull was the port through which the majority of the North European Jewish immigrants came and so an important Jewish settlement grew up there. The other towns mentioned are all major provincial centres in their own right and were also used as central bases by the Jews.

Smaller Jewish settlements of under 1,000 are also shown on Map 58. In all there are only eighty recognized communities in provincial England and the largest sixteen of these account for nearly two-thirds of the total provincial Jewry. Thus the Jews outside London are concentrated in relatively few places and tend to be in the larger rather than the smaller centres.

Many of the small provincial communities are now in danger of extinction. It requires a Jewish population of a reasonable size to support the necessities of Jewish life—a synagogue with a rabbi, a burial ground, kosher butchers, etc. Where a community lacks a minister or teacher the structure is liable to crumble. Some of its members will move to one of the larger Jewish centres while others will begin the drift which leads them away from Judaism.[11]

THE JEWS IN LONDON[12]

The Jewish community in London has dominated the life of English Jewry, numerically, economically and socially, since the Resettlement at the time of the Commonwealth. On returning to England the Jews found they were not confined by law to any ghetto area in London, although in practice they voluntarily created what was in all but name a ghetto on the eastern fringes of the City. As immigration continued this community overflowed into the adjacent parts of East London. The ghetto area of Whitechapel remained the basis of Jewish social life right up to recent times.

The first movement out of the ghetto area occurred in the early years of the 18th century when a few of the more affluent Jews bought country retreats in Hampstead and Highgate (Map 59). Stamford Hill and Streatham were similarly occupied later in the 18th century. These subsidiary settlements were of a high economic and social standing in comparison to the Whitechapel settlement, and quickly developed a Jewish life of their own.

The outbreak of persecution and violence against the Jews in Russia in the 1880s resulted in the beginning of a vast immigration of Jews into this country. The majority of them made for Whitechapel which became the main transit camp for the dispersion of East European Jewry to other parts of London, the main English provincial Jewish communities, the British Colonies, and the U.S.A. This immigration continued right up to the beginning of the First World War and during the peak time from 1883 to 1905[13] the Jewish population of London trebled. The leaders of Anglo-Jewry were extremely worried about the effects of over-population in the ghetto area and so they did all they could to encourage the immigrants to move on from Whitechapel and they even gave financial help to those who wished to settle in the New World.

Many Jews prospered with the expansion of the English economy during the First World War, and so began the first large-scale movement of Jews out of Whitechapel. The route was well defined (Map 59). First they moved north to Dalston and Hackney where the fares into the East End workshops were low, and then north again into Stoke Newington and Stamford Hill. The next stage was north-west, not to the older Jewish communities of Hampstead and Highgate, but into the more modest suburbs of north-west London.[14] This move was helped by the extension of the Northern Line of the Underground, and Jewish settlements grew up in Golders Green, Hendon, Edgware, Finchley and beyond. The final stage was to return to a Central London flat in St. John's Wood, the Hyde Park Estate or Mayfair. During the Second World War the price of property and rents fell and many Jews were able to short circuit the traditional route by moving straight from the East End to north-west London, missing out the north London stage. A further modification developed in the 1930s when many moved east from Whitechapel to the new suburban housing estates in Ilford and Woodford.

H. M. Brotz[15] emphasizes that this route is primarily a quest for prestige. At the bottom of the hierarchy is Whitechapel and a flat in the West End represents the ultimate achievement. However, the prestige sought is essentially prestige within a Jewish context and so the route is well defined and dependent on the existence of Jewish communities. A Jew who took a flat in a high status area such as Chelsea where there is no Jewish community, would be seen as opting out of Jewish society and would thus acquire little status among his co-religionists.

The Whitechapel area, almost all Jews agree, is of very low status value, and it has been the ambition of most to move out and start on the upward prestige route. In 1889 about 90% of London's Jewry was to be found in the Whitechapel area, but by 1929 this figure had fallen to 60%. Since the Second World War there has been little Jewish immigration into England and hence little into Whitechapel. As the old ghetto area is not being replenished, and as most of the Jews who formerly inhabited Whitechapel have been able to move out, the ghetto is in the final stages of decline, even though it has not completely vanished.

Anglo-Jewry is still dominated by London. Although accurate figures are not possible, there are probably between 270,000 and 280,000 Jews in London, out of a total English Jewish population of around 428,000.

THE ECONOMIC STRUCTURE OF JEWISH SOCIETY
IN ENGLAND

Traditionally the Jews are associated with certain trades and industries. Christians in the Pre-Reformation period were forbidden to act as moneylenders, and as economic life could not function without usury, this field of operations was undertaken by the Jews. Although this established the Jews as leading financiers, their influence in this sphere has now declined.

The Jews of the 19th century and 20th century immigrations into England found they were restricted in practice to trades which were peripheral to the English economy. The majority began to make livings through such immigrant trades and crafts as peddling and tailoring. Little capital was required to start up in light industry so many Jews moved into this field. A dominant Jewish trait is the desire to be self-dependent and hence self-employed. This partly accounts for the large number of Jews in the professions, as well as in trades like hairdressing and taxi-driving.[16] The main Jewish trades are clothing, furniture and footwear, along with the development of chain stores for the distribution of consumer goods (Marks and Spencer, Burtons, J. Lyons, Great Universal Stores), and also property development. Jewish involvement in agriculture, shipbuilding, the car industry, aircraft manufacture and heavy industry has been slight.

In recent years, however, there seems to have been a general decline in the typically Jewish trades. The tailoring trade in London is losing thousands of workers per year and even in Leeds it is experiencing a decline. Similarly the number of Jews in the East End furniture trade has dropped alarmingly from between 6,000 and 8,000 Jewish workers in 1930 to under 1,000 in 1957.[17] It is necessary however to differentiate between Jewish workers and Jewish employers, for while the number of Jewish employees in the traditional Jewish trades has been decreasing, the number of Jewish employers has remained fairly constant. There are still large numbers of Jewish employers in the clothing trades of London and Leeds and in the East End furniture trade, but the majority of the Jewish workers have now moved into the middle class.[18]

This socio-economic move into the middle class has had profound effects upon the geographical pattern of Jewish settlement. The former ghetto areas of Whitechapel in London, Cheetham in Manchester and Chapeltown in Leeds have now been almost totally abandoned, and certain suburban clusters have taken their place in Moortown for Leeds,[19] Prestwich for Manchester, and the north-west suburbs for London. These new areas of Jewish settlement are not nearly so cohesive and self-contained as the old. Many Jews, when they move out of the old areas, settle in districts where there is no organized Jewish life, and thus also move out of Judaism.

The socio-economic shift of Anglo-Jewry into the middle class has produced the geographical result of a move into the suburbs. This movement into the more affluent areas of towns, and into the new towns designed to relieve urban over-crowding, is clearly seen in the successive siting of synagogues.

THE JEWISH RELIGION AND ITS EFFECTS ON THE GEOGRAPHY OF JEWISH SETTLEMENT PATTERNS

Orthodox Judaism is more than a religion, it is also a way of life. Its religious ritual and rules spill over into most aspects of everyday life. The religious life of Judaism centres round the synagogue and so it was essential for Jews to live near to a synagogue. Furthermore Jewish law forbids the use of any form of transport on the Sabbath and on Holy Days and so it was necessary to live within walking distance of a synagogue. This rule alone meant that Jews could only live in a town where there was a synagogue and only in a small area around the synagogue—hence the ghetto-like groupings.

In addition to the necessity of being near a synagogue, provision had to be made for the religious education of children; a Jewish cemetery was required for burial; meat and poultry had to be slaughtered according to Jewish ritual prescription (Shechita). All these necessities required a Jewish community of a reasonable size for them to be economically possible. Observance of the Jewish Sabbath (i.e. Saturday, not Sunday), the limited group of occupations open to them, their mainly immigrant origin, and the tightly knit Jewish social life further helped to draw together and isolate the Jews from the general community in which they were living. This was further enforced by their economic self-sufficiency and the frequent hostility which they met from the host community. It is small wonder that the Jews normally formed completely organized and enclosed communities whose members were shut off from the outside world.

The established pattern of Jewish settlement in England can be explained largely as the result of controls laid down by orthodox Judaism. In recent years however Judaism has been subject to the same secularizing forces which have been at work on the Christian churches in this country. Increasingly the strict religious rules of orthodox Judaism are being viewed in a more liberal light by the average Jew, if not by the more orthodox religious hierarchy. Among the Jews there has been a loss of cultural self-sufficiency and a gradual assimilation of standards and ideas from the non-Jewish world.

In the past the ethnic distinctiveness of its members enabled Judaism to keep its ranks closed. Like any immigrant group most of the Jews were outside traditional English society and this had the inevitable consequence of turning them in on themselves. The last major immigration of Jews into this country was in the period 1933–9 when 60,000 Jews entered. They were very different in origin and outlook from the Jews of the previous major immigration (1883–1914). They came from Central Europe and had already gone through a period of assimilation in their countries of origin, and this had loosened their ties with Judaism. Socially many of them were from the upper strata of society and a considerable number were members of the professions. Religiously they were already far from orthodox and on arrival into this country they were quickly absorbed into English society.

Thus while the Jewish community dating from the period prior to the First World War had been gradually assimilated and thereby lost many of its distinctively Jewish characteristics, recent immigration has done nothing to bolster the separatist features of Anglo-Jewry. The Jews in England have become progressively less Jewish.

The drift away from strict orthodox Judaism has had profound effects on the Jewish settlement pattern. Many Jews no longer feel the need to cluster in the immediate vicinity of a synagogue and an increasing number are living many miles away. Dispersed residence has now become an accepted feature of Anglo-Jewish life.

Jews who move to new areas outside the reach of any Jewish social or religious organization are likely to quickly sever all connection with Judaism. This movement away from the large Jewish centres to suburban and rural areas has taken place in recent years. The chief obstacles to dispersion (the need for religious services, kosher food, Jewish education of children, etc.) have been partially eliminated by growing assimilation and the fall off in interest in religious Judaism.

JEWISH COMMUNITIES IN RESORT TOWNS [20]

The foundation and growth of Jewish communities in the resort and spa towns of England is a feature of the last forty years. In 1930 there were approximately 3,200 Jews [21] in these towns, whereas by 1967 the numbers had grown to over 21,000.

It is possible to group these towns into three distinct categories according to the date of the foundation of the Jewish community (Table 14). The category of old-established communities which were in existence before 1930 contains four out of the five largest resort town communities—Blackpool, Brighton and Hove, Southend, and Southport. A second group of communities was founded in the six years immediately prior to the Second World War. All these communities are firmly established and of medium size, with the one exception of Bournemouth whose number has grown to about 2,500. Between them these two groups of towns account for over 95% of the Jewish population in resort towns. A third category of nine towns possesses Jewish communities founded during or after the Second World War. With the exception of Wallasey they are all numerically small (under 130 members) and are still struggling for permanent establishment.

Most resort towns have a dual function; they provide places

of retirement for the more prosperous section of the community, and they also cater for holiday makers.

Function as Holiday Centres

Orthodox Jews who wish to go on holiday and also to observe their religious duties are very limited in their choice. Few non-Jewish-owned hotels would serve kosher food and observe the duties and obligations of ritual Judaism. An orthodox Jew would therefore wish to stay at a Jewish hotel, preferably in a town where there was already a settled Jewish community with its own synagogue.

The Jewish Travel Guide[22] publishes a list of Jewish hotels, classified according to strictness, for the various resort towns. The three-star hotels are the strictest, and they are under the supervision of a recognized religious authority, serving strictly kosher food, and meticulously observing the Sabbath, other Holy Days, and the various rules of Judaism. Two-star hotels make the same claims as three-star hotels but they do not come under any official supervision. One-star hotels, while not insisting on their guests observing the Jewish festivals, claim to serve exclusively kosher food.

For the purposes of this analysis only the starred hotels have been included. The *Guide* also lists other hotels and guest houses which are pleased to welcome Jews but which do not make any special dietary provision. However, it was decided to exclude these as they are not of a sufficiently Jewish character and are unlikely to have an overwhelming proportion of Jews among their guests.

Although the actual number of hotels is a useful criterion, the number of bedrooms is of greater value as this tells the quantity of accommodation available. Taking the figures for 1967 Bournemouth comes out as the premier Jewish resort, accounting for 27% of the total number of Jewish hotels and 40% of the bedrooms. Southend, Margate and Brighton each account for 10–14% of both the number of bedrooms and the number of hotels. All the resort towns with Jewish hotels, marked on Map 57 also have well-established settled Jewish communities—Clacton and Perranporth being the only exceptions.

A comparison between the figures for 1956 and 1967 for all the leading Jewish holiday resorts reveals a decline both in the number of hotels and in the number of bedrooms. Bognor, Colwyn Bay and Llandudno lost their only Jewish hotels between 1956 and 1967, although paradoxically Llandudno and Colwyn Bay gained permanent Jewish communities in the 1950s.

While the estimated Jewish population has increased by around 35% in the last twelve years, the number of bedrooms offered by Jewish hotels has fallen by 22%. This decline is yet another indicator of the changing attitude which many Jews are showing towards their religion. Increasing numbers of Jews feel it is no longer necessary to stay in hotels which serve strictly kosher food and observe the religious festivals. Assuming this trend continues it will greatly assist in the process of Jewish assimilation into English society and will gradually eliminate concentrations of Jewish holiday makers in particular resorts. Despite this recent decline, however, Jews still gather at certain popular resorts and stay at particular hotels catering for their religious needs.

Function as Retirement Centres

Any conclusions based on Jewish demographic data have to be treated with caution owing to the basic uncertainty surrounding much of the information. Nevertheless it does seem that the Jewish birthrate and the average size of the Jewish family are both lower than the average rates for the population as a whole. Neustatter comes to the conclusion that Anglo-Jewry is biologically on the decline. There is an even greater proportion of Jews in the over 65 age group than in the general population base. The Jews have an ageing population structure which gives them a top-heavy age pyramid and hence a large number of people of retiring age. The prime reason for this is that a large proportion of the Jewish immigrants came in between 1890 and the First World War and many of these were single men. They are all now in the over 65 age group.

The older members of the Jewish community naturally tend to be religiously conservative and more bound up with Jewish social life and would therefore wish to retire to a Jewish community. The increasing affluence of many Jews and their wholesale movement into the middle class has given them the necessary economic and social qualifications for retirement to the resort towns.

Why have Jewish communities grown up at some resorts and not at others? For a fully accurate answer to this question a detailed survey of each community would be necessary. However it is possible for us to draw certain conclusions from the information available.

The largest Jewish resort town in terms of its settled community is Brighton (it is also the third largest Jewish community outside London). Brighton's Jewish community had an early origin and by 1802 there were already many Jews here.[23] The first English Jewish school was opened in Brighton by Emmanuel Cohen and to this day Brighton continues to be the focal point for Britain's private Jewish schools. Why has the community at Brighton grown to such a size? In the first place Brighton became a fashionable retirement town for Londoners, and as over half the Jewish community are found in Greater London it is hardly surprising that many Jews found their way down to Brighton. Secondly, Brighton acts in part as a dormitory town for some of the more affluent who work in London, numbered among whom would be many Jews. Finally, part of the answer lies in the fact that in the late 19th century a large number of the wealthy element of London Jewry used to travel down to Brighton for the month of July. Thus right from the end of the 19th century Brighton played an integral part in London Jewry's pattern of life and she still continues this role today. It has been Brighton in preference to some of the other south coast resorts largely because Brighton is London's nearest point on the English Channel.

The second coastal focus for London Jewry has been Southend (Map 57). The Jewish community here has increased rapidly since the Second World War and caters for both the affluent commuters and the retired. Eight exclusively Jewish hotels form the basis of its Jewish holiday trade. Bournemouth is the other main coastal centre for London's Jewry. In spite of there being no settled Jewish community here until the early years of this century, Bournemouth is now the ninth largest Jewish provincial centre with a resident Jewish population of around 2,500. She heads the list both in the number and in the size of the Jewish hotels and is well patronized by London Jewry.

Margate has a sizeable Jewish holiday trade along with a settled community of about 300. Eastbourne's only two Jewish hotels closed in the early 1950s, but a small community has been in existence there since the war. The community founded at Bognor coincided with the closure of its only Jewish hotel. Small post-war settlements have been started at Worthing, Jersey, Torquay and Paignton and there has been a community at Ramsgate for many years although it has been declining since the war. Basically, however, when London Jewry goes on holiday and when some of its wealthier element retires, they make for Southend, Brighton or Bournemouth.

The situation in the north is somewhat complicated by the existence of two large nuclei of Jewish population, Manchester-Salford and Leeds, along with several subsidiary centres. Blackpool and Southport are the northern equivalents in Jewish society of Southend, Brighton and Bournemouth. Although the growth of Blackpool and Southport was already in full swing at the beginning of this century the big expansion of the Jewish communities in these two towns did not occur until after the Second World War. This may reflect the slower economic and social development of northern Jewry compared to the south, but more intensive investigation would be needed to establish this.

A feeling of corporate solidarity with their fellow Lancashire Jews may have made the Jews of Leeds look to Blackpool and Southport rather than to the east coast resorts of Scarborough, Whitby and Bridlington. There is a strong link between the Jews of Leeds and the inland spa of Harrogate. A Jewish community of around 300 has been in existence at Harrogate since the late 1930s and two Jewish hotels serve Leeds's Jewry. Apart from its other attractions as a resort, the existence of a Jewish settlement with Jewish hotels and restaurants has made

Harrogate a favourite centre for Jewish day trippers from Leeds. In addition to their links with Harrogate, the Jews of Leeds patronize the same two western resorts as do their Lancashire brethren.

The increasing prosperity of Liverpool Jewry is reflected in the establishment of a community at Wallasey on the Cheshire side of the Mersey, and also at Hoylake, a very exclusive suburb at the mouth of the Dee. Both communities are the product of the 1960s. Further evidence of the increasing affluence and top-heavy age structure of northern urban Jewry is seen in the establishment of communities at Rhyl, Colwyn Bay and Llandudno on the North Wales coast, all of which are resorts with a considerable population over 65 years of age.

Whitley Bay has been described by E. W. Gilbert[24] as the seaside playground of the north-east industrial region. Although the three Jewish hotels have closed early in the 1950s, there has been a Jewish settlement of around 150 in existence since before the Second World War. No doubt the more prosperous members of the large Jewish communities in Newcastle and Sunderland look to Whitley Bay as a good retirement centre.

One group of resort towns, the inland spas, deserve special mention as they are places to which the elderly retire in order to improve their health. Of the seven inland spas listed by Gilbert there are Jewish communities in three—Cheltenham, Harrogate and Tunbridge Wells. A small ephemeral community was started in a fourth, Bath, just prior to the Second World War, but it failed to survive through into the post-war era.

While it is undoubtedly true that the majority of the Jewish communities in resort towns consist of the more successful elderly and retired, it could well be that a small proportion of them come to work in the service industries. Resort towns have a significant percentage of their population in service industries and we have already seen that Jews tend to prefer self-employment where they are economically self-dependent. Although the service industries suffer from seasonal fluctuations in demand, attempts have been made to introduce light industry into resort towns and this again is a field in which the Jewish employer has found good openings. It would seem therefore that the resort town would be an ideal habitat for the ambitious young Jew. Unfortunately this will have to remain a theory, for we have as yet no information on the socio-economic composition of the Jewish resort communities.

CONCLUSION

The social geography of the Jews in England is quite distinctive. Traditionally they have always formed close-knit nucleated communities. Over half of the English Jews are in London and the majority of the rest are in Leeds, Manchester, certain major provincial centres, and a few other smaller towns. The most recent development has been the establishment of thriving communities in many of the resort towns.

However, all the signs point towards an accelerating disintegration of the distinctive Jewish settlement pattern. Slowly but inevitably the Jews are being absorbed into the prevailing national culture and in time there will be little left in England which is specifically Jewish in character. Eventually English Judaism is likely to become the concern of the historical geographer.

TABLES

Table 1

DEGREES OF MEMBERSHIP OF
THE CHURCH OF ENGLAND – 1962

100% | 41,299,000 total pop. born and resident in England

66% | 27,384,000 persons baptized in the C.of E.

24% | 9,842,000 Confirmed members

7% | 2,793,200 Electoral roll members

6% | 2,347,200 Easter communicants

5% | 1,892,700 Christmas communicants

Table 2

Attendances at all places of worship on Census Sunday 1851—England

A = Based on Mann's figures which exclude estimates for defective returns.
B = Based on Mann's figures which include estimates for defective returns.
C = Mann's original figures, with estimates added based on the percentage of churches not making returns.

Denomination	A Index of Attendance	B Total number of Attenders at all Services	B Index of Attendance	C Index of Attendance
All Denominations	56·3	9,910,928	59·1	58·8
Church of England	28·3	5,102,805	30·4	30·2
Roman Catholic	2·1	375,257	2·2	2·2
Free Church	25·8	4,432,866	26·4	26·4
Baptist	4·4	759,508	4·5	4·5
Independent	5·8	997,830	5·9	5·9
Presbyterian	0·5	80,510	0·5	0·5
Methodist	13·7	2,343,975	14·0	14·0
Others	1·4	251,043	1·5	1·5
Original Connexion	8·4	1,441,232	8·6	8·6
New Connexion	0·6	97,628	0·6	0·6
Primitive Methodists	2·9	497,111	2·9	3·0
Bible Christians	0·4	72,638	0·4	0·4
Methodist Association	0·5	92,541	0·6	0·6
Methodist Reformers	0·5	89,875	0·5	0·5
Calvinistic Methodists	0·3	52,949	0·3	0·3
Total population		16,764,470		

Table 3

Results of 1851 Census for England and Wales (including estimates for the defective returns—after Mann)

Denomination	Morning	Afternoon	Evening	Total
All denominations	4,647,482	3,184,135	3,064,449	10,896,066
Church of England	2,541,244	1,890,764	860,543	5,292,551
Roman Catholic	252,783	53,967	76,880	383,630
Others	1,853,455	1,239,404	2,127,026	5,219,885

Table 4

Nonconformist attendances expressed as a percentage of total attendances on Census Sunday

Town	Total Nonconformists	Congregationalists	Baptists	Methodists
Rochdale	75·3	8·2	13·2	37·8
Dudley	68·6	6·8	9·0	47·7
Bradford	68·0	13·1	11·5	37·6
Sunderland	67·7	9·5	7·8	37·2
South Shields	64·5	5·2	4·6	40·1
Tynemouth	61·1	9·2	3·7	35·5
Leeds	59·4	7·5	5·6	41·9
Wolverhampton	56·8	6·0	7·0	41·9
Ashton-under-Lyne	53·7	19·9	3·6	22·7

Table 5

Percentage of total Roman Catholic population

Province	*1851*	*1911*	*1961*
Westminster	17·6	15·2	26·6
Birmingham and Cardiff	17·8	15·5	20·0
Liverpool	57·4	58·4	37·8
Southwark	7·3	11·0	15·6

Table 6

Roman Catholics in certain cities and surrounding administrative counties
% Catholic = Catholics as a % of total population, April 1961,
estimated by the Newman Demographic Survey.
% Mass = Catholic Mass Attendance as a % of total
population, 1962.

City	% Catholic	% Mass	Admin. County	% Catholic	% Mass
Liverpool	41·5	13·8	Lancashire	20·4	7·4
Manchester	31·7	10·9	Cheshire	9·1	4·0
Leeds	15·2	5·9	West Riding	6·7	2·7
Sheffield	7·8	3·0			
Bradford	17·2	6·5			
Birmingham	19·6	6·5	Warwick	7·7	3·1
Coventry	21·3	6·9	Worcester	4·8	2·2
			Staffs	6·3	2·8
Nottingham	8·5	2·6	Notts	5·1	1·4
Bristol	9·4	3·6	Gloucestershire	5·4	2·0
			Somerset	4·1	1·8
			Wilts	7·3	3·1
London	23·0	6·9	Middlesex	13·4	5·2
			Hertfordshire	9·6	3·8
			Essex	7·4	3·2
			Kent	6·8	2·7
			Surrey	9·3	4·5

Table 7

Percentage of Roman Catholics in the total population, 1962

County Borough	Percentage	County Borough	Percentage
Bootle	19·2	Warrington	12·1
St. Helens	18·6	Manchester	10·9
Preston	18·2	Blackburn	10·8
Wigan	16·9	Birkenhead	10·2
Liverpool	13·8	Salford	9·1

Table 9

Census of religious attendance 1851

	Index of Attendance
Total England	58·8
Nonconformists	26·4
Methodists (all branches)	14·0
Original Connexion	8·6
New Connexion	0·6
Primitive Methodists	3·0
Bible Christians	0·4
Wesley Methodist Association	0·6
Wesley Methodist Reformers	0·5
Calvinistic Methodists	0·3

Table 10

Percentage of total Quaker membership for England, 1967

London and Middlesex	16·6	Gloucestershire	4·3
Yorkshire	12·9	Sussex	4·1
Lancashire	6·3	Hampshire	3·0
Warwickshire	5·8	Somerset	2·9
Hertfordshire	4·3	Essex	2·8

(Total membership for England was 19,800 in 1967)

Table 8

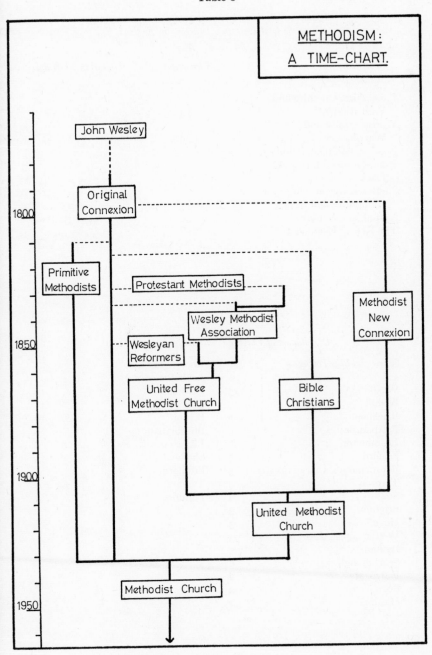

METHODISM:
A TIME-CHART.

John Wesley

Original
Connexion

1800

Primitive
Methodists

Protestant Methodists

Wesley Methodist
Association

Methodist
New
Connexion

1850

Wesleyan
Reformers

United Free
Methodist Church

Bible
Christians

1900

United Methodist
Church

Methodist Church

1950

Table 11

*Unitarian allegiance by county groups as a percentage
of the total Unitarian following in England*

	1851 Attendances	1952 Unitarian Marriages
Lancashire, Cheshire and West Riding	38·4	71·5
Worcestershire and Warwickshire	12·0	6·0
London, Middlesex, Surrey, Kent, Hertfordshire and Essex	7·3	4·8
Somerset, Devon, Dorset, Hampshire and Sussex	17·5	0·9
Norfolk and Suffolk	5·0	0·3
The Rest of England	19·8	16·5

Table 12

Distribution of Christian Scientist practitioners, 1967

Resort and Spa Towns		Main Urban Centres (excluding London)	
Worthing	13	Manchester	13
Bexhill	7	Leeds	11
Blackpool	6	Bristol	10
Eastbourne	6	Birmingham	9
Leamington	6	Liverpool	8
Seaford	5	Sheffield	5
Bournemouth	5	Bradford	4
Torquay	4	Tyneside	4
Southport	4	Potteries	2
Brighton	3		
Hove	3		
Weston-super-Mare	3		
Lytham	3		
Scarborough	2		
Harrogate	2		
Bognor	2		
Hastings	2		

Table 13

Size of the major provincial Jewish communities—1967

Community	Population
Manchester, Salford and District	28,000
Leeds	18,000
Liverpool	7,500
Brighton and Hove	7,500
Birmingham	6,300
Southend and Westcliff	4,000
Southport	3,000
Newcastle	3,000
Hull	2,500
Bournemouth	2,500
Blackpool	2,000
Sheffield	1,600
Nottingham	1,500
Sunderland	1,350
Luton and Dunstable	1,160
Leicester	1,100

(Population totals are taken from *The Jewish Yearbook 1967*)

Resort town communities are in italics.

Table 14
*A classification of Jewish resort communities
according to date of foundation*

1. *Communities in existence in 1930*
   Blackpool, Brighton and Hove, Ramsgate, Southend and Southport.
   Total population in 1967—16,565

2. *Communities founded immediately before the Second World War*
   Bournemouth, Eastbourne, Harrogate, Margate, St. Anne's and Whitley Bay.
   Total population in 1967—3,830

3. *Communities founded during and after the Second World War*
   (a) Founded before 1960—Cheltenham, Worthing, Torquay and Paignton.
   (b) Founded after 1960—Bognor Regis, Hoylake, Isle of Man, Jersey, Tunbridge Wells and Wallasey.
   Total population in 1967—780

ABBREVIATIONS

Abbreviations used in the references and the bibliography are
as follows:

A.A.A.G.	= Annals of the Association of American Geographers.
B.J.S.	= British Journal of Sociology.
C.H.S.T.	= Congregational Historical Society Transactions.
C.Q.R.	= Church Quarterly Review.
J.E.H.	= Journal of Ecclesiastical History.
J.F.H.S.	= Journal of the Friends Historical Society.
Trans. I.B.G.	= Transactions of the Institute of British Geographers.

REFERENCES

CHAPTER ONE   The Geography of Religion

1. Sopher, D. E., *Geography of Religions*, Englewood Cliffs, New Jersey, 1967, p. vii.
2. Isaac, E., 'Religious geography and the geography of religion', in *University of Colorado Studies, Series in Earth Sciences*, July 1965, p. 1.
3. Stamp, L. D. (editor), *A Glossary of Geographical Terms*, London, 1961.
   Stamp, L. D. (editor), *Longmans Dictionary of Geography*, London, 1966.
   Monkhouse, F. J., *A Dictionary of Geography*, London, 1965.
4. James, P. E. and Jones, C. F., *American Geography: Inventory and Prospect*, Syracuse, U.S.A., 1954.
5. Broek, J. O. M., 'Progress in human geography', in James, P. E. (editor), *New Viewpoints in Geography*, Washington, 1959.
6. Pahl, R. E., 'Trends in social geography', in Chorley, R. J. and Haggett, P., *Frontiers in Geographical Teaching*, London, 1965, p. 81.
7. Ibid., p. 96.
8. Watson, J. W., 'The Sociological Aspects of Geography', in Taylor, G. T. (editor), *Geography in the Twentieth Century*, London, 1957.
9. Ibid., p. 465.
10. Sopher, D. E., op. cit.
11. See Bibliography for a list of his works.
12. Boulard, F., *An Introduction to Religious Sociology*, London, 1960.
13. Godin, H. and Daniel, Y., *France, Pays de Mission?*, Paris, 1943.
14. Boulard, F., op. cit., pp. 13 and 14.
15. Vogt, E., 'The sociology of Protestantism in Norway', in *Social Compass*, 1966, p. 439.
16. Gustafsson, B., *Svensk Kyrkogeografi*, Lund, 1957.
17. Gustafsson, B., 'The state of the sociology of Protestantism in Scandinavia', in *Social Compass*, 1965, pp. 359–65.

18. Collard, E. A., *Carte de la Pratique Dominicale en Belgique, par Commune*, Mons Editions, Dimanche, 1952.

19. Fogarty, M. P., *Christian Democracy in Western Europe 1820–1953*, London, 1957.

20. Strietelmeier, J. H. and Meyer, A. H., *Geography in World Society*, New York, 1963, pp. 361–78.

21. Ibid., p. 366.

22. Sopher, D. E., op. cit.

23. Hotchkiss, W. A., *Areal Pattern of Religious Institutions in Cincinnati*, University of Chicago, Dept. of Geography, Research Paper No. 13, Chicago, 1950.

24. Ibid., p. 1.

25. Ibid., p. 1.

26. Douglass, H. P., *The Greater Cincinnati Church Study*, Cincinnati, 1947.

27. Hotchkiss, W. A., op. cit., p. 33.

28. Hartshorne, R., 'The nature of geography', in *A.A.A.G.*, 1939, p. 418. '. . . (1) the interrelation of different kinds of phenomena that are directly or indirectly tied to the earth,

    (2) the *differential* character of these phenomena and the complexes they form in different areas of the earth,

    (3) the areal expression of the phenomena or complexes.'

29. Hotchkiss, W. A., op. cit., p. 98.

30. Zelinsky, W., 'An approach to the religious geography of the United States: patterns of church membership in 1952', in *A.A.A.G.*, 1961, pp. 139–93.

31. O'Dea, T. F., 'Geographical position and Mormon behaviour', in *Rural Sociology*, 1954, pp. 358–64.

32. Zelinsky, W., op. cit., pp. 166–7.

33. Jones, E., *Social Geography of Belfast*, London, 1960.

34. Ibid., p. 177.

35. Evans, E. E., 'Belfast—the site and the city', reprinted in 1945 from *The Ulster Journal of Archaeology*, 3rd Series, Vol. 7.

36. Jones, E., op. cit., p. 204.

37. Bowen, E. G., *Wales: A Study in Geography and History*, Cardiff, 1941.

38. Bowen, E. G., *The Settlements of the Celtic Saints in Wales*, Cardiff, 1954. Bowen, E. G., *Saints, Seaways and Settlements in the Celtic Lands*, Cardiff, 1969.

39. Sylvester, D., 'The church and the geographer: an introduction to the ecclesiastical geography of Britain', in Steel, R. W., and Lawton, R., *Liverpool Essays in Geography*, London, 1967.

40. Sylvester, D., *The Rural Landscape of the Welsh Border*, London and Toronto, 1969, pp. 164–89.

41. Lewis, G. J., *A Study of Socio-Geographical Change in the Central Welsh Borderland since the mid-Nineteenth Century*, Ph.D. Thesis, Leicester, 1969.

42. Daniel, J. E., *The Distribution of Religious Denominations in Wales*, M.Sc. Thesis, University of Wales, 1928.

43. Huntington, E., *Principles of Human Geography*, London, 1951, p. 18.

44. Semple, E. C., *Influences of Geographic Environment*, London, 1911.
45. Ibid., p. 41.
46. Kuriyan, G., 'Geography and religion', in *Indian Geographical Journal*, Jan.–March 1961, pp. 46–51.
47. Strietelmeier, J. H. and Meyer, A. H., *Geography in World Society*, New York, 1963, pp. 361–78.
48. Fickeler, P., 'Fundamental questions in the geography of religions', in Wagner, P. L. and Mikesell, M. W., *Readings in Cultural Geography*, Chicago, 1962, pp. 94–117.
49. Deffontaines, P., *Géographie et Religions*, Paris, 1948.
50. Fickeler, P., op. cit.
51. Isaac, E., 'Religion, landscape and space', in *Landscape*, Winter 1959–1960, p. 14.
52. Isaac, E., 'The act and the covenant: the impact of religion on the landscape', in *Landscape*, Winter 1961–2, p. 12.
53. Sievers, A., 'Christentum und Landschaft in Südwest Ceylon (eine sozialgeographische Studie),' in *Erkunde*, Vol. 12, 1958, p. 107.
54. Mecking, L., 'Kult und Landschaft in Japan', in *Geographischer Anzeiger*, Vol. 30, 1929, pp. 137–46.
55. Credner, W., 'Kultbauten in der hinterindischen Landschaft', in *Erkunde*, Vol. 1, 1947, pp. 48–61.
56. Hahn, H., 'Konfession und Sozialstruktur—Vergleichende Analysen auf geographischer Grundlage', in *Erkunde*, Dec. 1958, p. 241.
57. Klaer, W., 'Vergleichende sozialgeographische Untersuchungen in einigen christlichen und mohammedanischen Gemeinden von Lebanon', in *Heidelberger Geographische Arbeiten*, 1966, pp. 331–9.
58. Warkentin, J., 'Mennonite agricultural settlements of Southern Manitoba', in *The Geographical Review*, 1959, pp. 342–68.
59. Ibid., p. 367.
60. Gentilcore, R. L., 'Missions and mission lands of Alta California' in *A.A.A.G.*, 1961, p. 46.
61. Zimpel, H. G., 'Vom Religionseinfluss in den Kulturlandschaften zwischen Taurus und Sinai', in *Mitteilungen der Geographischen Gesellschaft in München*, 1963.
62. Sopher, D. E., op. cit., pp. 24–46.

CHAPTER TWO   *The Sources*

1. Matthijssen, M. A. J. M., 'Catholic intellectual emancipation in the Western countries of mixed religion', in *Social Compass*, Vol. 6, No. 3, p. 104.
2. For example the Canadian Population Census. The results can be seen on Map 55 of *The Atlas of Canada*, 1957. The Census of Northern Ireland also asks for religious affiliation to be stated: *Northern Ireland—Census of Population 1961, General Report*, Belfast, 1965. Similarly in Eire: *Census of Population of Ireland, 1961, Vol. VII, Part 1, Religions*, Dublin, 1965. In view of the controversy raised by the collection of information on

religious affiliation, it is worth noting that although the enumerators were instructed not to insist on the completion of this section, only 0·2% of the population failed to declare their allegiance.

3. A third occasion used to be on reporting for National Service.
4. This is particularly applicable in urban and central city parishes.
5. The Enabling Act of 1919.
6. Theoretically a person living outside of the geographical parish can only be placed on the Electoral Roll if he looks on that church as his regular place of worship. In practice many incumbents are prepared to accept vague promises of attendance in the future and immediately place one or both partners on the Electoral Roll in order that they may be married in that church.
7. *Facts and Figures about the Church of England,* London, Church Information Office, 1965.
8. Spencer, A. E. C. W., 'The Newman demographic survey, 1953–64: reflection on the birth, life and death of a Catholic institute for socio-religious research', in *Social Compass,* Vol. 11, No. 3/4, 1964, pp. 31–7.
9. Spencer, A. E. C. W., *Statistical Definitions of Belonging to the Church,* 1962, p. 5.
10. In principle Catholics are supposed to attend Mass every Sunday although there are a number of acceptable excuses.
11. An estimate supplied by the Convener of the Publicity and Publications Committee.
12. There is a high status value attached to Congregationalism which attracts certain members from lower status denominations such as the Baptists and the Methodists.
13. See *Church Membership*—an official publication of the Congregational Church.
14. Perkins, E. B., *Discipline—with Special Reference to the Methodist Church,* London, 1966, Chapter 4.
15. *Minutes of the Methodist Conference*—an official publication.
16. A circuit is a geographical area containing a number of chapels. In scale it approximates to an Anglican rural deanery.
17. For the two main viewpoints see Wilson, B. R., *Religion in Secular Society,* London, 1966, and Martin, D. A., *A Sociology of English Religion,* London, 1967.
18. Martin, B., 'Comments on some Gallup poll statistics', in Martin, D. A. (editor), *A Sociological Yearbook of Religion in Britain,* London, 1968, pp. 146–97.
19. The cost of collecting such information would be extremely high and would have to be met by the churches themselves. As yet the churches in this country are sceptical about the value of any market research into religious attitudes and practices.
20. Gorer, G., *Exploring English Character,* London, 1955, Chapter 14.
21. The Registrar General, *Annual Report,* 1844–1914.
22. The Registrar General, *Annual Report.* 1919. The Registrar General, *Statistical Review,* 1924, 1929, 1934, 1952, 1957, 1962, 1967.

23. *The Reader's Digest Complete Atlas of the British Isles*, London, 1965, pp. 121–2.

24. Many Free Church ministers will remarry divorcees in church, but most divorcees are deterred because of the predominant view on marriage held by Christians.

25. Legal steps are now being taken to simplify this procedure.

26. It is curious how often people who have generously supported the work and running of a church in their lifetime, fail to make any continuing provision in their will.

27. Williams, W. M., *Gosforth: the Sociology of an English Village*, London, 1956.

28. See Martin, D. A., *A Sociology of English Religion*, London, 1967, pp. 15–16.

29. Usher, R. G., *The Reconstruction of the English Church*, 2 vols., London, 1910.

CHAPTER THREE   The 1851 Census of Church Attendance

1. Mann, H., 'On the statistical position of religious bodies in England and Wales', in *The Journal of the Statistical Society*, Vol. XVIII, 1855, p. 155.

2. *Census of Great Britain 1851: Religious Worship: England and Wales*, London, 1853. See also Mann, H., *Report upon Religious Worship in England and Wales, founded upon the 1851 Census*, London, 1854.

3. The two methods are not mutually exclusive and could easily be used to complement each other. At the time, however, it appears that this possibility was not considered.

4. Mann, H., *Report upon Religious Worship*, op. cit., p. viii.

5. Mudie-Smith, R., *The Religious Life of London*, London, 1904.

6. Mann, H., in *The Journal of the Statistical Society*, op. cit.

7. The attendances, expressed as a proportion of the sittings, were as follows:

	Church of England	*Dissenters*	
Morning	52·4	53·4	(per 100 sittings)
Afternoon	50·3	51·6	
Evening	49·5	54·6	

The slight differential in the evening proportions was due to the Dissenting tradition of evening attendance.

8. It was on this point that the Census came in for a great deal of criticism.

9. Mann, H., in *The Journal of the Statistical Society*, op. cit., p. 147.

10. *The Times*, 9th January 1854, p. 6.

11. Inglis, K. S., *English Churches and the Working Classes 1880–1900*, D.Phil. Thesis, Oxford, 1956, pp. 64–101, and pp. 652–70.

12. Pickering, W. S. F., 'The 1851 Religious Census—a useless experiment?', in *B.J.S.*, Dec. 1967, pp. 382–407.

13. See the detailed tables at the end of the Census report.

14. Mann, H., *Report on Religious Worship*, op. cit., p. clxx.
15. See Chapters 5 and 7.
16. For an explanation of the Index of Attendance, see p. 54.
17. In most of the summary tables compiled by Mann it was necessary to deduct the Welsh totals to arrive at the figures for England only.
18. Mann, H., in *The Journal of the Statistical Society*, op. cit.
19. Mann, H., ibid., p. 152—the 'total worshipping community' is the total number of people who are in the habit of worshipping, more or less regularly, with some particular communion.
20. i.e. the number of attenders as calculated by using Mann's formula.
21. Mann, ibid, p. 152.
22. Hume, A., *Remarks on the Census of Religious Worship for England and Wales, with suggestions for an Improved Census in 1861, and a Map Illustrating the Religious Condition of the Country*, London, 1860, p. 17.
23. He calculated the denominational percentages as follows:

Independents	7·35
Baptists	5·45
Wesleyans	12·84
Other Nonconformists (excluding R.C.s)	3·85
Total Nonconformists	29·50
Church of England	42·00
Roman Catholics	3·50
Total worshipping community	75·00
Balance non-worshipping	25·00

24. Inglis, K. S., *English Churches and the Working Classes*, op. cit.
25. Example of the calculation of an Index of Attendance: Denom: Anglican. County: Devon. Total pop.: 567,908

Morning Attendance	Afternoon Attendance	Evening Attendance	Total
103,301	93,972	30,171	227,444

Index of Attendance = 40·1

26. The Index of Attendance has a slight advantage over Pickering's method of taking the maximum-minimum figure in that it takes into account all the services held on Census Sunday, and not just the most popular.
27. Mann, H., *Report on Religious Worship*, op. cit., p. clviii.
28. Mann, H., ibid., p. clviii.
29. Engels, F., *The Condition of the Working Class in England in 1844*, London, 1892, p. 125.
30. Wickham, E. R., *Church and People in an Industrial City*, London, 1957.
31. Inglis, K. S., op. cit. The majority of his thesis, although not the detailed sections concerning the 1851 Census, has been published; Inglis K. S., *Churches and the Working Classes in Victorian England*, London, 1963.
32. Some conflicting evidence on this point appears in: Walker R. B., 'Religious changes in Cheshire 1750–1850', in *J.E.H.*, April 1966, pp. 77–94.

33. Southampton, York, Leicester, Northampton, Worcester, Dover, Cheltenham, Cambridge, Reading, Wakefield and Ipswich.
34. This is an official classification used by the Census.
35. Rochdale, Portsmouth, King's Lynn, Brighton, Devonport, Bristol, Chester, Nottingham, Great Yarmouth, Wigan, Wolverhampton, Kidderminster, Chatham, Plymouth, Dudley, Derby, Warrington, Newport, Oxford, Huddersfield and Maidstone.
36. Hull, Gravesend, Sunderland, Leeds, Ashton-under-Lyne, South Shields, Norwich, City of London, Liverpool, Tynemouth, Bury, Macclesfield, Walsall, Greenwich, Stockport, Bradford, Halifax, Stoke-on-Trent, Coventry, Newcastle upon Tyne, Marylebone, Westminster, Blackburn, Southwark, Finsbury, Bolton, Salford, Birmingham, Carlisle, Manchester, Gateshead, Sheffield, Oldham, Lambeth, Tower Hamlets and Preston.
37. Mann blamed poverty and bad housing for the poor attendances and thought that better housing would stimulate churchgoing.
38. Sopher, D. E., *Geography of Religions*, Englewood Cliffs, New Jersey, 1967, p. 109.
39. Hume, A., *Remarks on the Census of Religious Worship*, op. cit., p. 33.
40. Rogan, J., 'The Religious Census of 1851', in *Theology*, 1963, pp. 11–15.
41. Pickering, W. S. F., in *B.J.S.*, op. cit.
42. Pickering, W. S. F., ibid., p. 387.

CHAPTER FOUR   The Church of England

1. Paul, L., *The Deployment and Payment of the Clergy*, London, 1964, p. 26.
2. For example see Bulloch, J., *The Life of the Celtic Church*, Edinburgh, 1963; Deanesly, M., *The Pre-Conquest Church in England*, London, 1961; Godfrey, C. J., *The Church in Anglo-Saxon England*, Cambridge, 1962; Moorman, J. R. H., *Church Life in England in the Thirteenth Century*, Cambridge, 1946.
3. Gay, J. D., *The Geography of Religion in England*, D. Phil. Thesis, Oxford, 1969, pp. 156–87.
4. Carpenter, S. C., *The Church in England 597–1688*, London, 1954, Chapter 9.
5. The term 'secular' is used here in its strictly technical sense to indicate a member of the priesthood who does not belong to one of the monastic orders.
6. Hart, A. T., *The Country Clergy in Elizabethan and Stuart Times 1558–1660*, London, 1958.
7. The Act of Uniformity is published in full at the beginning of *The Book of Common Prayer 1662*. For details of the church's 'Establishment' see: Mayfield, G., *The Church of England: Its Members and its Business*, Oxford, 1963, pp. 3–15.
8. Usher, R. G., *The Reconstruction of the English Church*, London, 1910, 2 vols.

9. Deane, P. and Cole, W. A., *British Economic Growth 1688–1959*, Cambridge, 1962.

10. King, G., *Natural and Political Observations and Conclusions upon the State and Condition of England, 1696*, London, 1810.

11. Ashton, T. S., *An Economic History of England—the Eighteenth Century*, London, 1955, Chapter 1.

12. Addison, J. and Steele, R., *Sir Roger de Coverley and Other Papers from the 'Spectator'*, London, 1932.

13. Constable, G., *Monastic Tithes*, Cambridge, 1964.

14. Greaves, B., *An Analysis of the Spread of Methodism in Yorkshire during the 18th and early 19th Century, 1740–1831, with special reference to the Environment of this Movement*, M.A. Thesis, Leeds, 1960–1, p. 44.

15. Deane, P. and Cole, W. A., op. cit.

16. For a case study of Sheffield see Wickham, E. R., *Church and People in an Industrial City*, London, 1957.

17. Law, C. M., 'The growth of urban population in England and Wales, 1801–1911', in *Trans. I.B.G.*, No. 41, June 1967, pp. 125–43.

18. Inglis, K. S., *English Churches and the Working Classes 1880–1900*, D.Phil. Thesis, Oxford, 1956.

19. The only exception was in London where the Church of England was more successful than the Nonconformists. Even so percentage attendances were low.

20. Ward, W. R., 'The tithe question in England in the early 19th Century', in *J.E.H.*, April 1965, p. 67.

21. Hart, A. T. and Carpenter, E. F., *The Nineteenth Century Country Parson*, Shrewsbury, 1954, p. 2.

22. Walker, R. B., 'Religious changes in Cheshire 1750–1850', in *J.E.H.*, April 1966, pp. 77–94.

23. Hart, A. T., *The Country Priest in English History*, London, 1959, p. 19.

24. *Facts and Figures about the Church of England, Number 3*, Church Information Office, London, 1965.

25. The complete reversal of the position in the north-west between 1851 and 1962 calls for a detailed local investigation.

26. The most far-reaching of these being Paul, L., *The Deployment and Payment of the Clergy*, London, 1964.

CHAPTER FIVE   The Roman Catholics

1. Smith, H. M., *Pre-Reformation England*, London, 1938.

2. Usher, R. G., *The Reconstruction of the English Church*, London, 1910, 2 vols.

3. The recusancy returns for 1603 gave the total number of Roman Catholics in England as 8,570—the highest number being in Lancashire and Cheshire. However the recusancy returns indicated the degree to which the recusancy laws were applied and were not a true reflection of the strength of Catholicism. O. Chadwick, in *The Reformation*, London, 1964, is prepared to allow a further 100,000 or more who conformed

occasionally and so were not included in the recusancy returns. Chadwick's estimate is considerably smaller than Usher's.

4. Estimate given by Magee, B., *The English Recusants*, London, 1938. A much lower estimate was reached by Dr. Bentham in 1716 who calculated the total Catholic population to be about 80,000. See Watkin, E. I., *Roman Catholicism in England from the Reformation to 1950*, London, 1957, p. 111.

5. Magee, B., op. cit.

6. Berington, J., *The State and Behaviour of English Catholics from the Reformation to the Year 1780*, London, 1780.

7. Cragg, G. R., *The Church and the Age of Reason 1648–1789*, London, 1960, pp. 138–9.

8. Beck, G. A. (editor), *The English Catholics 1850–1950*, London, 1950, Chapter VII.

9. *Census of Great Britain 1841*, London 1843, Part I, p. 14.

10. *Census of England and Wales, 1861*, London, 1863, Vol. II. p. lxxii.

11. Beck, G. A., op. cit., pp. 265–6.

12. Detailed accounts can be studied in Hickey, J. V., *The Irish Rural Immigrant and British Urban Society*, Newman Demographic Survey, 1960, and Jackson, J. A., *The Irish in Britain*, London, 1963.

13. Although many of the immigrants are now bringing their families and dependants over with them and are settling permanently in England, the myth of temporary exile is still kept alive.

14. For an analysis of a downtown Catholic parish in Liverpool see Ward, C. K., *Priests and People*, Liverpool, 1961.

15. Halley, R., *Lancashire—Its Puritanism and Nonconformity*, Manchester, 1869, Vol. I, Chapter II.

16. Registrar General, *Annual Report*, 1851.

17. Registrar General, *Statistical Review*, Part II. Appendix B, Tables 1 and 2, 1962.

18. Lumley, W. G., 'The statistics of the Roman Catholics in England and Wales', in *The Journal of the Statistical Society*, Vol. XXVII, Sept. 1864, pp. 303–23. Spencer, A. E. C. W., *The Demography and Sociography of the Catholic Community of England and Wales*, 1965.

19. Spencer, A. E. C. W., ibid.

20. Figures were obtained from the Registrar General's *Statistical Reviews* for 1924, 1929, 1934, 1952, 1957 and 1962.

21. Berington, J., op. cit.

22. Spencer, A. E. C. W., op. cit.

23. Registrar General, *Statistical Review*, Part II, Appendix B, Table I, 1962.

24. Hulme, A., *Incidence of Catholicism in the Eastern District*, M.A. (External) Thesis, London, 1957–8.

CHAPTER SIX   *The Nonconformists*

1. Unfortunately there is no accurate nomenclature. The term 'Free Church' is essentially a 20th-century one referring primarily to the

9

Baptists, the Congregationalists, the Presbyterians and the Methodists. 'Dissent' is applied to the religious institutions which grew up as a result of the Great Ejection in 1662 and so would not include the Methodists. 'Nonconformity', although rather negative in meaning and having strong Victorian overtones, is the safest term as it can properly be used to cover the four main groups at any stage of their history.

2. Hughes, P., *The Reformation in England*, London, 1953, Vol. II, pp. 260–4. There appears to be a discrepancy of seven in the total.

3. Usher, R. G., *The Reconstruction of the English Church*, London, 1910, p. 255.

4. Corporate bodies such as town corporations could also buy the rights of presentation to particular livings.

5. Usher, R. G., op. cit., p. 271.

6. The two classic works on this are Tawney, R. H., *Religion and the Rise of Capitalism*, London, 1926, and Weber, M., *The Protestant Ethic and the Spirit of Capitalism*, translated by Parsons, T., London, 1930.

7. This was forced on Cromwell by the Scots in return for the help of their armies.

8. Bebb, E. D., *Nonconformity and Social and Economic Life*, London, 1935, Appendix II.

9. All three lists count only the number of separate congregations and do not give any indication as to size of membership.

10. This compulsory payment meant that not only did Nonconformists have to pay for the upkeep of their own chapels, but they also were contributing to the maintenance of the parish church.

11. In the Census report the term 'Nonconformist' was applied to all the Christian Groups not belonging to the Church of England or the Roman Catholic Church. Many of the small sects are not strictly within mainstream Nonconformity, but their numbers were so small as to be of little statistical account.

12. See Table 3.

13. Inglis, K. S., *English Churches and the Working Classes 1880–1900*, D.Phil. Thesis, Oxford, 1956, Chapter 2.

14. Briggs, A., *Victorian Cities*, London, 1963, p. 206.

15. The Methodists played a minor role in Birmingham life. By the time they were properly organized, Birmingham was already a closed shop with the older Dissenting groups in firm control.

16. Halley, R., *Lancashire—Its Puritanism and Nonconformity*, Manchester, 1869, 2 vols. Saxelby, C. H., *Bolton Survey*, Bolton, 1953.

17. The theology faculty of the university was established and run by the Nonconformists—a challenge to the Anglican monopoly of Oxbridge.

18. Pelling, H., *The Social Geography of British Elections, 1885–1910*, London, 1967.

19. Ward, W. R., 'The tithe question in England in the early nineteenth century', in *J.E.H.*, April 1965, pp. 67–81.

20. Driver, C., 'The Nonconformist Conscience', in *New Society*, 27th June 1963, pp. 6–8.

21. Brogan, D. W., *The English People*, London, 1943, p. 121.
22. Martin, D. A., *A Sociology of English Religion*, London, 1967, p. 41.
23. Driver, C., *A Future For the Free Churches?*, London, 1962, pp. 16 and 17.
24. Williams, W. M., *The Sociology of an English Village*, London, 1956.
25. Pons, V. G., *The Social Structure of a Hertfordshire Parish: A Study in Rural Community*, Ph.D. Thesis, London, 1955.
26. Shippey, F. A., *Protestantism in Suburban Life*, New York, 1964. Winter, G., *The Suburban Captivity of the Church*, New York, 1961.
27. Tillyard, F., 'Distribution of the Free Churches in England', in *The Sociological Review*, 1935, pp. 1–18.

CHAPTER SEVEN   The Baptists, the Presbyterians and the Congregationalists

1. Troeltsch, E., *The Social Teaching of the Christian Churches*, London, 1931, pp. 706–9.
2. The Brownists were the original group, named after a certain Robert Browne, from whom the Independents evolved.
3. The Calvinists held that particular individuals had been predestined for salvation from the very beginning. By contrast the Arminian viewpoint was that salvation was designed for all men in general without any pre-ordination of a special number.
4. Chadwick, O., *The Reformation*, London, 1964, p. 207.
5. The traditional method of Christian baptism is effusion, whereby water is poured on to the head of the person being baptized. The Baptist rite of immersion involves the person being completely immersed in water.
6. Bebb, E. D., *Nonconformity and Social and Economic Life*, London, 1935, Chapter 2.
7. Rippon, J., *The Baptist Register*, London, 1793, Vol. I.
8. 'Open' communion meant communion with those who had not been baptized by the rite of immersion.
9. This feature of congregational independence is still very much present within the Baptist Union.
10. 'The Religious Census of London', in *The British Weekly*, London, 1886.
11. Mudie-Smith, R., *The Religious Life of London*, London, 1904.
12. This contrasts with the normal three-fold order of bishop-priest-deacon. The name Presbyterian was derived from the New Testament Greek word for minister.
13. Hart, A. T., *The Man in the Pew 1558–1660*, London, 1966, Chapter 6.
14. Milton, J., *Sonnet: On The Forces of Conscience under the Long Parliament*.
15. Bebb, E. D., *Nonconformity and Social and Economic Life*, London, 1935, Chapter 2.
16. Vidler, A., *The Church in an Age of Revolution*, London, 1961, Chapter 5.
17. The change of preposition from *in* to *of* was highly significant and marked a radical change in outlook and approach.
18. 'The Report of the Statistical Committee', in *The Minutes of the Synod of the Presbyterian Church of England*, 1877.

19. The counties of Nottinghamshire, Norfolk, Kent and Hereford were omitted from the Report.
20. The British Council of Churches, *The Land, the People, and the Churches*, London, 1945.
21. Some of the early separatist leaders eventually gave up waiting for a more tolerant religious climate in England and made for the New World. Of particular note was the voyage of the Pilgrim Fathers. The role of religious persecution and missionary outreach in the exploration and development of countries forms a vast subject in its own right.
22. Bebb, E. D., op. cit.
23. Pelling, H., *Social Geography of British Elections 1885–1910*, London, 1967, p. 61.
24. Most of these congregations were extremely narrow and revivalist. Once the initial flush of enthusiasm had died down, they were keen to join part of a more permanent structure.
25. For a contemporary comment on the Census results respecting the Congregationalists see an article by Kennedy, J., in *The Congregational Yearbook 1855*, pp. 33–47.
26. The Baptists exerted the greatest influence to the south of the Thames and it was here that Spurgeon, the renowned Baptist preacher, set up his headquarters.
27. Taylor, J. H., 'London Congregational churches since 1850', in *C.H.S.T.*, May 1965.
28. A certain degree of error was inevitable in the density calculations, for the County Unions do not always coincide exactly with the geographical counties. The densities for Devon and Cornwall had to be taken together as separate figures were not available.
29. Geographical mobility often points to upward social mobility as well. Free Church members, when they achieve a higher social standing, frequently join the Church of England.
30. Many of these rural chapels were inherited from the Presbyterians during the 18th century.
31. Jenkins, D., *Congregationalism: a Restatement*, London, 1954, pp. 29–30.
32. Based on information supplied in the *Congregational Yearbook*, 1966.

CHAPTER EIGHT   The Methodists

1. Walsh, J. D., 'Origins of the Evangelical movement', in Bennett, G. V. and Walsh, J. D., *Essays in Modern Church History*, London, 1966, p. 160.
2. Wesley, J., *Journal*, 11th June 1739.
3. Greaves, B., *An Analysis of the Spread of Methodism in Yorkshire during the 18th century and early 19th century, with Special Reference to the Environment of this Movement*, M.A. Thesis, Leeds, 1960–1.
4. For a discussion of the use made by the Methodists of the turnpike road system see Sylvester, D., 'The Church and the Geographer', in Steel, R. W. and Lawton, D., *Liverpool Essays in Geography*, London, 1967.

5. Kent, J., *The Age of Disunity*, London, 1966.
6. Davies, R. E., *Methodism*, London, 1963, p. 136.
7. Shaw, T., *The Bible Christians 1815–1907*, London, 1965.
8. Martin, E. W., *The Shearers and the Shorn*, London, 1965.
9. Kent, J., op. cit., Chapter 1. Wearmouth, R. F., *The Social and Political Influence of Methodism in the 20th Century*, London, 1957, pp. 59–80.
10. Currie, R., *Methodism Divided*, London, 1968.
11. Pocock, W. W., *A Sketch of the History of Wesley Methodism in some of the Southern Counties of England*, London, 1885.
12. Dyson, J. B., *Methodism in the Isle of Wight*, Ventnor, Isle of Wight, 1865, p. 251.
13. Balchin, W. G. V., *Cornwall*, London, 1954, pp. 53–4.
14. Taylor, E. R., *Methodism and Politics 1791–1851*, Cambridge, 1935, p. 55.
15. Harris, T. R., 'Methodism and the Cornish miner', in *The Cornish Methodist Historical Association, Occasional Publication No. 1*, 1960.
16. Probert, J. C. C., 'The sociology of Cornish Methodism', in *The Cornish Methodist Historical Association, Occasional Publication No. 8*, 1964.
17. Hoskins, W. G., *Devon*, London, 1954, Chapter 12.
18. Baker, W. P., *The English Village*, London, 1953, Chapter 5.
19. Tillyard, F., 'The Distribution of the Free Churches in England', in *The Sociological Review*, 1935, pp. 1–18.
20. *Rural Methodism*. A Commission Report to the 1958 Methodist Conference.
21. Edwards, M. L., *Methodism and England*, London, 1943, Chapter 2. Edwards, M. L., *After Wesley*, London, 1935, Part V.
22. *Report of the Church Membership Committee*, The Methodist Church, 1964.
23. The Registrar General, *Statistical Review, Part II*, 1924, 1929, 1934, 1952, 1957, 1962.

CHAPTER NINE   The Smaller Christian Groups

1. In this and the following chapter an attempt has been made to classify the miscellaneous collection of other religious groups (see contents pages). The Welsh and Scottish churches are included with the other European ethnic churches as they exhibit a similar set of features and fulfil the same functions. It can be argued that the Unitarians are not specifically Christian at all, but it was decided to include them with the Christian groups. While some of the finer points of this classification can be disputed, its basic aim is to provide a reasoned and convenient framework within which to discuss the whole medley of religious bodies which lie outside the umbrella of the main English denominations.
2. Herberg, W., *Protestant Catholic Jew*, New York, 1960, especially pp. 6–45.
3. The transient nature of the Greek Cypriot community discourages parish priests from keeping proper statistics.
4. *Lutheran Directory of Great Britain*, 1966.

5. Pearce, E. G., *The Lutheran Church in Great Britain*, a pamphlet published by the Evangelical Lutheran Church of England.
6. The Lutheran Council of Great Britain, *Sociological Self Study, 1966.*
7. Patterson, S., 'Polish London', in *London, Aspects of Change*, Centre for Urban Studies, London, 1964.
8. *The Lutheran*, Easter 1966, p. 4.
9. It is estimated that about 75% of the German Synod membership is female.
10. *The Church of Scotland Yearbook*, 1968.
11. This is a model illustration of how an apparently extraneous factor can completely upset the denominational distribution pattern.
12. For the history and theology of the Moravians see their official publication: *An Introduction to the Moravian Church*, London, 1939.
13. Armytage, W. H. G., 'The Moravian Communities in Britain', in *C.Q.R.*, 1957, pp. 141–52.
14. In that they are both episcopal churches the Moravians are very akin to the Church of England.
15. *The Statistical Returns of the Moravian Church 1967.*
16. In particular the Moravian ideal of community led to the great emphasis placed by Wesley on the Class Meetings.
17. Coxill, H. W. and Grubb, K., *World Christian Handbook*, London, 1967, pp. 194–5.
18. The subject of sectarian religion is a great favourite among sociologists and a large amount has been written on it. For a representative collection see Wilson, B. R. (editor), *Patterns of Sectarianism*, London, 1967.
19. The latest addition to the sectarian churches is the West Indian Pentecostal Church which thrives wherever there are large concentrations of West Indians. See Calley, M. J. C., *God's People*, London, 1965, and Hill, C. S., *West Indian Migrants and the London Churches*, London, 1963.
20. Cole, A., 'The social origins of the early Friends', in *J.F.H.S.*, Vol. 48, No. 3, 1957, pp. 99–118.
21. Marshall, D., *English People in the Eighteenth Century*, London, 1956, p. 225 ff.
22. Marwick, W. H., 'Some Quaker firms of the nineteenth century', in *J.F.H.S.*, Vol. 48, No. 6, 1958, pp. 239–59.
23. *Friends' Book of Meetings*, 1967.
24. Barr, J., 'Amongst Friends', in *New Society*, 1.12.66, p. 821.
25. *The Yearbook of the Independent Methodist Churches*, 1966–7.
26. *The Wesleyan Reform Union Yearbook*, 1961–2.
27. Wilbur, E. M., *A History of Unitarianism in Transylvania, England and America*, Cambridge, Mass., 1952.
28. Its correct name was 'The Unitarian Society for Promoting Christian Knowledge and the Practice of Virtue by the Distribution of Books'.
29. Because of the endless procession of Unitarian mayors in Leicester, the chapel became known as 'the mare's nest'.

30. The Unitarians do not publish any membership or attendance figures.
31. The Unitarian and Free Christian Churches, *Yearbook of the General Assembly*.
32. Wilson, J., *The History and Organization of British Israelism: Aspects of the Religious and Political Correlates of Changing Social Status*, D.Phil. Thesis, Oxford, 1966, especially chapters 1, 2, and 5.
33. For the lists of meeting places see *The National Message of the British Israel World Federation*.

CHAPTER TEN   Quasi-Christian Groups and Eastern Religions

1. *The Watchtower*, 1st January 1969, pp. 21–5.
2. See *The Christian Science Journal*.
3. These are the dedicated 'nuclear' members.
4. Wilson, B. R., *Sects and Society*, London, 1961, p. 200.
5. *The Christian Science Journal*, January 1967, pp. 5–9, and pp. 48–53.
6. Moser, C. A. and Scott, W., *British Towns*, London, 1961. The towns included are Worthing, Hove, Bournemouth, Hastings, Eastbourne, Harrogate, Southport, Torquay, Cheltenham, Blackpool, Brighton, Southend, and Wallasey. The absence of practitioners in Wallasey, Southend and Cheltenham is probably due to their respective proximity to Liverpool, London, and Bristol.
7. Wilson, B. R., op. cit., pp. 121–215.
8. Davies, H., *Christian Deviations*, London, 1965, p. 97.
9. Nelson, G. K., *The Development and Organization of the Spiritualist Movement in Britain*, Ph.D. Thesis, London, 1967.
10. Nelson, H., ibid., p. 332.
11. Membership figures were privately supplied by the Church.
12. This is the official title, although they are normally referred to as the Mormons. The term 'saint' is used in the original sense of a follower of Christ, and is not meant to imply canonization.
13. Chadwick, O., *The Victorian Church*, Part I, London, 1966, p. 438.
14. Linforth, L., *Route from Liverpool to Great Salt Lake City*, Liverpool, 1855.
15. This estimate is provided by officials of the Mormon Church in this country.
16. Considering the rigorous obligations and requirements imposed upon their members this is a very high percentage.
17. As the enumerating method fails to distinguish between different nationalities there is no way of separating out the number of Americans from the overall total.
18. The Mormons divide England into five independent Missions. However there are also four 'stake' areas (the three named here and London) which operate as separate units, although they are geographically inside Mission areas.
19. Quoted from the famous missionary hymn 'Thy Kingdom come, O God' by L. Hensley.

20. Strictly speaking it is the Middle East and North Africa which is the cradle of Islam.
21. This forms the Islamic headquarters in Britain and incorporates the Central London Mosque.
22. Collins, S., *Coloured Minorities in Britain*, London, 1957, Chapter 10.
23. For a detailed study of the Islamic community in Bradford see Butterworth, E., *A Muslim Community in Britain*, London, 1967.
24. Coxill, H. W. and Grubb, K., *World Christian Handbook*, London, 1968, pp. 233–5.
25. Information supplied by the Buddhist Society of London.
26. Desai, R., *Indian Immigrants in Britain*, London, 1963.
27. An estimate given by the editor of the *Sikh Courier* in 1967.
28. The Maidenhead community is a breakaway movement outside of mainstream Sikhism.
29. Many of these Associations are cultural and political in their objectives. However, it is impossible to disentangle the social from the religious aspects.

CHAPTER ELEVEN   The Jews

1. Neustatter, H., 'Demographic and other statistical aspects of Anglo-Jewry', in Freedman, M. (editor), *A Minority in Britain*, London, 1955, p. 133.
2. Prais, S. J., 'Statistical research: needs and prospects', in Gould, J. and Esh, S. (editors), *Jewish Life in Modern Britain*, London, 1964, pp. 111–35.
3. *The Jewish Yearbook*, 1967.
4. Neustatter, H., op. cit.
5. Trachtenberg, H. L., 'Estimate of the Jewish population of London 1929', in *The Journal of the Royal Statistical Society*, Vol. XCVI, Part I, 1933. Kantorowitsch, M., 'Estimate of the Jewish population of London 1929–1933', in *The Journal of the Royal Statistical Society*, Vol. XCIX, Part II, 1936.
6. However, see the letter from Dr. Ernest Krausz in *The Times*, 9th February 1970.
7. Davies, W. D., *Paul and Rabbinic Judaism*, London, 1962.
8. Hyamson, A. M., *The Jews of England*, London, 1947. Hyamson estimates there were 16,000 Jews in this country at the time of the expulsion decree.
9. Roth, C., *A History of the Jews in England*, Oxford, 1964.
10. Summary details of all the major Jewish communities in England are available in *The Jewish Yearbook*, 1967.
11. Brotman, A. G., 'Jewish communal organization', in Gould, J. and Esh, S. (editors), *Jewish Life in Modern Britain*, London, 1964, pp. 1–17.
12. Adler, E. N., *History of the Jews in London*, London, 1930.
13. There were 47,000 Jews in London in 1883, and by 1905 this figure had risen to about 150,000. These estimates are confirmed by the increase

in the proportion of Jewish marriages over this period. The proportion rose from 12·1 per 1,000 total marriages in 1884 to 35·5 per 1,000 total marriages in 1904. See The Registrar General, *Statistical Review*, 1934, text volume.

14. Brixton and Tottenham were also settled by Jews.

15. Brotz, H. M., 'The outlines of Jewish society in London', in Freedman, M. (editor), *A Minority in Britain*, London, 1955, pp. 137–97.

16. Krausz, E., 'The economic and social structure of Anglo-Jewry', in Gould, J. and Esh, S. (editors), *Jewish Life in Modern Britain*, London, 1964, pp. 27–40.

17. Unfortunately there are no estimates for the years after 1957.

18. This accounts for the disappearance of the Jewish trade unions.

19. The Jewish community in Leeds has been well documented geographically in an unpublished work, Connell, J. H., *The Jewish Population of Leeds*, University of Leeds, 1967.

20. For a full classification and discussion of the larger resort towns see Moser, C. A. and Scott, W., *British Towns*, London, 1961.

21. All the population totals are taken from the appropriate editions of *The Jewish Yearbook*.

22. *The Jewish Chronicle Travel Guide*, 1951 and 1956. *The Jewish Travel Guide*, 1961 and 1967.

23. Gilbert, E. W., *Brighton, Old Ocean's Bauble*, London, 1954. See also the review article by Soref, H. in *The Jewish Chronicle*, 22.10.54.

24. Gilbert, E. W., op. cit., p. 26.

BIBLIOGRAPHY

All those works which were of particular value in the production of this book are listed on the following pages. To facilitate easy reference the works are grouped under their most relevant chapter headings. If a title has been cited in a reference, and it has no further general relevance, it has not been included in the bibliography. In the first section an attempt has been made to include a comprehensive list of the works on the geography of religion.

1. THE GEOGRAPHY OF RELIGION

(a) General works

Baker, C. A., 'Geography and the church register', in *Geography*, 1966, pp. 50–2.

Clarke, J. I., *Population Geography*, London, 1965, Chapter 6.

Fickeler, P., 'Fundamental questions in the geography of religions', in Wagner, P. L. and Mikesell, M. W., *Readings in Cultural Geography*, Chicago, 1962, pp. 94–117.

Fischer, E., 'Religions: their distribution and role in political geography', in Weigert, H. W., *Principles of Political Geography*, New York, 1957, pp. 405–39.

Fischer, E., 'Some comments on a geography of religions', in *A.A.A.G.*, 1956, pp. 246–7.

Fleure, H. J., 'The geographical distribution of the major religions', in *Bulletin Soc. Royale de Géographie d'Egypte*, 1951.

Humphrey, B., 'Geography and the churchyard', in *Geography*, 1965, pp. 145–7.

Jones, E., *Human Geography*, London, 1965, pp. 53–6.

Perpillou, A. V., *Human Geography*, London, 1966, pp. 38–42.

Sopher, D. E., *Geography of Religions*, New Jersey, U.S.A., 1967.

Strietelmeier, J. H., and Meyer, A. H., *Geography in World Society*, New York, 1963, pp. 361–78.

(b) Religion and the environment

Credner, W., 'Kultbauten in der Hinterindischen Landschaft', in *Erkunde*, 1947, pp. 48–61.

Deffontaines, P., *Géographie et Religions*, Paris, 1948.

Hahn, H., 'Konfession und Sozialstruktur—Vergleichende Analysen auf geographischer Grundlage', in *Erkunde*, 1958, pp. 241–53.

Huntington, E., *Civilization and Climate*, Yale, 1924.

Huntington, E., *Mainsprings of Civilization*, New York, 1945.

Huntington, E., *Principles of Human Geography*, London, 1951.

Isaac, E., 'The influence of religion on the spread of citrus', in *Science*, 23rd January 1959, pp. 179–86.

Isaac, E., 'Religion, landscape and space', in *Landscape*, Winter 1959–60, Vol. 9, No. 2, pp. 14–17.

Isaac, E., 'The act and the covenant: the impact of religion on the landscape,' in *Landscape*, Winter 1961–2, Vol. 11, No. 2, pp. 12–17.

Isaac, E., 'God's Acre—Property in Land—a Sacred Origin?', in *Landscape*, Winter 1964–5, Vol. 14, No. 2, pp. 28–32.

Isaac, E., 'Religious geography and the geography of religion', in *University of Colorado Studies, Series in Earth Sciences*, July 1965, pp. 1–14.

Klaer, W., 'Vergleichende sozialgeographische Untersuchungen in einigen christlichen und mohammedanischen Gemeinden von Lebanon', in *Heidelberger Geographische Arbeiten*, 1966, pp. 331–9.

Kuriyan, G., 'Geography and religion', in *Indian Geographical Journal*, Vol. 36, 1961, pp. 46–51.

Mecking, L., 'Kult und Landschaft in Japan', in *Geographischer Anzeiger*, 1929, pp. 137–46.

Semple, E. C., *Influences of Geographic Environment*, London, 1911.

Sievers, A., 'Christentum und Landschaft in Sudwest-Ceylon, eine sozialgeographische Studie', in *Erkunde*, 1958, pp. 107–20.

Zimpel, H. G., 'Vom Religionseinfluss in den Kulturlandschaften zwischen Taurus und Sinai', in *Mitteilungen der Geographischen Gesellschaft in München*, 1963, pp. 136 ff.

(c) France

Le Bras, G., 'Statistique et histoire religieuse', in *Revue d'Histoire de l'Eglise de France*, 1931, pp. 425–49.

Le Bras, G., 'Premiers traits d'une carte de la pratique religieuse dans les campagnes françaises', in *Revue de Folklore Français*, pp. 159–167.

Le Bras, G., 'Un Programme: la géographie religieuse', in *Annales d'Histoire Economique et Sociale*, 1945, pp. 87–111.

Le Bras, G., 'Proof by religious maps', in *Lumen Vitae*, 1951, pp. 23–40.

Le Bras, G., *Etudes de Sociologie Religieuse*, Paris, 1956, 2 vols.

Boulard, F., 'Carte religieuse de la france rurale', in *Cahiers du Clergé Rural*, 92, 1947, pp. 403–14.

Boulard, F., 'La pratique religieuse: une méthode de réprésentation graphique', in *Cahiers du Clergé Rural*, 115, 1950, pp. 69–76.

Boulard, F. and le Bras, G., *Carte Religieuse de la France Rurale*, Paris, 1952.

Boulard, F., *An Introduction to Religious Sociology*, London, 1960.

Delprat, R., Géographie et sociologie religieuse', in *Economie et Humanisme*, 30, 1951, pp. 176–9.

Diebold, E., *La Pratique Dominicale. Carte Religieuse du Diocèse de Nice*, Nice, 1955.

Godin, H. and Daniel, Y., *France, Pays de Mission?*, Paris, 1943.

Gros, L., *La Pratique Religieuse dans la Diocèse de Marseilles*, 1954.

Lebret, L. J., 'Etude statistique et géographique des actes religieux', in *Efficacité*, 1951, pp. 121–43.

Léonard, E. G., 'Travaux de sociologie religieuse sur le protestantisme français', in *Archives de Sociologie des Religions*, 1956', No. 2. pp. 39–44.

Lestringant, P., Géographie du protestantisme français', in *Protestantisme Français*, Paris, 1945.

Winninger, P., 'Eléments de géographie religieuse de l'agglomeration strasbourgeoise. Le Catholicisme', in *Bulletin de l'Association Géographique d'Alsace*, 1956, pp. 16–20.

(d) Scandinavia

Fur, G., 'Frikyrklighet och socialgeografiska regioner i Smaland', in *Svensk Geografisk Arsbok*, 1952.

Gustafsson, B., 'The state of the sociology of Protestantism in Scandinavia', in *Social Compass*, 1965, pp. 359–65.

Gustafsson, B., *Svensk Kyrkogeografi*, Lund, 1957.

Lundman, B., *Sveriges Religiösa Geografi*, Malmo, 1942.

Rokhan, S., 'Geography, religion and social class, cross-cutting cleavages in Norwegian politics', in Lipset, S. M., and Rokhan, S., *Party Systems and Voter Alignments*, New York, 1964.

Vogt, E. A., 'The sociology of Protestantism in Norway', in *Social Compass*, 1966, pp. 439–41.

(e) The rest of Europe

Bedeschi, L., *Geografia del Laicismo*, Rome, 1957.

Carrier, H. and Pin, E., *Sociology of Christianity, International Bibliography*, Rome, 1964, pp. 175–201.

Centre de Recherches Socio-Religieuses, *La Pratique Religieuse en Wallonie*, Brussels, 1956.

Collard, E., 'Commentaire de la Carte de la Pratique Dominicale en Belgique', in *Lumen Vitae*, 1952, pp. 644–52.

Collard, E. A., *Carte de la Pratique Dominicale en Belgique, par Commune*, Mons Editions, Dimanche, 1952.

Duocastella, R., 'Géographie de la pratique religieuse en Espagne', in *Social Compass*, 1965, pp. 253–303.

Fogarty, M. P., *Christian Democracy in Western Europe*, London, 1957.

Gramatica, L., *Testo e Atlante di Geografia Ecclesiastica*, Bergamo, 1927.

Imbrighi, G., *Lineamenti di Geografia Religiosa*, Rome, 1961.

Moberg, D. O., 'Sociology of religion in the Netherlands', in *Review of Religious Research*, 1960, pp. 1–7.

Oudshoorn, H., *Les jardiniers en Wateringen et au Lièr: contribution à la géographie religieuse de l'Ouest du Pays*, Assen, 1957.

'The geography of religion in Spain', in *Social Compass*, 1965, p. 253.

Zeegers, G. H. L., 'Sociological analyses of the religious and social position in the Netherlands', in *Lumen Vitae*, 1951, No. 1–2, pp. 41–54.

(f) North America

Atlas of Canada, 1957, Map 55.

Bogue, D. J., *The Population of the U.S.A.*, New York, 1959, pp. 688–709.

Clark, A. H., 'Old World origins and religious adherence in Nova Scotia', in *Geographical Review*, 1960, pp. 317–44.

Douglass, H. P., *The Greater Cincinnati Church Study*, Cincinnati, 1947.

Gaustad, E. S., *Historical Atlas of Religion in the U.S.A.*, New York, 1962.

Gentilcore, R. L., 'Missions and mission lands of Alta California', in *A.A.A.G.*, 1961, pp. 46–72.

Hotchkiss, W. A., *Areal Pattern of Religious Institutions in Cincinnati*, University of Chicago, Dept. of Geography, Research Paper No. 13, Chicago, 1950.

Houtart, F., 'The religious practice of Catholics in the U.S.A.', in *Lumen Vitae*, 1954, No. 3, pp. 459–76.

Johnson, P. T., *An Analysis of the Spread of the Church of Jesus Christ of Latter Day Saints from Salt Lake City, Utah, utilizing a diffusion model*, Ph.D. Thesis, Iowa, 1966.

Meinig, D. W., 'The Mormon culture region: strategies and patterns in the geography of the American West, 1847–1964', in *A.A.A.G.*, 1965, pp. 191–220.

O'Dea, T. F., 'Geographical position and Mormon behaviour', in *Rural Sociology*, 1954, pp. 358–64.

Roucek, J. S., 'Census data on religion in the U.S.', in *Sociologia Religiosa*, 1964, pp. 50–60.

Warkentin, J., 'Mennonite agricultural settlements of Southern Manitoba', in *Geographical Review*, 1959, pp. 342–68.

Zelinsky, W., 'The religious composition of the American population', in *Geographical Review*, 1960, pp. 272–3.

Zelinsky, W., 'An approach to the religious geography of the U.S.: patterns of church membership in 1952', in *A.A.A.G.*, 1961, pp. 139–193.

(g) Great Britain

Bowen, E. G., 'Early Christianity in the British Isles', in *Geography*, 1932, pp. 267–76.

Bowen, E. G., *Wales: A Study in Geography and History*, Cardiff, 1941.

Bowen, E. G., *The Settlements of the Celtic Saints in Wales*, Cardiff, 1954.

Bowen, E. G., 'The Baptists in South West Wales in 1715', in *The Discussions of the Historical Society of the Welsh Baptists*, 1957, pp. 5–14.

Bowen, E. G., *Saints, Seaways and Settlements in the Celtic Lands*, Cardiff, 1969.

Daniel, J. E., *The Distribution of Religious Denominations in Wales*, M.Sc. Thesis, University College of Wales, 1928.

Evans, E. E., 'Belfast—The site and the city', reprinted in 1945 from *The Ulster Journal of Archaeology*, 3rd Series, Vol. 7.

Gay, J. D., 'Some aspects of the social geography of religion in England: the Roman Catholics and the Mormons', in Martin, D. A. (editor), *A Sociological Yearbook of Religion in Britain*, London, 1968, pp. 47–76.

Jones, E., *Social Geography of Belfast*, London, 1960.

Lewis, G. J., *A Study of Socio-geographical Change in the Central Welsh Borderland since the mid-nineteenth Century*, Ph.D. Thesis, Leicester, 1969.

Reader's Digest Complete Atlas of the British Isles, London, 1965, pp. 120–21.

Sylvester, D., 'The church and the geographer: an introduction to the ecclesiastical geography of Britain', in Steel, R. W. and Lawton, R., *Liverpool Essays in Geography*, London, 1967.

Sylvester, D., *The Rural Landscape of the Welsh Border*, London and Toronto, 1969, pp. 164–89.

(h) Other works

Bowman, I., 'The Mohammedan world', in *Geographical Review*, 1924, pp. 62–74.

Brush, J. E., 'The distribution of religious communities in India', in *A.A.A.G.*, June 1949, pp. 81–98.

D'Souza, S., 'Some demographic characteristics of Christianity in India', in *Social Compass*, 1966, pp. 415–29.

Friedrich, E., 'Religionsgeographie Chile', in *Petermanns Mitteilungen*, 1917, pp. 183–6.

Johnson, H. B., 'The location of Christian missions in Africa', in *Geographical Review*, 1967, pp. 168–202.

Lautensach, H., 'Religion und Landschaft in Korea', in *Nippon. Zeitschrift fur Japanologie*, 1942, pp. 204–19.

Scott, G. P., 'The population structure of Australian cities', in *Geographical Journal*, 1965, pp. 470–5.

2.   SOURCE MATERIAL

(a) Religion in England

Argyle, M., *Religious Behaviour*, London, 1958.

Blackham, H. J., *Religion in Modern Society*, London, 1966.

British Council of Churches, *The Land, The People and the Churches*, London, 1945.

British Weekly, The Religious Census of London, London, 1886.

Brothers, J. B., 'Recent developments in the sociology of religion in England and Wales', in *Social Compass*, 1964, pp. 13–19.

'How many in the pew?' *The Economist*, 30.8.58.

Gorer, G., *Exploring English Character*, London, 1955.

Hoggart, R., *The Uses of Literacy*, London, 1957.

Johns, E. A., *The Social Structure of Modern Britain*, London, 1965.

MacLeod, R. D., 'Church statistics for England', in *The Hibbert Journal*, 1948, pp. 351–7.

Martin, D. A., 'Towards eliminating the concept of secularization', in Gould, J. (editor), *Penguin Survey of the Social Sciences*, London, 1965, pp. 169–82.

Martin, D. A., *A Sociology of English Religion*, London, 1967.

Martin, D. A., *A Sociological Yearbook of Religion in Britain*, London, 1968.

Martin, D. A., *A Sociological Yearbook of Religion in Britain, No. 2*, London, 1969.

Mass Observation, *Puzzled People*, London, 1947.

Mass Observation, *Meet Yourself on Sunday*, London, 1959.

Masterman, C. F. G., *The Condition of England*, London, 1909.

Mayor, S. H., 'The religion of the British people', in *The Hibbert Journal*, Oct. 1960, pp. 38–43.

Mudie-Smith, R., *The Religious Life of London*, London, 1904.

Oldham, A. L., *The Census and the Church*, London, 1882.

Rowntree, B. S., and Lavers, G. R., *English Life and Leisure, A Social Study*, London, 1951.

Sampson, A., *Anatomy of Britain*, London, 1962, Chapter 11.

Sandhurst, B. G., *How Heathen is Britain*, London, 1948.

Simey, T. S., 'The Church of England and English society', in *Social Compass*, No. 3–4, 1964, pp. 5–12.

Simey, T. S., and Simey, M. B., *Charles Booth: Social Scientist*, Oxford, 1960.

Snape, H. C., 'The Church in Britain and its social environment', in *Modern Churchman*, 1958–9, pp. 9–16.

Social Surveys (Gallup Polls) Ltd., *Television and Religion*, London, 1964.

Spencer, A. E. C. W., *Statistical Definitions of Belonging to the Church*, Newman Demographic Survey Report, 1962.

Spinks, G. S., *Religion in Britain since 1900*, London, 1957.

Ward, C. K., 'Sociological research in the sphere of religion in Great Britain', in *Sociologia Religiosa* No. 3–4, 1959, pp. 79–94.

Wilson, B. R., *Religion in Secular Society*, London, 1966.

Walters, G. (editor), *Religion in a Technological Society*, Bath, 1968.

(b) Local surveys

Baker, W. P., *The English Village*, Oxford, 1953, pp. 101–30.

Balchin, W. G. V., *Cornwall*, London, 1954.

Birch, A. H., *Small Town Politics*, Oxford, 1959, Chapter 12.

Bonham-Carter, V., *The English Village*, London, 1952.

Booth, C., *Life and Labour of the People in London, 3rd Series, Religious Influences*, London, 1902.

Bracey, H. E., *English Rural Life*, London, 1959, Chapter 12.

Bracey, H. E., *Social Provision in Rural Wiltshire*, London, 1952.

Caradog-Jones, D. (editor), *A Social Survey of Merseyside*, London, 1934, Vol. 3, pp. 321–42.

Cauter, T. and Downham, J. S., *The Communication of Ideas*, London, 1954.

Durant, R., *Watling—A Social Survey*, London, 1939, pp. 52–8.

Frankenberg, R., *Village on the Border*, London, 1957, Chapter 2.

Frankenberg, R., *Communities in Britain*, London, 1966.

Harrison, T., *Britain Revisited*, London, 1961.

Hawksley, R. E., *A Sociological Study of a Suburban Church*, M. A. Thesis, Liverpool, 1962–3.

Hoskins, W. G., *Devon*, London, 1954, Chapter 12.

Jones, M., *Potbank*, London, 1961.

Kaim-Caudle, P., *Religion in Billingham*, Durham, 1962.

Littlejohn, J., *Westrigg—The Sociology of a Cheviot Parish*, London, 1963.

Mess, H., *Industrial Tyneside: a Social Survey*, London, 1928, Chapter 9.

Millward, R., *Lancashire*, London, 1955.

Langdale, E., 'Survey of Eastcote Parish', in *New Life*, May-June 1955, pp. 109–14.

Pickering, W. S. F., *The Place of Religion in the Social Structure of Two English Industrial Towns*, Ph.D. Thesis, London, 1957–8.

Pickering, W. S. F., 'Religious movements of church members in two working class towns in England', in *Archives de Sociologie des Religions*, 1961, pp. 129–40.

Pons, V. G., *The Social Structure of a Hertfordshire Parish: Study in Rural Community*, Ph.D. Thesis, London, 1955.

Saxelby, C. H., *Bolton Survey*, Bolton, 1953.

Stacey, M., *Tradition and Change: A Study of Banbury*, Oxford, 1960, Chapter 4.

Wickham, E. R., *Church and People in an Industrial City*, London, 1957.

Williams, W. M., *The Sociology of an English Village*, London, 1956.

3. THE 1851 CENSUS OF CHURCH ATTENDANCE

Census of Great Britain 1851: Religious Worship: England and Wales, London, 1853.

Hume, A., *A Clergyman's Account of a Portion of the Town of Liverpool*, London, 1850.

Hume, A., *Remarks on the Census of Religious Worship for England and Wales, with Suggestions for an Improved Census in 1861, and a Map Illustrating the Religious Condition of the Country*, London, 1860.

Inglis, K. S., *English Churches and the Working Classes 1880–1900*, D.Phil. Thesis, Oxford, 1956.

Inglis, K. S., 'Patterns of religious worship in 1851', in *J.E.H.*, 1960, pp. 74–86.

Inglis, K. S., *Churches and the Working Classes in Victorian England*, London, 1963.

Kennedy, J., 'On the Census returns respecting Congregational worship,' in *The Congregational Yearbook*, 1855, pp. 33–47.

Mann, H., *Report upon Religious Worship in England and Wales, Founded upon the 1851 Census*, London, 1854.

Mann, H., 'On the statistical position of religious bodies in England and Wales,' in *The Journal of the Statistical Society*, 1855, pp. 141–60.

Pickering, W. S. F., 'The 1851 Religious Census—a useless experiment?', in *B.J.S.*, Dec. 1967, pp. 382–407.

Rogan, J., 'The Religious Census of 1851', in *Theology*, 1963, pp. 11–15.

Walker, R. B., 'Religious changes in Cheshire 1750–1850', in *J.E.H.*, April 1966, pp. 77–94.

Goodridge, R. M., 'The religious condition of the West Country in 1851', in *Social Compass*, 1967, pp. 285–96.

4. HISTORY

The following historical works have a general relevance. Others of a more specific nature are listed under the denominational headings.

Ashton, T. S., *An Economic History of England: the 18th Century*, London, 1955.

Carpenter, C. S., *18th Century Church and People*, London, 1959.

Chadwick, O., *The Victorian Church (Part 1)*, London, 1966.

Chadwick, O., *The Reformation*, London, 1964.

Cragg, G. R., *The Church and the Age of Reason, 1648–1789*, London, 1966.

Deane, P. and Cole, W. A., *British Economic Growth 1688–1959. Trends and Structures*, Cambridge, 1962.

Deane Jones, I., *The English Revolution*, London, 1931.

Elliott-Binns, L. E., *Religion in the Victorian Era*, London, 1936.

Ensor, R. C. K., *England 1870–1914*, Oxford, 1936.

Ernle, Lord, *English Farming, Past and Present*, London, 1961, 6th Edition.

Fussell, G. E., 'English countryside and population in the 18th century', in *Economic Geography*, 1936, pp. 294–310 and 411–30.

Hill, J. E. C., *Economic Problems of the Church from Archbishop Whitgift to the Time of the Long Parliament*, Oxford, 1956.

Hoskins, W. G., *Local History in England*, London, 1959.

Hoskins, W. G., *The Making of the English Landscape*, London, 1955.

Laslett, P., *The World We Have Lost*, London, 1965.

Law, C. M., 'The growth of urban population in England and Wales 1801–1911', in *Trans. I.B.G.*, No. 41, June 1967, pp. 125–43.

Lynd, H. M., *England in the Eighteen-Eighties*, Oxford, 1945, pp. 299–348.

Moorman, J. R. H., *A History of the Church in England*, London, 1953.

Slack, K., *The British Churches Today*, London, 1961.

Smith, H. M., *Pre-Reformation England*, London, 1938.

Sykes, N., *The Crisis of the Reformation*, London, 1938.

Usher, R. G., *The Reconstruction of the English Church*, London, 1910, 2 vols.

Vidler, A., *The Church in an Age of Revolution*, London, 1961.

Ward, W. R., 'The tithe question in England in the early 19th century', in *J.E.H.*, April 1965, pp. 67–81.

Wrigley, E. A. (editor), *An Introduction to English Historical Demography*, London, 1966.

5. THE CHURCH OF ENGLAND

Andrews, J. H. B., 'The country parson 1969', in *Theology*, March 1969, pp. 103–8.

Archbishops of Canterbury and York, Commission on Evangelism, *Towards the Conversion of England*, London, 1945.

Carpenter, S. C., *Church and People 1789–1889*, London, 1933.

Clark, D. B., *Survey of Anglicans and Methodists in Four Towns*, London, 1965.

Commission on the Deployment and Payment of the Clergy, *Partners in Ministry*, Church Information Office, London, 1967.

Commission on the Organization of the Church, *Diocesan Boundaries (London and the Southeast)*, Church Information Office, London, 1967.

Facts and Figures about the Church of England, No. 3, Church Information Office, London, 1965.

Ferris, P., *The Church of England*, London, 1964.

Hart, A. T. and Carpenter, E., *The 19th Century Country Parson*, Shrewsbury, 1954.

Hart, A. T., *The 18th Century Country Parson*, Shrewsbury, 1955.

Hart, A. T., *The Country Clergy in Elizabethan and Stuart Times, 1558–1660*, London, 1958.

Hart, A. T., *The Country Priest in English History*, London, 1959.

Hart, A. T., *The Man in the Pew, 1558–1660*, London, 1966.

Jackson, M. J., 'Church and city', in *C.Q.R.*, 1961, pp. 476–88.

Lloyd, R., *The Church of England 1900–1965*, London, 1965.

McClatchey, D., *Oxfordshire Clergy, 1777–1869*, Oxford, 1960.

Mayfield, G., *The Church of England: Its Members and Its Business*, Oxford, 1963.

Neill, S., *Anglicanism*, London, 1965.

Paul, L., *The Deployment and Payment of the Clergy*, London, 1964.

Thompson, R. H. T., *The Church's Understanding of Itself*, London, 1957.

Wilson, B., 'The Paul Report examined', in *Theology*, February 1965, pp. 89–103.

6. *THE ROMAN CATHOLICS*

Beck, G. A. (editor), *The English Catholics 1850–1950*, London, 1950.

Berington, J., *The State and Behaviour of English Catholics from the Reformation to the Year 1780*, London, 1780.

Bullough, S., *Roman Catholicism*, London, 1963.

Halley, R., *Lancashire—Its Puritanism and Nonconformity*, Manchester, 1869, 2 vols.

Hickey, J. V., *Urban Catholics*, London, 1967.

Hickey, J. V., *The Irish Rural Immigrant and British Urban Society*, Newman Demographic Survey Publication, 1960.

Hughes, P., *Rome and the Counter Reformation in England*, London, 1942.

Hughes, P., *The Reformation in England*, London, 1953.

Hulme, A., *Incidence of Catholicism in the Eastern District*, M.A. (External) Thesis, London, 1957–8.

Jackson, J. A., *The Irish in Britain*, London, 1963.

Leys, M. D. R., *Catholics in England*, London, 1961.

Lumley, W. G., 'The statistics of the Roman Catholics in England and Wales', in *The Journal of the Statistical Society*, Vol. XXVII, Sept. 1864, pp. 303–23.

Magee, B., *The English Recusants*, London, 1938.

O'Dwyer, M., *Catholic Recusants in Essex 1580–1600*, M.A. Thesis, London, 1959–60.

Scott, G., *The Roman Catholics*, London, 1967.

Spencer, A. E. C. W., *The Demography and Sociography of the Catholic Community of England and Wales*, 1965.

Spencer, A. E. C. W., *Sociology and the Structure of the Catholic Church in England*, 1965.

Spencer, A. E. C. W., 'The Newman Demographic Survey, 1953–1964: Reflection on the birth, life and death of a Catholic Institute for socio-religious research', in *Social Compass*, Vol. II, No. 3/4, 1964, pp. 31–7.

Walker, R. B., 'Religious changes in Liverpool in the 19th century', in *J.E.H.*, Oct. 1968, pp. 195–211.

Ward, C. K., *Priests and People*, Liverpool, 1961.

Watkins, E. I., *Roman Catholicism in England from the Reformation to 1950*, Oxford, 1957.

7. THE NONCONFORMISTS

Bebb, E. D., *Nonconformity and Social and Economic Life*, London, 1935.

Briggs, A., *Victorian Cities*, London, 1963.

British Weekly, 1955, 10th March and 17th March.

Cowherd, R. G., *The Politics of English Dissent*, London, 1959.

Driver, C., *A Future for the Free Churches?*, London, 1962.

Hill, J. E. C., *Society and Puritanism in Pre-Revolutionary England*, London, 1964.

Nuttall, G. F., 'Dissenting churches in Kent before 1700', in *J.E.H.*, 1963, pp. 175–89.

Payne, E., *The Free Church Tradition in the Life of England*, London, 1965.

Pelling, H., *Social Geography of British Elections 1885–1910*, London, 1967.

Routley, E., *English Religious Dissent*, Cambridge, 1960.

Tawney, R. H., *Religion and the Rise of Capitalism*, London, 1926.

Thompson, E. P., *The Making of the English Working Class*, London, 1963.

Tillyard, F., 'Distribution of the Free Churches in England', in *Sociological Review*, 1935, pp. 1–18.

Walsh, J. D. and Bennett, G. V. (editors), *Essays in Modern Church History*, London, 1966.

Weber, M., *The Protestant Ethic and the Spirit of Capitalism*, translated by Parsons, T., London, 1930.

Wilkinson, J. T., *1662 and After—Three Centuries of English Nonconformity*, London, 1962.

8.   THE BAPTISTS, THE PRESBYTERIANS AND THE CONGREGATIONALISTS

(a) The Baptists
Catherall, G. A., 'Baptists of North Northumberland', in *The Baptist Quarterly*, Oct. 1965, pp. 169–73.
Rippon, J., *The Baptist Register Vol. 1*, London, 1793.
Underwood, A. C., *A History of the English Baptists*, London, 1956.
The Baptist Handbook—various years.

(b) The Presbyterians
Bolam, C. G. et al., *The English Presbyterians*, London, 1968.
Presbyterian Church of England, *Official Handbook*—various years.
Presbyterian Church of England, *The Minutes of the Synod*.
Ross, H. S., 'Some aspects of the development of Presbyterian polity in England', in *The Journal of the Presbyterian Historical Society of England*, May 1964, pp. 3–17.

(c) The Congregationalists
The Congregational Yearbook—various years.
Jenkins, D., *Congregationalism: A Restatement*, London, 1954.
Jones, R. T., *Congregationalism in England*, London, 1962.
Map of the Congregational Churches in London and its Suburbs, available at Mansfield College, Oxford.
Peel, A., *A Brief History of English Congregationalism*, London, 1931.
Routley, E., *The Story of Congregationalism*, London, 1961.
Sellers, I., 'Congregationalists and Presbyterians in 19th Century Liverpool', in *C.H.S.T.*, Oct. 1965, pp. 74–85.
Taylor, J. H., 'London Congregational Churches since 1850', in *C.H.S.T.*, May 1965, p. 22 ff.

9.   THE METHODISTS

Chamberlayne, J. H., 'From sect to church in British Methodism', in *B.J.S.*, Vol. 15, No. 2, 1964, pp. 139–49.
Commission Report to the 1958 Conference, *Rural Methodism*, London, 1958.
Currie, R., *Methodism Divided*, London, 1968.
Davies, R. E., *Methodism*, London, 1963.
Dyson, J. B., *Methodism in the Isle of Wight*, Ventnor, I.O.W., 1865.
Edwards, M. L., *After Wesley*, London 1935.
Edwards, M. L., *Methodism and England*, London, 1943.
Edwards, M. S., 'The divisions of Cornish Methodism', in *The Cornish Methodist Historical Association, Occasional Publication No. 7*, 1964.
Greaves, B., *An Analysis of the Spread of Methodism in Yorkshire during the 18th Century and early 19th Century, 1740–1831, with special reference to the Environment of this Movement*, M.A. Thesis, Leeds, 1960–1.
Harris, T. R., 'Methodism and the Cornish miner', in *The Cornish Methodist Historical Association; Occasional Publication No. 1*, 1960.

Hobsbawm, E., 'Methodism and the threat of revolution', in *History Today*, Feb. 1957.

Kent, J., *The Age of Disunity*, London, 1966.

Perkins, E. B., *Discipline—With Special Reference to the Methodist Church*, London, 1966.

Pickering, W. S. F. (editor), *Anglican-Methodist Relations: Some Institutional Factors*, London, 1961.

Pocock, W. W., *A Sketch of the History of Wesley Methodism in some of the Southern Counties of England*, London, 1885.

Price, H., 'The Wesleyan movement and the Church of England', in *Concept*, Nov. 1965, pp. 17–26.

Probert, J. C. C., 'The sociology of Cornish Methodism', in *The Cornish Methodist Historical Association, Occasional Publication No. 8*, 1964.

Probert, J. C. C., *Primitive Methodism in Cornwall*, privately circulated, 1966.

Rowe, W. J., *Cornwall in the Age of the Industrial Revolution*, Liverpool, 1953.

Rupp, E. G. and Davies, R. E. (editors), *A History of the Methodist Church in Great Britain, Vol. 1*, London, 1965.

Shaw, T., *The Bible Christians, 1815–1907*, London, 1965.

Taylor, E. R., *Methodism and Politics 1791–1851*, Cambridge, 1935.

Tindall, E. H., *Section No. 1 of the Wesley Methodist Atlas*, London, 1873.

Wearmouth, R. F., *Methodism and the Working Class Movements of England, 1800–80*, London, 1937.

Wearmouth, R. F., *Methodism and the Common People of the 18th Century*, London, 1945.

Wearmouth, R. F., *Methodism and the Struggle of the Working Classes 1850–1900*, London, 1954.

Wearmouth, R. F., *The Social and Political Influence of Methodism in the 20th Century*, London, 1957.

Wearmouth, R. F., *Methodism and the Trade Unions*, London, 1959.

Report of the Church Membership Committee, The Methodist Church, 1964.

10. OTHER RELIGIOUS GROUPS

Armytage, W. H. G., 'The Moravian communities in Britain', in *C.Q.R.*, 1957, pp. 141–52.

Barr, J., 'Amongst Friends', in *New Society*, 1.12.66, p. 821.

Bloch-Hoell, N., *The Pentecostal Movement*, London, 1964.

Braden, C. S., *Christian Science Today*, Dallas, U.S.A., 1958.

Braithwaite, W. C., *The Beginnings of Quakerism*, London, 1955.

Butterworth, E., *A Muslim Community in Britain*, London, 1967.

Calley, M. J. C., *God's People*, Oxford, 1965.

Cole, A., 'The social origins of the early Friends', in *J.F.H.S.*, 1957, pp. 99–118.

Collins, S., *Coloured Minorities in Britain*, London, 1957.

Coxill, H. W. and Grubb, K. (editors), *World Christian Handbook*, London, 1967.

Davies, H. *Christian Deviations*, London, 1965.

Davison, R. B., *Black British*, Oxford, 1966.
Davison, R. B., *Commonwealth Immigrants*, Oxford, 1964.
Desai, R., *Indian Immigrants in Britain*, Oxford, 1963.
Giffith, J. A. G. *et al*, *Coloured Immigrants in Britain*, Oxford, 1960.
Herberg, W., *Protestant, Catholic, Jew*, New York, 1960.
Hill, C. S., *How Colour Prejudiced is Britain?*, London, 1965.
Hill, C. S., *West Indian Migrants and the London Churches*, Oxford, 1963.
Isichei, E. A., 'From sect to denomination in English Quakerism, with special reference to the 19th century', in *B.J.S.*, 1964, pp. 207–22.
James, E. O., *History of Religions*, London, 1964.
Lewis, A. J., *Zinzendorf—The Ecumenical Pioneer*, London, 1962.
Linforth, L., *Route from Liverpool to Great Salt Lake City*, Liverpool, 1855.
Loukes, H., *The Quaker Contribution*, London, 1965.
Lutheran Directory of Great Britain, London, 1966.
The Lutheran—various editions.
Marwick, W. H., 'Some Quaker firms of the 19th century', in *J.F.H.S.*, 1958, pp. 239–59.
The Moravian Church, *An Introduction to the Moravian Church*, London, 1938.
Mullen, R. R., *The Mormons*, London, 1967.
Neatby, W. B., *A History of the Plymouth Brethren*, London, 1901.
Nelson, G. K., *The Development and Organization of the Spiritualist Movement in Britain*, Ph.D. Thesis, London, 1967.
Niebuhr, H. R., *The Social Sources of Denominationalism*, New York, 1929.
O'Dea, T., *The Mormons*, Chicago, 1957.
Patterson, S., 'Polish London', in *London, Aspects of Change*, Centre for Urban Studies, Report No. 3, London, 1964.
Peach, G. C. K., 'Factors affecting the distribution of West Indians in Great Britain', in *Trans. I.B.G.*, June 1966, pp. 151–63.
Pearce, E. G., *The Lutheran Church in Great Britain*, a pamphlet published by the Evangelical Lutheran Church of England.
Ross, K. N., *Dangerous Delusions*, London, 1961.
Sikh Courier—various editions.
Smith, J. F., *Essentials in Church History*, Utah, U.S.A., 1946.
Taylor, P. A. M., *Expectation Westward*, London, 1965.
Warburton, T. R., *A Comparative Study of Minority Religious Groups: With Special Reference to Holiness and Related Movements in Britain in the last 50 years*, Ph.D. Thesis, London, 1966.
Whalen, W. J., *The Latter Day Saints in the Modern Day World, An Account of Contemporary Mormonism*, U.S.A., 1964.
Wilbur, E. M., *A History of Unitarianism in Transylvania, England and America*, Cambridge, Mass., 1952.
Wilbur, S., *The Life of Mary Baker Eddy*, Boston, Mass., 1938.
Wilson, B. R. (editor), *Patterns of Sectarianism*, London, 1967.
Wilson, B. R., *Sects and Society*, London, 1961.
Wilson, J., *The History and Organization of British Israelism: Some Aspects of the Religious and Political Correlates of Changing Social Status*, D.Phil. Thesis, Oxford, 1966.

11. THE JEWS

Adler, E. N., *History of the Jews in London*, London, 1930.

Connell, J. H., *The Jewish Population of Leeds*, unpublished study, 1967.

Freedman, M. (editor), *A Minority in Britain*, London, 1955.

Gartner, L. P., 'From Jewish immigrant to English Jew', in *New Society*, 2.9.65.

Geographical Review, 1930, pp. 515–16, 'Movements of the Jewish population during the last century'.

Gilbert, E. W., *Brighton, Old Ocean's Bauble*, London, 1954.

Gould, J. and Esh, S., *Jewish Life in Modern Britain*, London, 1964.

Hyamson, A. M., *The Jews of England*, London, 1947.

Hyamson, A. M., *A History of the Jews in England*, London, 1928.

The Jewish Journal of Sociology, Dec. 1967, pp. 149–74, 'The Statistics of Jewish Marriages in Great Britain'.

The Jewish Chronicle Travel Guide, 1951 and 1956.

The Jewish Travel Guide, 1961 and 1967.

Kantorowitsch, M., 'Estimate of the Jewish population of London 1929–33' in *The Journal of the Royal Statistical Society*, Vol. XCIX, Part II, 1936.

Kantorowitsch, M., 'On the statistics of Jewish marriages in England and Wales', in *Population*, 1936, pp. 75–83.

Lipman, V. D. (editor), *Three Centuries of Anglo-Jewish History*, Cambridge, 1961.

Moser, C. A. and Scott, W., *British Towns*, London, 1961.

Prais, S. J. and Schmool, M., 'The size and structure of the Anglo-Jewish population 1960–65'. in *The Jewish Journal of Sociology*, June 1968, pp. 5–34.

Roth, C., *The Rise of Provincial Jewry*, London, 1950.

Roth, C., *History of the Jews in England*, Oxford, 1964.

Salaman, R. N., 'Anglo-Jewish vital statistics', in *The Jewish Chronicle Supplement*, 1921, No. 4–8.

Schmool, M., 'Register of research on the Anglo-Jewish community', in *The Jewish Journal of Sociology*, Dec. 1968, pp. 281–6.

Trachtenberg, H. L., 'Estimate of the Jewish population of London 1929', in *The Journal of the Royal Statistical Society*, Vol. XCVI, Part I, 1933.

Wanklyn, H. G., 'Geographical aspects of Jewish settlement east of Germany,' in *Geographical Journal*, 1940, pp. 175–90.

MAPS

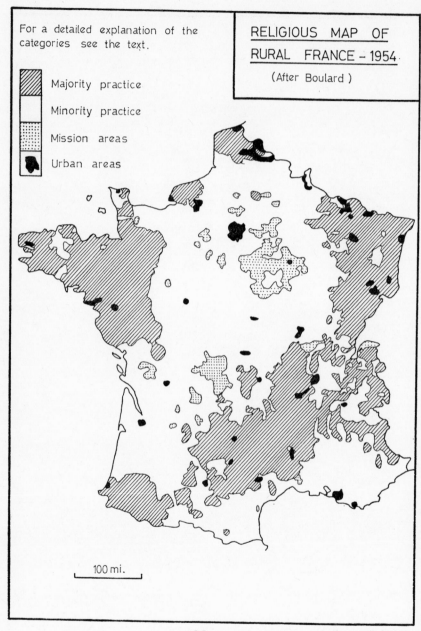

For a detailed explanation of the categories see the text.

RELIGIOUS MAP OF RURAL FRANCE – 1954.

(After Boulard)

Majority practice

Minority practice

Mission areas

Urban areas

100 mi.

Map I

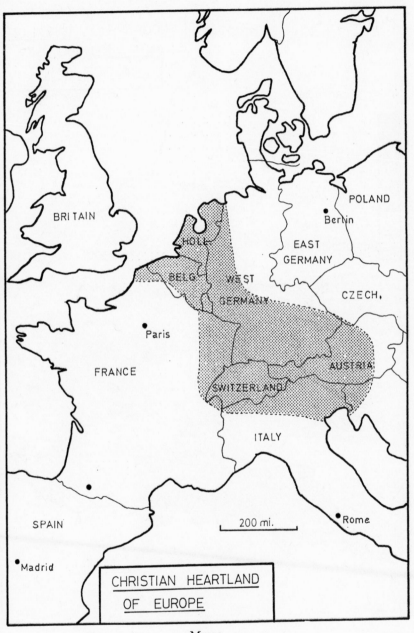

CHRISTIAN HEARTLAND

OF EUROPE

Map 2

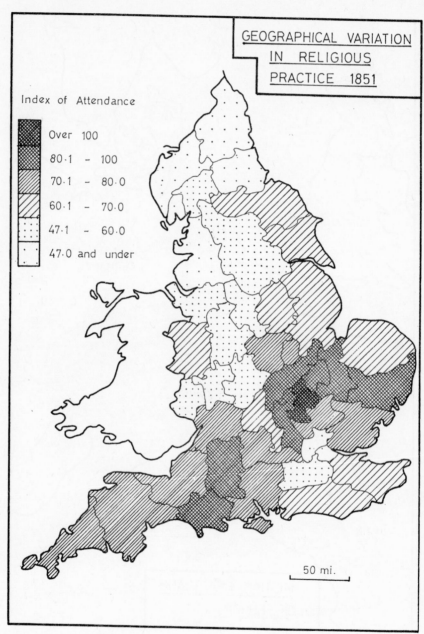

Map 3

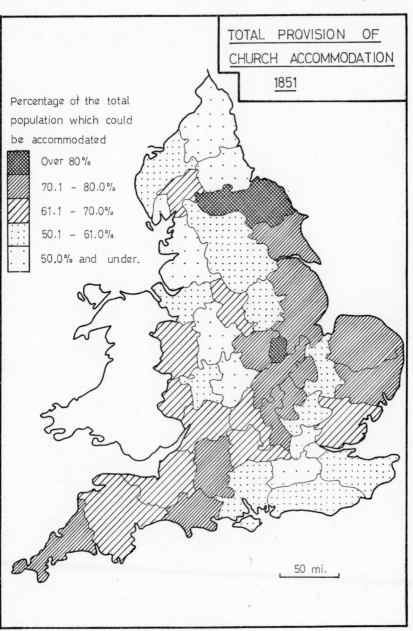

Map 4

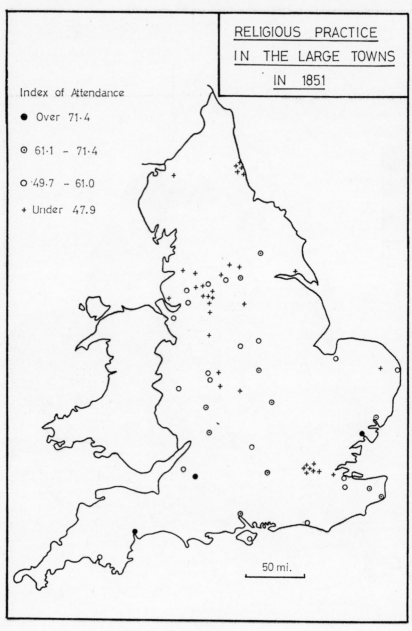

RELIGIOUS PRACTICE
IN THE LARGE TOWNS
IN 1851

Index of Attendance

● Over 71·4

◉ 61·1 – 71·4

○ ·49·7 – 61.0

+ Under 47.9

50 mi.

Map 5

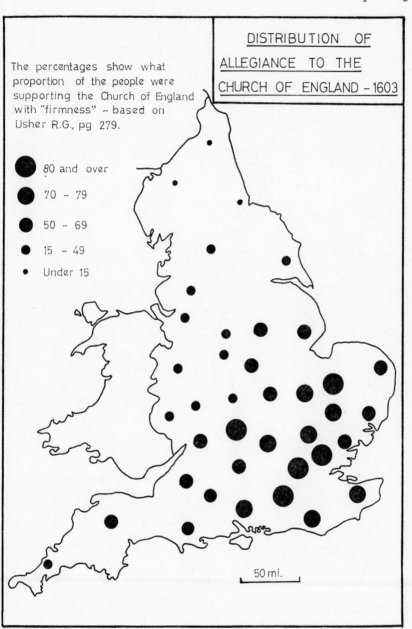

DISTRIBUTION OF ALLEGIANCE TO THE CHURCH OF ENGLAND – 1603

The percentages show what proportion of the people were supporting the Church of England with "firmness" – based on Usher R.G., pg 279.

- 80 and over
- 70 – 79
- 50 – 69
- 15 – 49
- Under 15

50 mi.

Map 6

THE DIOCESES
1541 – 1834

Durham

Carlisle

York

Chester

Lincoln
(north)

Lichfield
and
Coventry

Norwich

Peterborough

Worc.

Ely

Here.

Oxford

Lincoln
(south)

Bristol

Glouc.

London

Salisbury

Roch

Bath
and Wells

Winchester

Cant.

Chichester

Exeter

Bristol

50 mi.

Map 7

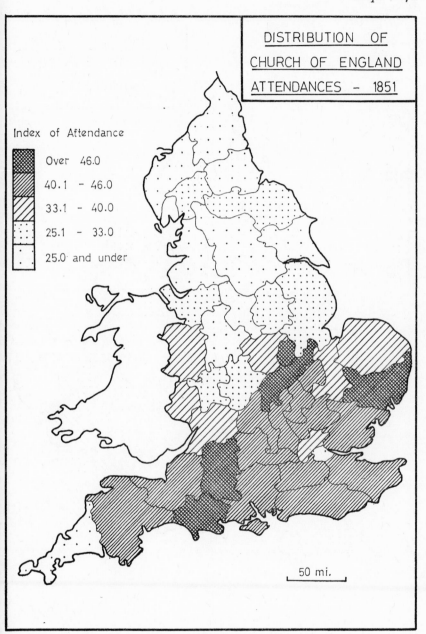

Map 8

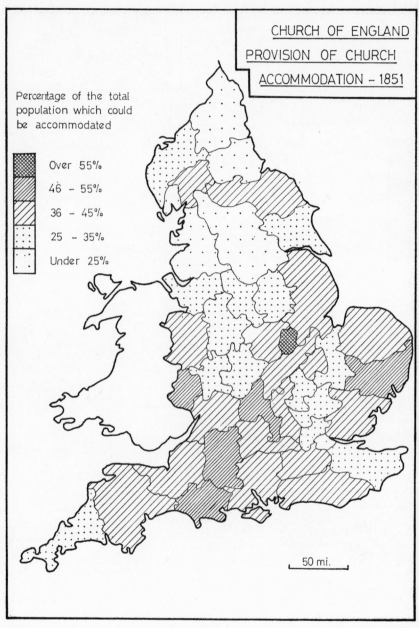

Map 9

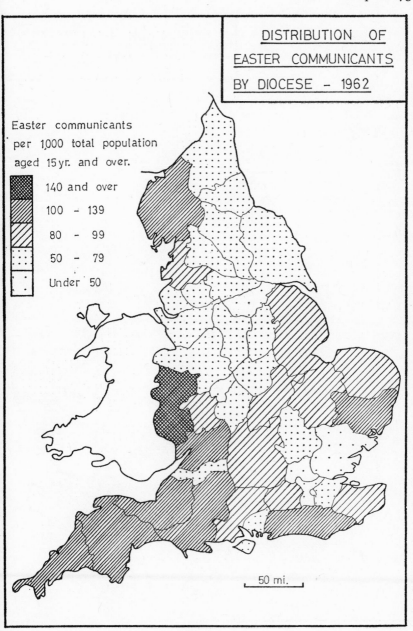

DISTRIBUTION OF
EASTER COMMUNICANTS
BY DIOCESE – 1962

Easter communicants
per 1,000 total population
aged 15 yr. and over.

140 and over
100 – 139
80 – 99
50 – 79
Under 50

50 mi.

Map 10

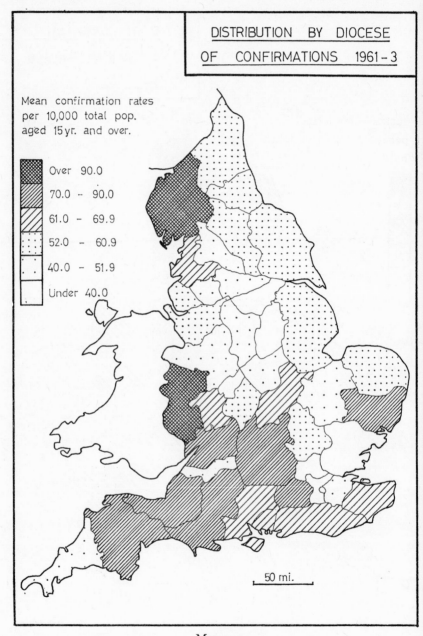

DISTRIBUTION BY DIOCESE
OF CONFIRMATIONS 1961-3

Mean confirmation rates
per 10,000 total pop.
aged 15 yr. and over.

Over 90.0

70.0 - 90.0

61.0 - 69.9

52.0 - 60.9

40.0 - 51.9

Under 40.0

50 mi.

Map 11

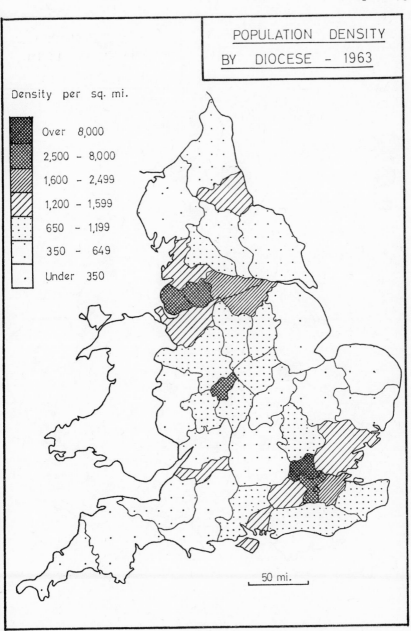

POPULATION DENSITY
BY DIOCESE – 1963

Density per sq. mi.

Over 8,000
2,500 – 8,000
1,600 – 2,499
1,200 – 1,599
650 – 1,199
350 – 649
Under 350

50 mi.

Map 12

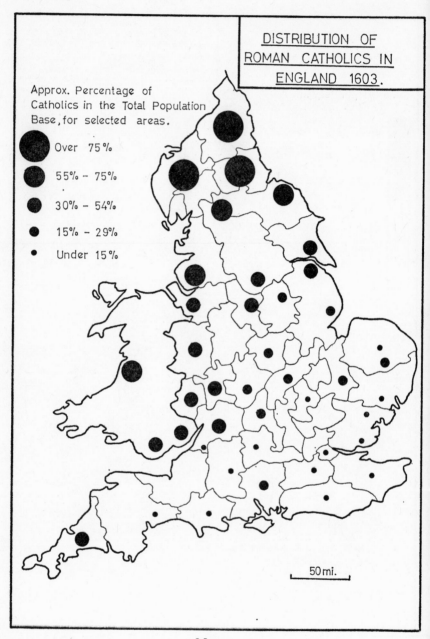

Map 13

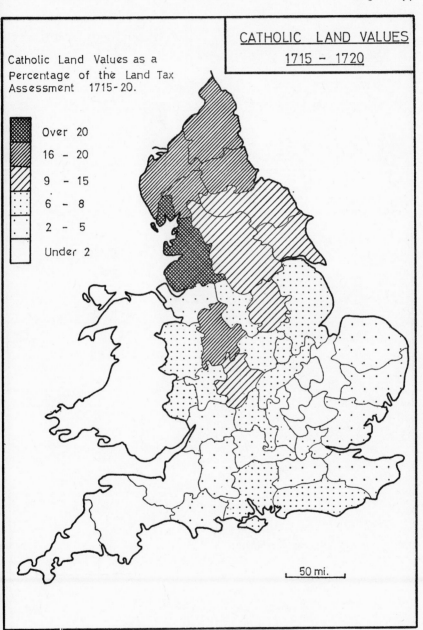

Catholic Land Values as a
Percentage of the Land Tax
Assessment 1715-20.

CATHOLIC LAND VALUES
1715 - 1720

Over 20
16 - 20
9 - 15
6 - 8
2 - 5
Under 2

50 mi.

Map 14

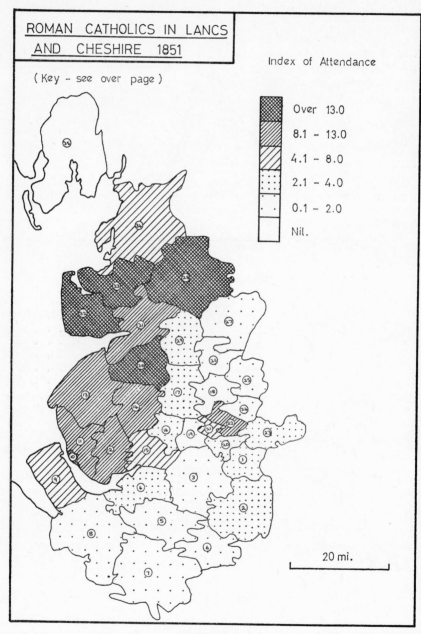

Map 15

Key to Map 15

Registration Districts or Poor Law Unions

1. Stockport
2. Macclesfield
3. Altrincham
4. Runcorn
5. Northwich
6. Congleton
7. Nantwich
8. Great Broughton
9. Wirral
10. Liverpool
11. West Derby
12. Prescot
13. Ormskirk
14. Wigan
15. Warrington
16. Leigh
17. Bolton
18. Bury
19. Barton-upon-Irwell
20. Chorlton
21. Salford
22. Manchester
23. Ashton-under-Lyne
24. Oldham
25. Rochdale
26. Haslingden
27. Burnley
28. Clitheroe
29. Blackburn
30. Chorley
31. Preston
32. Fylde
33. Garstang
34. Lancaster
35. Ulverston

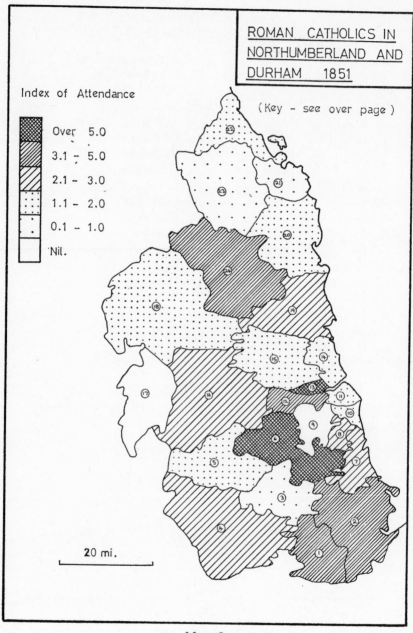

ROMAN CATHOLICS IN
NORTHUMBERLAND AND
DURHAM 1851

(Key - see over page)

Index of Attendance

Over 5.0
3.1 - 5.0
2.1 - 3.0
1.1 - 2.0
0.1 - 1.0
Nil.

20 mi.

Map 16

Key to Map 16

Registration Districts or Poor Law Unious

1. Darlington	13. Newcastle
2. Stockton	14. Tynemouth
3. Auckland	15. Castle Ward
4. Teesdale	16. Hexham
5. Weardale	17. Haltwhistle
6. Durham	18. Bellingham
7. Easington	19. Morpeth
8. Houghton-le-Spring	20. Alnwick
9. Chester-le-Street	21. Belford
10. Sunderland	22. Berwick-on-Tweed
11. South Shields	23. Glendale
12. Gateshead	24. Rothbury

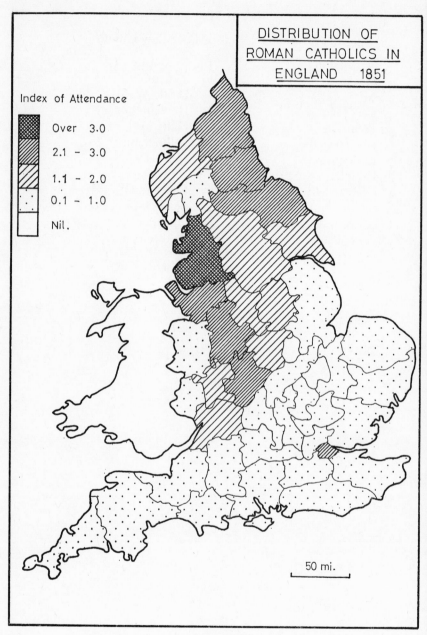

Map 17

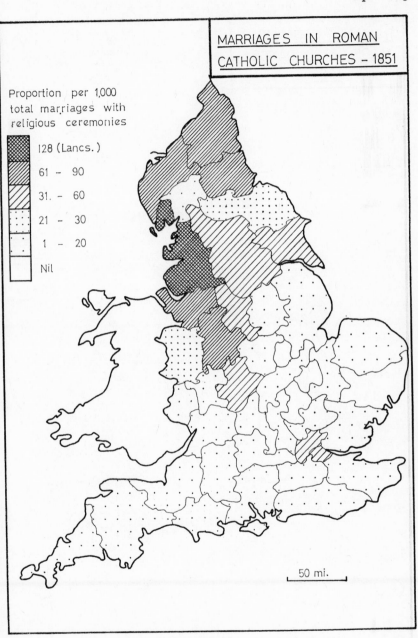

Map 18

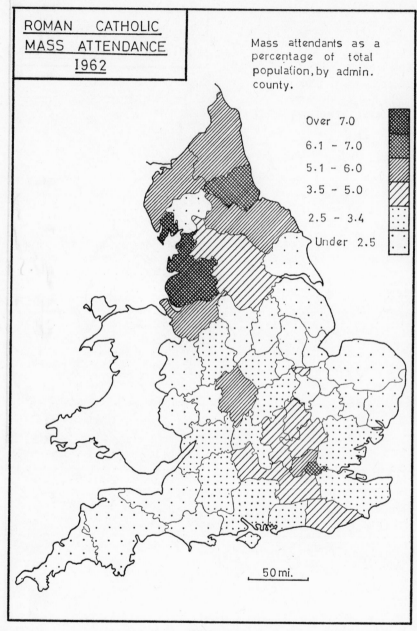

Map 19

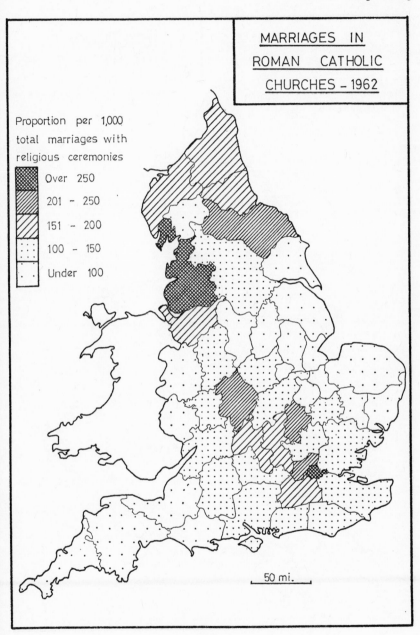

MARRIAGES IN
ROMAN CATHOLIC
CHURCHES - 1962

Proportion per 1,000
total marriages with
religious ceremonies

Over 250
201 - 250
151 - 200
100 - 150
Under 100

50 mi.

Map 20

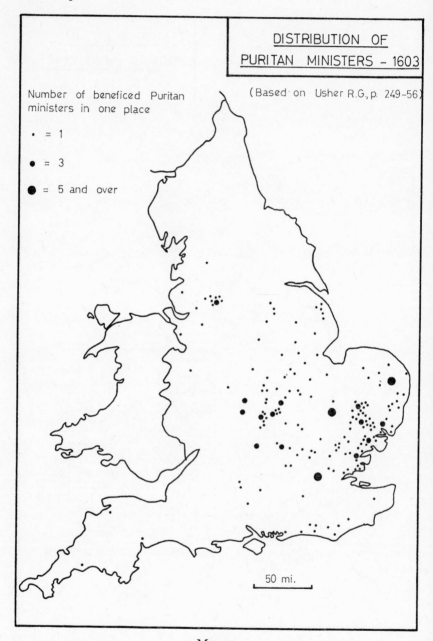

DISTRIBUTION OF
PURITAN MINISTERS - 1603

Number of beneficed Puritan
ministers in one place

(Based on Usher R.G., p. 249-56)

• = 1

● = 3

⬤ = 5 and over

50 mi.

Map 21

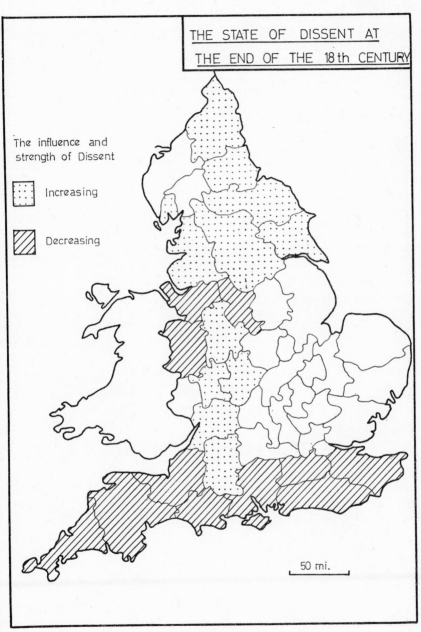

Map 22

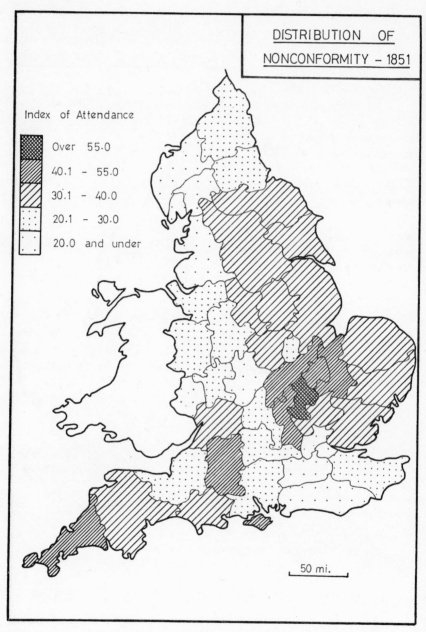

Map 23

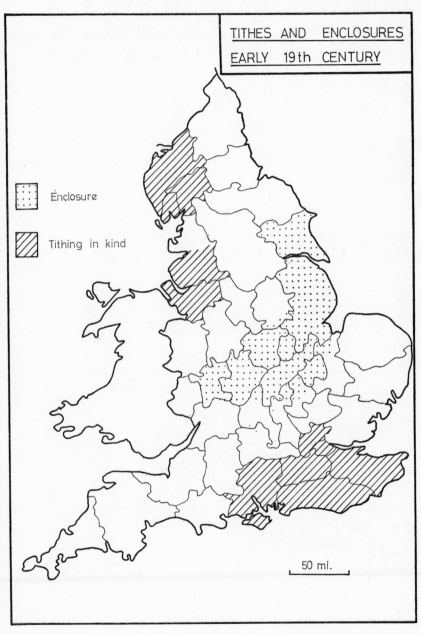

Map 24

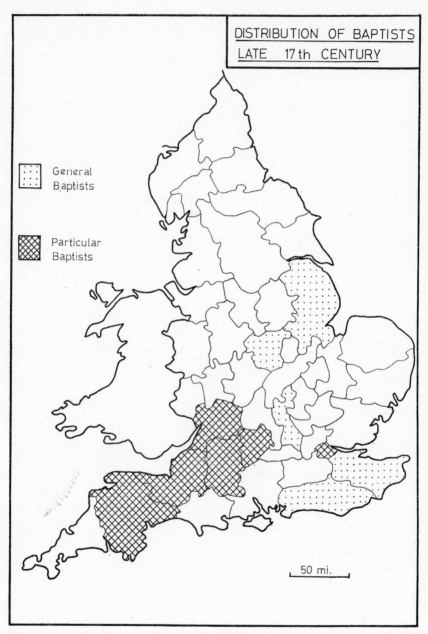

Map 25

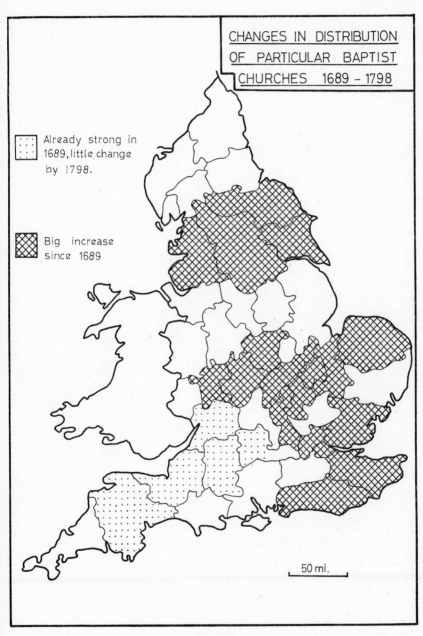

Map 26

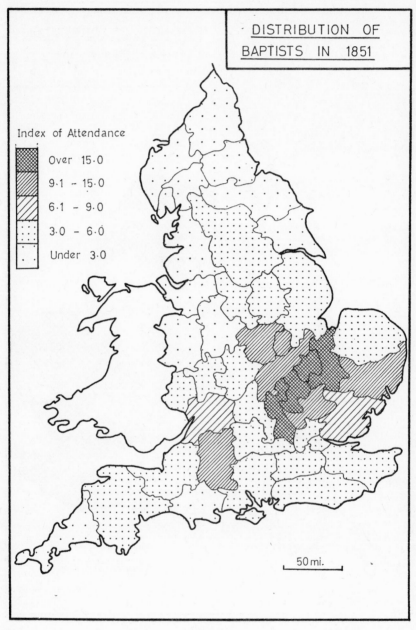

Map 27

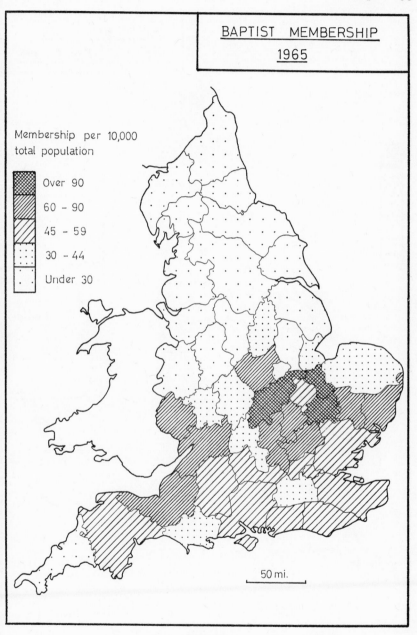

BAPTIST MEMBERSHIP
1965

Membership per 10,000
total population

Over 90
60 - 90
45 - 59
30 - 44
Under 30

50 mi.

Map 28

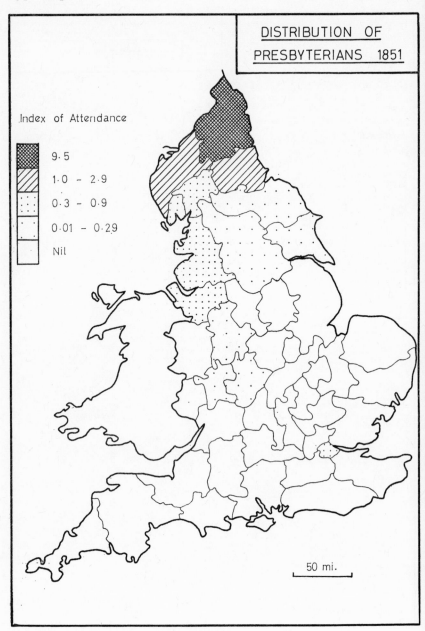

Map 29

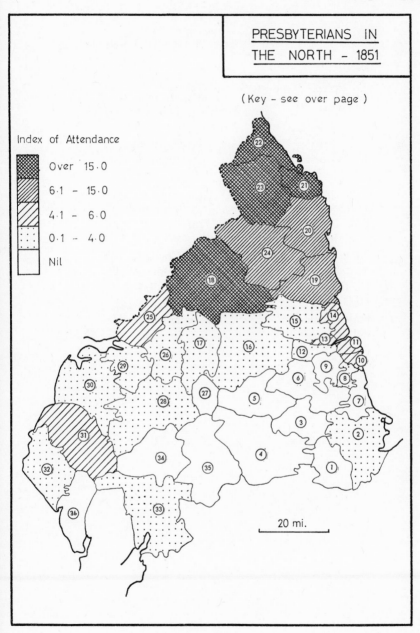

PRESBYTERIANS IN
THE NORTH – 1851

(Key – see over page)

Index of Attendance

Over 15.0
6.1 – 15.0
4.1 – 6.0
0.1 – 4.0
Nil

20 mi.

Map 30

Key to Map 30

Registration Districts or Poor Law Unions

1. Darlington	19. Morpeth
2. Stockton	20. Alnwick
3. Auckland	21. Belford
4. Teesdale	22. Berwick-on-Tweed
5. Weardale	23. Glendale
6. Durham	24. Rothbury
7. Easington	25. Longtown
8. Houghton-le-Spring	26. Brampton
9. Chester-le-Street	27. Alston
10. Sunderland	28. Penrith
11. South Shields	29. Carlisle
12. Gateshead	30. Wigton
13. Newcastle	31. Cockermouth
14. Tynemouth	32. Whitehaven
15. Castle Ward	33. Kendal
16. Hexham	34. West Ward
17. Haltwhistle	35. East Ward
18. Bellingham	36. Bootle

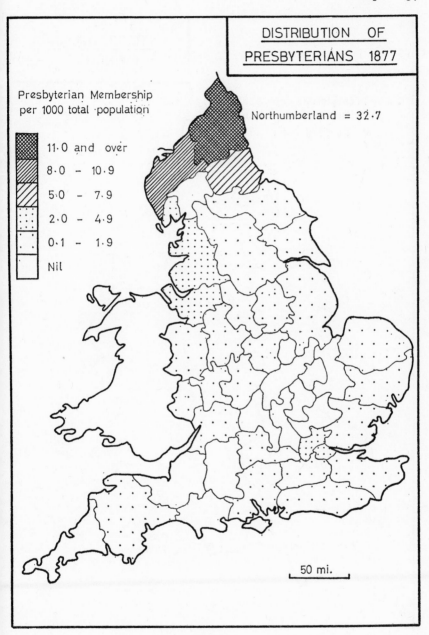

Map 31

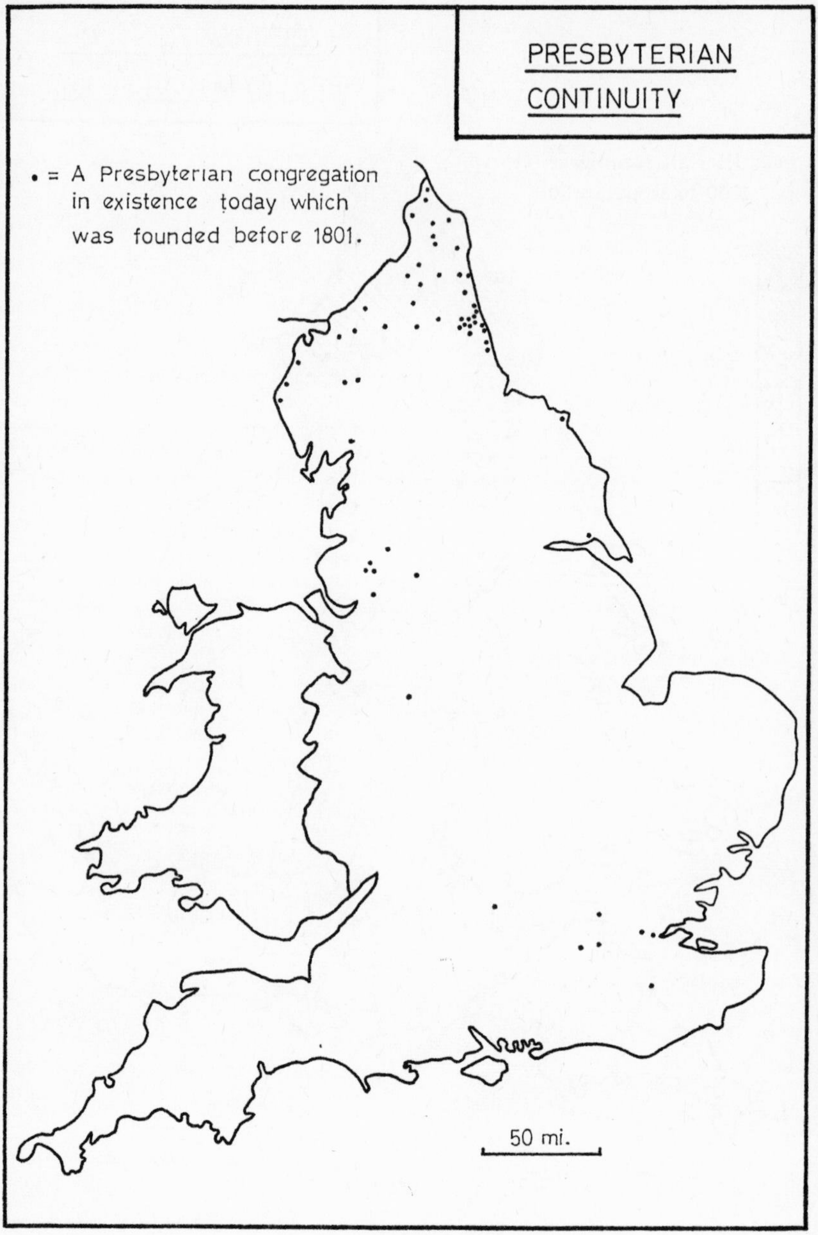

PRESBYTERIAN
CONTINUITY

• = A Presbyterian congregation
in existence today which
was founded before 1801.

50 mi.

Map 32

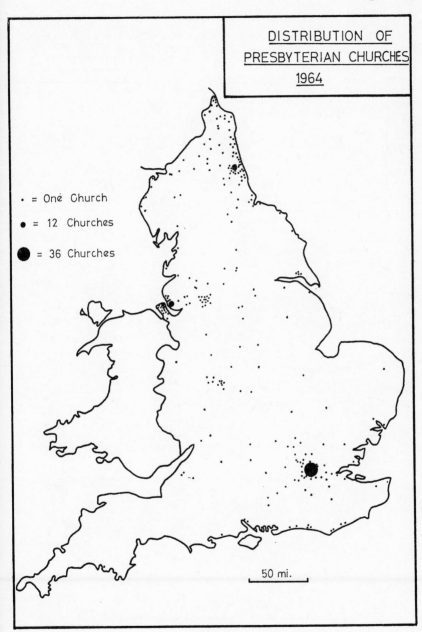

DISTRIBUTION OF
PRESBYTERIAN CHURCHES
1964

• = One Church

● = 12 Churches

⬤ = 36 Churches

50 mi.

Map 33

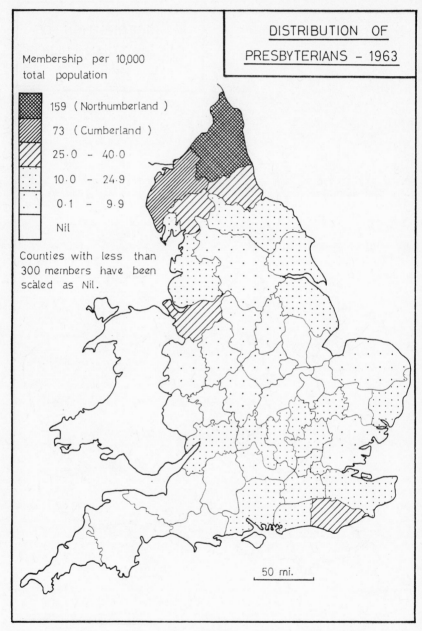

Map 34

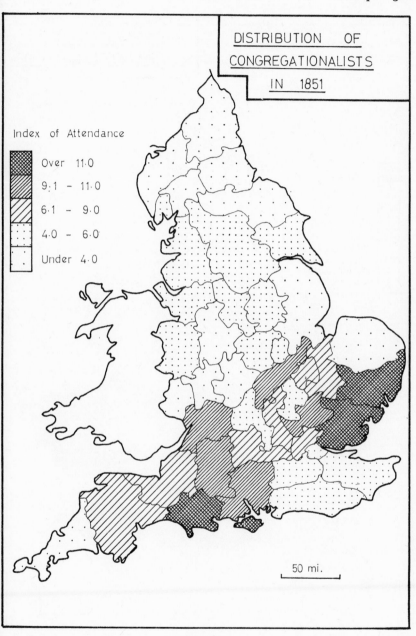

Index of Attendance

Over 11.0
9.1 – 11.0
6.1 – 9.0
4.0 – 6.0
Under 4.0

50 mi.

Map 35

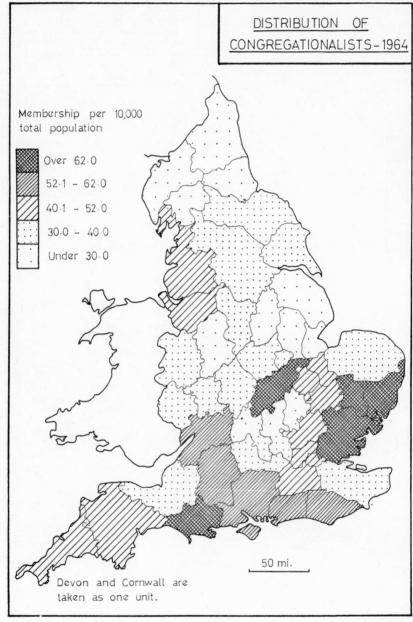

Map 36

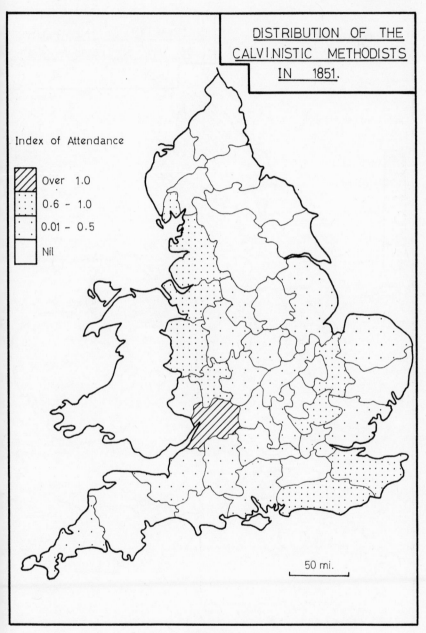

Index of Attendance

- Over 1.0
- 0.6 – 1.0
- 0.01 – 0.5
- Nil

DISTRIBUTION OF THE
CALVINISTIC METHODISTS
IN 1851.

50 mi.

Map 37

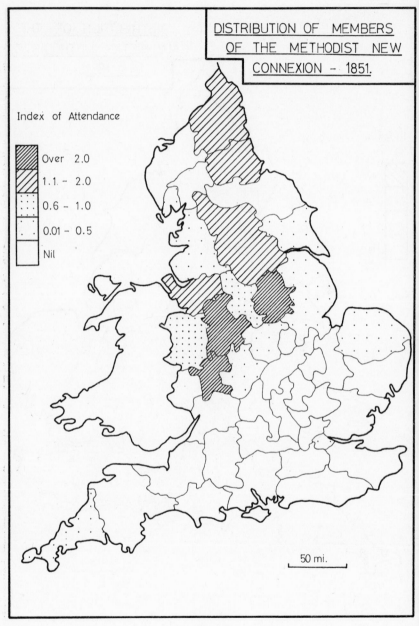

Map 38

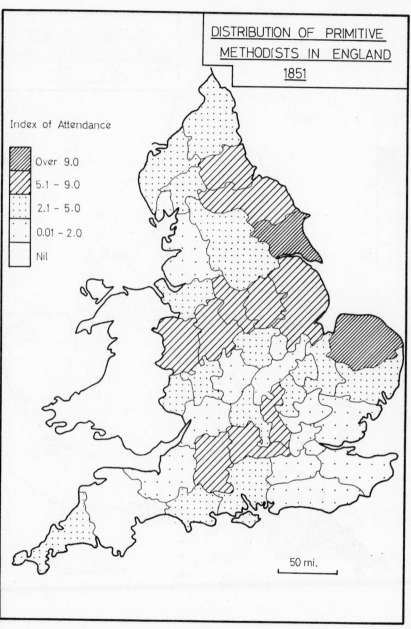

Map 39

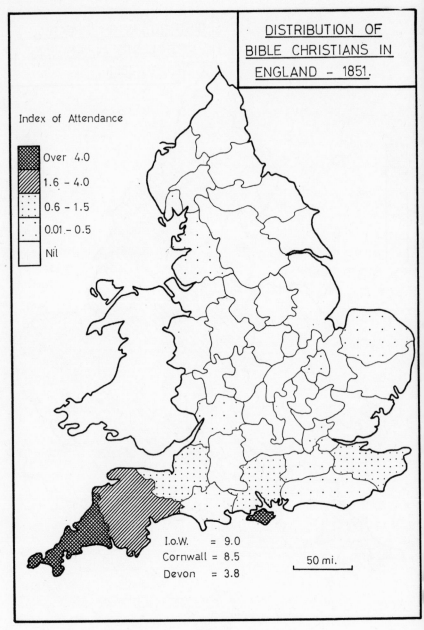

Map 40

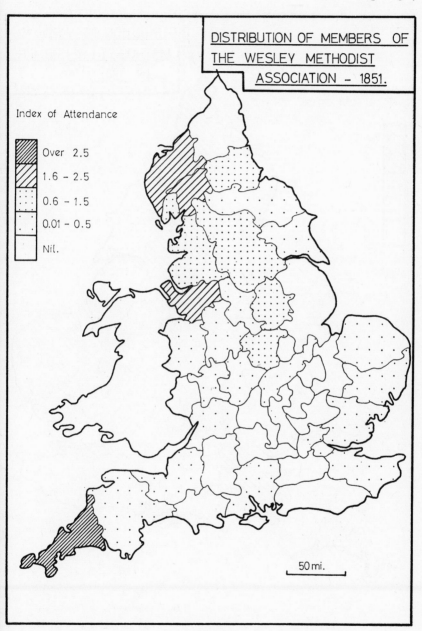

DISTRIBUTION OF MEMBERS OF
THE WESLEY METHODIST
ASSOCIATION - 1851.

Index of Attendance

Over 2.5
1.6 - 2.5
0.6 - 1.5
0.01 - 0.5
Nil.

50 mi.

Map 41

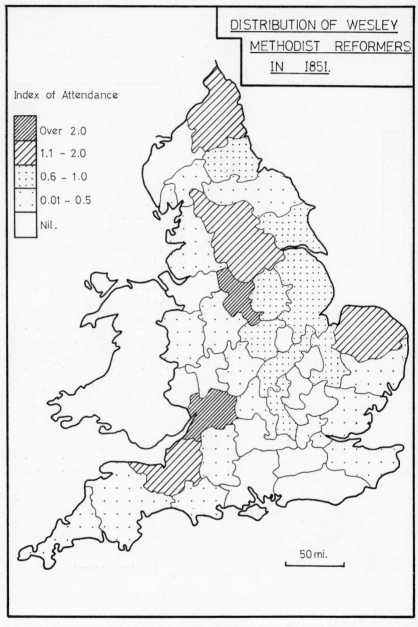

Index of Attendance

Over 2.0
1.1 - 2.0
0.6 - 1.0
0.01 - 0.5
Nil.

DISTRIBUTION OF WESLEY
METHODIST REFORMERS
IN 1851.

50 mi.

Map 42

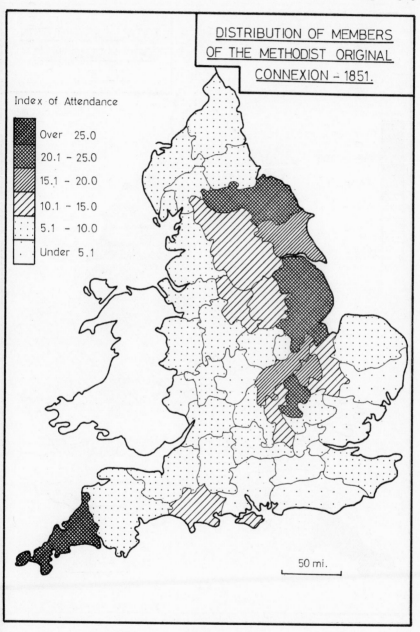

Map 43

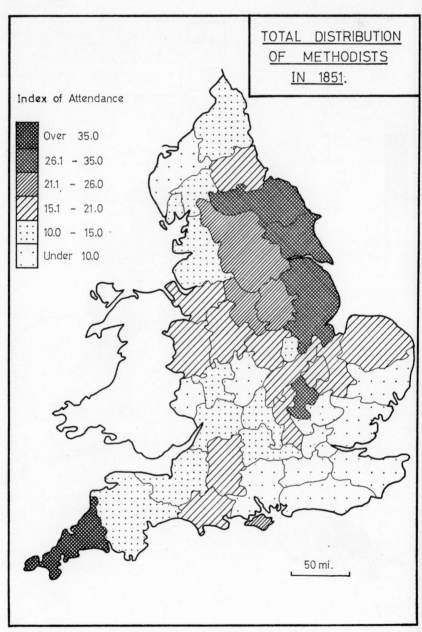

Map 44

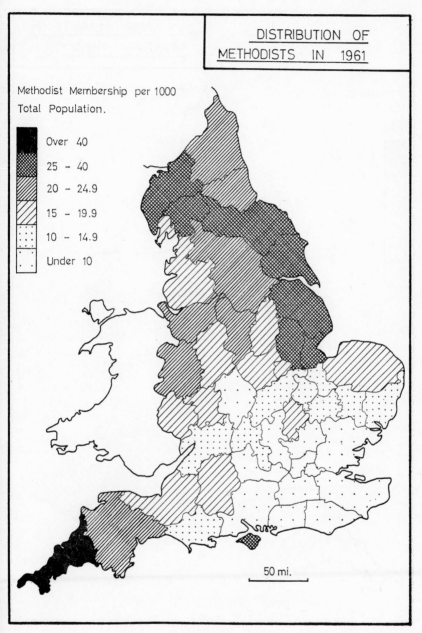

DISTRIBUTION OF
METHODISTS IN 1961

Methodist Membership per 1000
Total Population.

Over 40

25 – 40

20 – 24.9

15 – 19.9

10 – 14.9

Under 10

50 mi.

Map 45

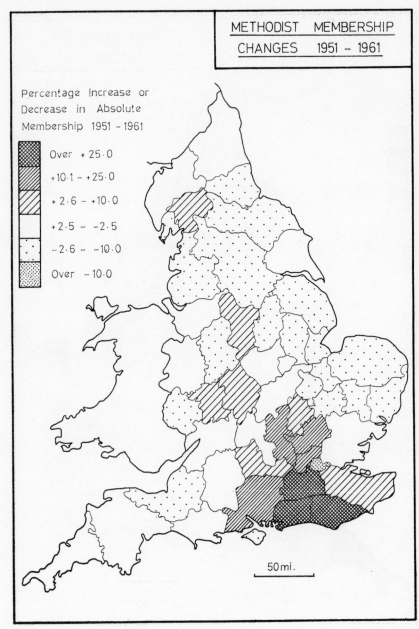

METHODIST MEMBERSHIP
CHANGES 1951 – 1961

Percentage Increase or
Decrease in Absolute
Membership 1951 – 1961

Over + 25·0
+10·1 – +25·0
+ 2·6 – +10·0
+2·5 – –2·5
–2·6 – –10·0
Over – 10·0

50 mi.

Map 46

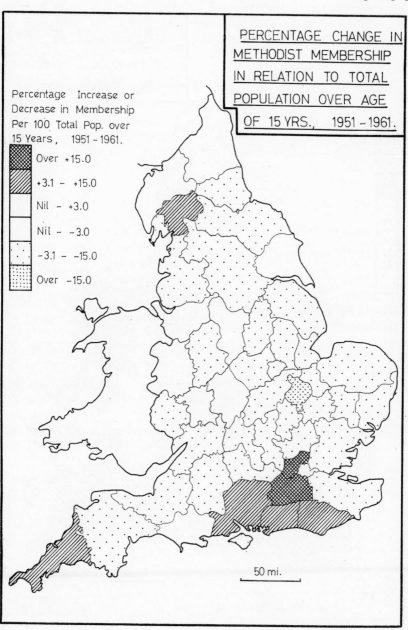

Percentage Increase or Decrease in Membership Per 100 Total Pop. over 15 Years, 1951-1961.

Over +15.0
+3.1 - +15.0
Nil - +3.0
Nil - -3.0
-3.1 - -15.0
Over -15.0

PERCENTAGE CHANGE IN METHODIST MEMBERSHIP IN RELATION TO TOTAL POPULATION OVER AGE OF 15 YRS., 1951-1961.

50 mi.

Map 47

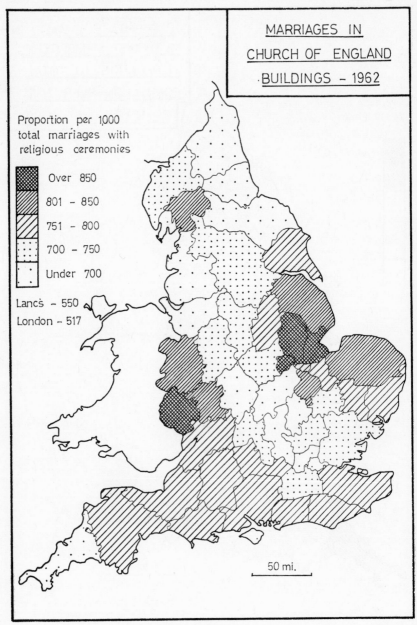

MARRIAGES IN
CHURCH OF ENGLAND
·BUILDINGS – 1962

Proportion per 1,000
total marriages with
religious ceremonies

Over 850

801 – 850

751 – 800

700 – 750

Under 700

Lancs – 550
London – 517

50 mi.

Map 48

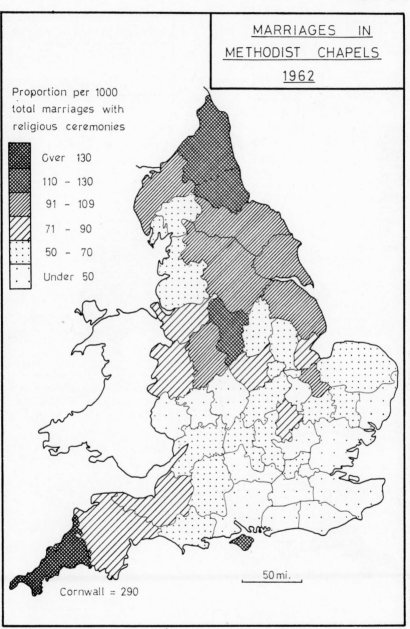

Proportion per 1000
total marriages with
religious ceremonies

Over 130
110 – 130
91 – 109
71 – 90
50 – 70
Under 50

MARRIAGES IN
METHODIST CHAPELS
1962

Cornwall = 290

50 mi.

Map 49

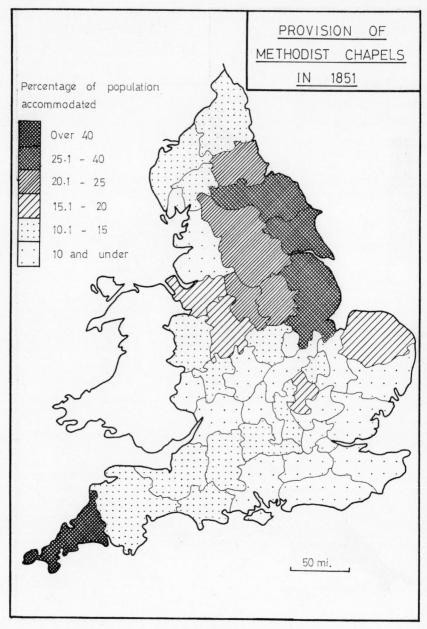

Map 50

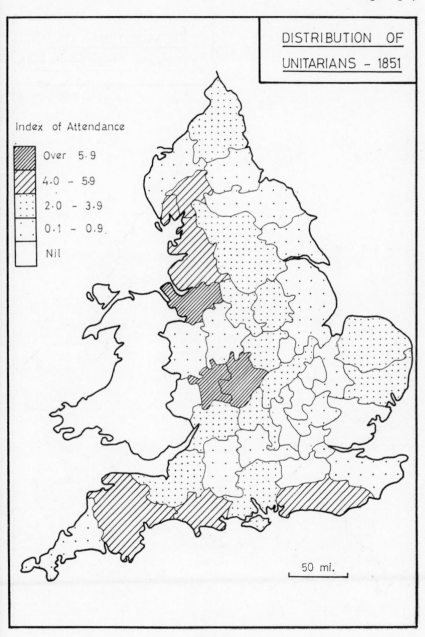

Map 51

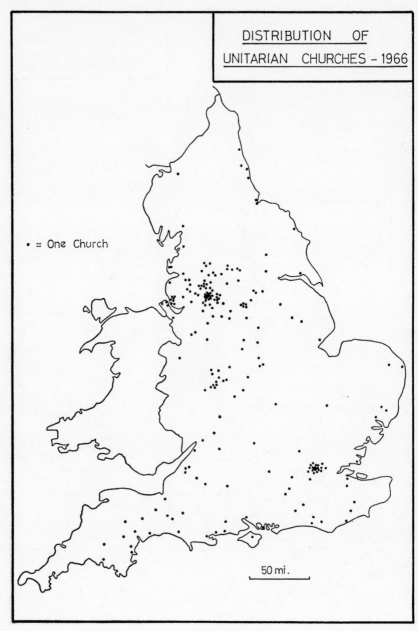

Map 52

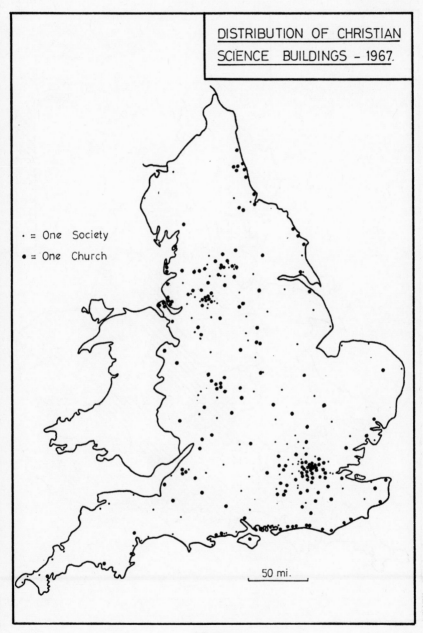

DISTRIBUTION OF CHRISTIAN
SCIENCE BUILDINGS - 1967.

· = One Society
● = One Church

50 mi.

Map 53

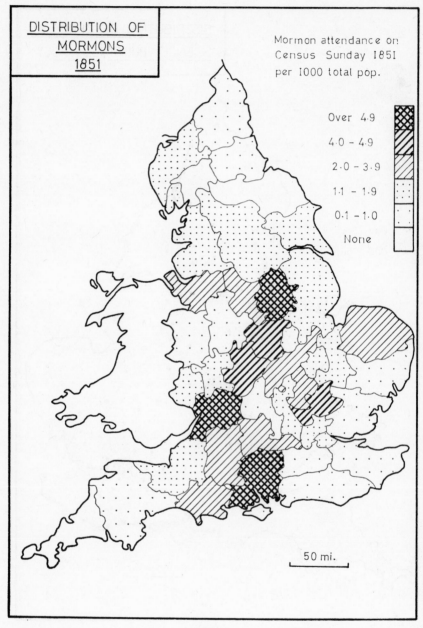

DISTRIBUTION OF
MORMONS
1851

Mormon attendance on
Census Sunday 1851
per 1000 total pop.

Over 4·9
4·0 - 4·9
2·0 - 3·9
1·1 - 1·9
0·1 - 1·0
None

50 mi.

Map 54

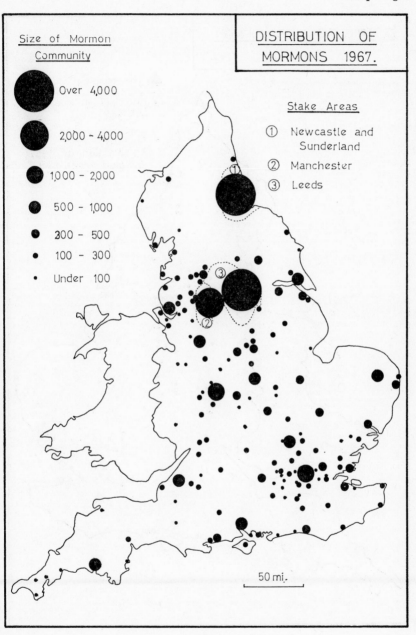

Map 55

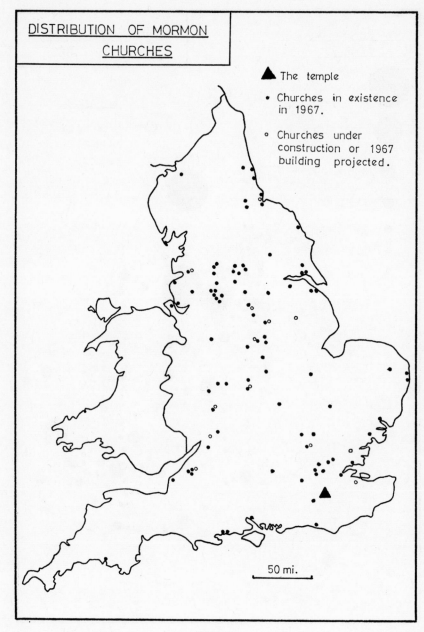

Map 56

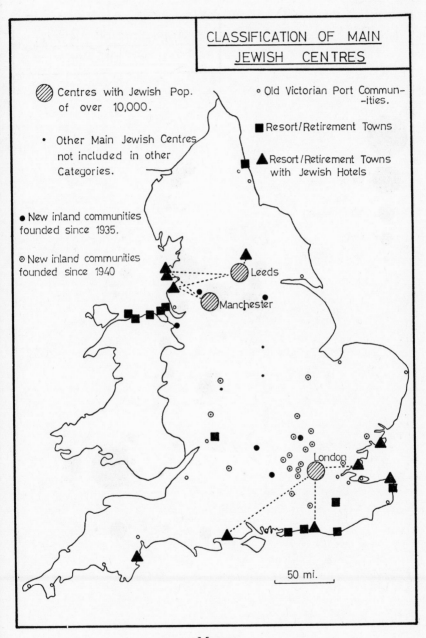

CLASSIFICATION OF MAIN
JEWISH CENTRES

Centres with Jewish Pop. of over 10,000.

Other Main Jewish Centres not included in other Categories.

New inland communities founded since 1935.

New inland communities founded since 1940

Old Victorian Port Commun- -ities.

Resort/Retirement Towns

Resort/Retirement Towns with Jewish Hotels

Leeds

Manchester

London

50 mi.

Map 57

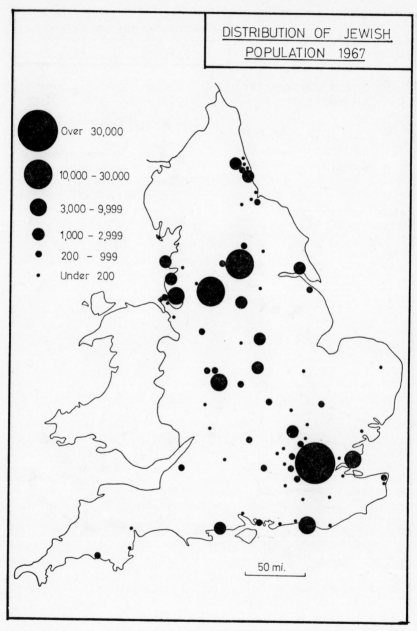

Map 58

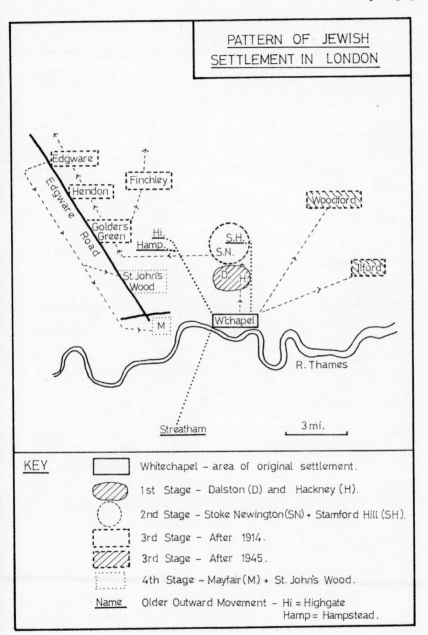

Map 59

Subject Index

Absenteeism of Anglican Clergy, 75
77, 146–7, 158, 160
Act of Supremacy, 66, 82
Act of Uniformity, 67, 101, 104, 125,
136
Adherents, 32, 113, 151
Agriculture, 2, 17, 20, 69, 71, 75–6, 89,
93, 99, 111–12, 147, 162–4; agri-
cultural communities, 105, 111–12,
151; agricultural settlements, 20
Anglican, see Church of England
Anglican-Methodist unity, 167
Anomie, 189
Arable economy, 111, 162–3, 164
Ashkenazi community, 206
Assimilation of immigrant groups, 100,
174, 201, 203, 213–14, 216, 220

Baptisms, statistics of, 26–7, 30, 34,
194–5
Baptists, 30–1, 110, 116–17, 118–23,
124, 138, 234
Bible Christians, 57, 150–1, 152–4
Bourne, H., 150
British Israel Movement, 183–4
Browne, R., 134
Buckingham, J. S., 177
Buddhists, 17, 19, 196, 198–9, 201
Buildings, churches and chapels, 41–3,
56–7, 75, 113, 115–16, 132–3, 156,
165, 166, 182
Bunyan, J., 119

Calvin, J., 124
Calvinist theology, 118, 120–1, 124,
126–7, 133, 135, 148–9, 241
Calvinistic Methodists, 148–9
Capitalism and Puritanism, 103
Caste, 199
Catchment areas, 147, 188
Celtic Church, 64
Celtic saints and settlement patterns,
15, 159–60
Charles II, 104–5, 119, 125, 136
Chief manufacturing districts, see
Urban and industrial areas
Christian Scientists, 185–8, 190
Church as a community centre, 65, 67,
115–16, 133, 141–3
Church attendance, 35–6, 45–63
Church of England, 23, 24–7, 36, 38–42,
45, 47, 50, 53–5, 57–62, 64–80,
101–2, 104, 106, 108–11, 114–17,

124, 138, 141, 144, 145–8, 153–4,
158, 159–62, 176 (see also Estab-
lishment)
Church rates, 107
Circuits, 34, 114, 147, 161, 163
Cities, see Urban and industrial areas
Civic Gospel, 110
Civic life, 181–2
Civil marriages, 39, 41
Civil War, 68, 103, 105, 118, 124, 133,
135, 178
Class Meetings, 34
Climatic effects on religion, 16–18
Clowes, W., 150
Coal towns, 59, 108, 152
Commercial links, 110, 170
Communicants, 25–7, 29–34, 36, 79
Communication links, 5, 7, 68, 89, 132,
135, 142, 171, 193–5, 206–8, 242
Community ideal, 176–7
Community life, 65, 67, 90–1, 104, 145,
163, 168, 197
Commuters, 79, 217; commuter areas,
163, 217
Competition among religious groups,
62
Confirmations in the Church of
England, 25–7, 79
Congregationalists, 32–3, 60, 103, 110,
116–17, 119, 124, 127–8, 130, 133,
134–43, 181
Conversions, 97, 202–3
Corn prices, 76
Cotton towns, 59, 108, 139
Cromwell, O., 68, 103–5, 119, 125, 135,
138
Cultural expressions, 18, 199, 213;
landscape, 3, 19; regions, 14

Declaration of Indulgence, 43, 105,
119, 126, 136
Desert environment and its effects on
religion, 17
Determinism, 6, 16
Diocesan system of territorial organiza-
tion, 64–5, 72–3, 80, 237
Dispersed residence patterns, 204, 207,
214
Dissenters, see Nonconformists

Eastern religions, 196–201
Economic factors, 7, 19, 110, 134, 137,
139–40, 144, 152–4, 160, 176, 179,
209, 211–13, 219

Place Index

Index of authors cited